CULINARY COMEDY IN MEDIEVAL FRENCH LITERATURE

Purdue Studies in Romance Literatures

Editorial Board

Patricia Hart, Series Editor
Jeanette Beer
Paul B. Dixon
Benjamin Lawton

Howard Mancing
Floyd Merrell
Allen G. Wood

Associate Editors

French
Paul Benhamou
Willard Bohn
Gerard J. Brault
Mary Ann Caws
Gérard Defaux
Milorad R. Margitić
Glyn P. Norton
Allan H. Pasco
Gerald Prince
David Lee Rubin
Roseann Runte
Ursula Tidd

Italian
Fiora A. Bassanese
Peter Carravetta
Franco Masciandaro
Anthony Julian Tamburri

Luso-Brazilian
Fred M. Clark
Marta Peixoto
Ricardo da Silveira Lobo Sternberg

Spanish and Spanish American
Maryellen Bieder
Catherine Connor
Ivy A. Corfis
Frederick A. de Armas
Edward Friedman
Charles Ganelin
David T. Gies
Roberto González Echevarría
David K. Herzberger
Emily Hicks
Djelal Kadir
Amy Kaminsky
Lucille Kerr
Alberto Moreiras
Randolph D. Pope
Francisco Ruiz Ramón
Elżbieta Skłodowska
Mario Valdés
Howard Young

PSRL volume 37

CULINARY COMEDY IN MEDIEVAL FRENCH LITERATURE

Sarah Gordon

Purdue University Press
West Lafayette, Indiana

Copyright © 2007 by Purdue University. All rights reserved.

♾ The paper used in this book meets the minimum requirements of American National Standard for Information Sciences—Permanence of Paper for Printed Library Materials, ANSI Z39.48-1992.

Printed in the United States of America
Design by Anita Noble

Library of Congress Cataloging-in-Publication Data
Gordon, Sarah, 1975–
   Culinary comedy in medieval French literature / Sarah Gordon.
     p.   cm. — (Purdue studies in romance literatures ; v. 37)
   Includes bibliographical references and index.
   ISBN-13: 978-1-55753-430-9 (alk. paper)
   ISBN-10: 1-55753-430-6
   1. French literature—To 1500—History and criticism. 2. Food in literature. I. Title II. Series.
   PQ155.F66G67 2006
   840.9'3559—dc22
                                    2006016917

To my sister, mother, and grandmother

Contents

ix **Acknowledgments**
  1 **Introduction**
 14 **Chapter One**
     Food Fight: Medieval Gastronomy and Literary Convention
 50 **Chapter Two**
     Uncourtly Table Manners in Arthurian Romance
 97 **Chapter Three**
     Much Ado about Bacon: The Old French Fabliaux
140 **Chapter Four**
     Hungry like the Wolf, Sly as a Fox: *Le Roman de Renart*
178 **Conclusion**
183 **Notes**
197 **Bibliography**
211 **Index**

Acknowledgments

I wish to acknowledge the College of HASS, Dean Gary Kiger, and the Women and Gender Research Institute at Utah State University for providing generous research and travel funding in support of this project. I am grateful to my department head, Charlie Huenemann, for his support of my research leave. Many thanks are due to Jeanette Beer for her support and insight, and to the PSRL reviewers for their interest and guidance in this interdisciplinary topic. Susan Clawson has been a pleasure to work with, and I value her careful readings, editorial expertise, and input.

I am thankful for the mentoring of Norris J. Lacy, for decades of support and inspiration. Tony Hunt, the late Elspeth Kennedy, the Oxford Old French Seminar, and members of the International Arthurian Society have also been influential and supportive in my research. I cherish Nancy Bell's sense of humor and value her research and scholarly opinions on humor theory. My warmest personal heartfelt thanks go to Benjamin Renard-Wiart, Christa Jones, Brett Jones, Liz Klein, Jeremy Bruskotter, Ann Gordon, David Shafie, Peter MacKinnon, Lisa Saunderson, Mark Anderson, and Mark Humphries for shared feasting, raucous laughter, inside jokes, and gentle encouragement during the writing of this book. I appreciate the continuing friendship of all my St. Peter's College, Oxford friends and relish our dining hall memories. I am grateful to Louise Deakin and my fellow food critics at Eat in Paris for helping me make the connection between gastronomy and comedy. Thanks also to Matt Klein and Nancy Peterson-Klein for the use of their culinary library. A nod goes out to my students, with whom I have had the pleasure of sharing countless spirited discussions, and even on occasion food fights, while analyzing medieval humor and verse in the classroom. This book is for all my foodie friends, family, students, and colleagues. Bon appétit.

Introduction

> Dis-moi ce que tu manges,
> je te dirai ce que tu es.
> —Brillat-Savarin
> *La physiologie du goût*

Long before tales of gargantuan gluttony regaled early modern audiences, and centuries before pie-in-the-face or banana peel gags enlivened vaudeville slapstick, medieval French poets employed food as a powerful device of humor and criticism. Food and humor both have the power to satisfy, to entertain, and to construct identity; this power is doubled when they are combined. Unexpected usages of food may be humorous to large numbers of people because food is a universal, necessary, and sometimes banal part of everyday life. However, eating and drinking represent more than just basic or mundane elements of survival. Food may be perceived as a coveted object of desire or may figure at the center of a traditional celebration or ritual. The consumption of food and drink defines cultures and periods. As suggested by the now ubiquitous adage "you are what you eat," alimentary customs may define an individual or a community. Diet and table manners are indicators of social status in a complex system of codified culinary norms. Food choice, preparation, and modes of consumption contribute to the construction of individual identities. Food and laughter, as two essential elements in human existence, can both be used to question and redefine meaning in culture—meaning linked to the role of the body and sexuality, to religion, to class hierarchies, and to gender relations. In general, both humor and food are identity markers; that is, they each entail belongingness to or exclusion from a given group. Because humor and food may

Introduction

be exclusionary, each defining group and community identity, humor about food in comic texts functions as effective social satire. Comedy about how one eats and what one eats (or does not eat) may involve self-evaluative humor for a given group, or on the other hand, may target members outside the group. Thus culinary comedy may mock either "us" or "them." Those who eat similar food and have similar manners are acceptable while those who differ in their foodways may be perceived as other, strange, even disgusting or vulgar. Foodways help to define social hierarchies and boundaries, also marking status within a given community. In the Middle Ages, these communities may be clergy, bourgeois, *vilains*, nobles, or several more exclusive communities, such as the knights of the Arthurian court. Culinary comedy both satirizes and reinforces the conventions of these groups and their food preferences and behaviors as distinct from other groups. Through examination of medieval conventions surrounding both food and narrative, we may better interpret what may have provoked laughter and invited criticism for audiences of courtly literature.

Gastronomy is beyond a doubt an integral element of French culture and history. Literary representations of food, eating habits, and drinking are central to centuries of French literature. Significant gastronomic elements in Rabelais, Molière, Brillat-Savarin, Balzac, Zola, Proust, Ponge, and countless others come to mind. Descriptions of symbolic foods and customary meals amplify themes. Protagonists are characterized by what and how they eat. Gastronomical discourse is rich in a broad spectrum of codes and symbols, particularly in medieval French art and literature. Medieval gastronomy is a complex form of material consumption; medieval culinary discourse consists of its conventional portrayal. In the Middle Ages consumption of food is marked by three very real possibilities of life: hunger, adherence to conventions of consumption, or gluttony. Extravagant feasting existed alongside voluntary fasting and catastrophic famine, any of which could be daily preoccupations, depending on one's status in society. Evidently both extremes of bounty and hunger were cause for humor and ridicule. The ritual of the communal medieval feast was an elite social event that constructed identity and modeled courtly conventions. In courtly literature, any unanticipated deviation from

Introduction

courtly conventions and practices, particularly at mealtime, is shown as a playful provocation of laughter or a grave infraction with negative consequences.

Because consumption was and is a powerful indicator of identity, medieval attitudes toward food are complex. Eating and fasting were tied to religion and morality. What one ate or abstained from eating could alter one's spiritual identity, most obviously in the case of the Eucharist, hermetic vegetarianism, or the observance of feast and fast days (Crossley-Holland counts between 182 and 227 meatless days per year during this period, depending on observance). Religious food symbols were mocked by many parodic ecclesiastical texts, mock sermons, and in fictional literature by such blasphemous comic images as Renart's holy andouille sausage. Pilgrims, hermits, and some clerics had ascetic diets, the physical manifestation of their spiritual devotion. Vegetables and grains or a vegetarian diet were seen as more pious fare than the courtly feasts of abundant roasted meat and game, the rich diet of aristocrats and knights.

Food could signify the self as distinct from members of other communities. This was especially true in the diets prescribed by different religions. Muslims, Christians, and Jews have dietary codes or food habits that set them apart. Fictional narratives often remark on the differences of the "Saracen" diet with wonder or scorn. The Muslim diet with its food restrictions was seen as exotic and other, and was used to represent cultural differences in literature. Outside of the ecclesiastical arena, socio-economic identity was dictated by food in both courtly and urban life. In short, much more so than in today's diverse and globalized world, what one consumed showed how one lived, worshipped, celebrated, and sinned in the Middle Ages.

Uniting the cultural and literary study of food with theoretical approaches to comedy, humor, and parody proves a fruitful methodology. Previous studies on medieval food have addressed primarily the socio-historical perspective, concentrating on the history of diet and alimentary practices. Though very successful in reconstructing a complex cultural history, they tend to overlook the considerable comic literary use of food in medieval French secular narrative literature. The chapters that follow reflect on ludic cultural representations of food and

Introduction

consumption in late-twelfth- through early-fourteenth-century French fictional verse narrative: epic chanson de geste, *chantefable*, verse romance, fabliau, and beast epic. Culinary comedy and non-humorous references to food nourish three highly conventional genres in particular during this period. Courtly romance, the fabliaux, and the multi-branch *Roman de Renart* contrast traditional convention with many levels of humorous and unexpected transgression, or contravention of the rules. The investigation of the way in which humor and the literary images of food interact in all of these genres, in conjunction with a discussion of didactic manuals and cultural expectations, will reveal much about medieval French literary production and reception.

As will be observed in further detail in the following chapters, specific foods were often considered funny, their mere presence in a scene lending the opportunity for laughter and the occasion to cross the boundaries and go beyond the limits of what is socially acceptable. In romance and epic, roast poultry can be comic, because it often figures in food fights with knights, and because such food fights are a waste of that which is traditionally considered an expensive food and cooking technique preferred by nobles. Statistically speaking, the most commonly consumed food items in the fabliaux are: bacon, capons and geese, cakes, bread, and wine; given their frequency and the potentially high cost in the diet, these items are often the main ingredients of culinary comedy. In the fabliaux, poultry, fish, and bacon also become objects in the endless gender tug-of-war, a sort of sexual currency. Appetite for poultry, such as roast chicken or partridge, is associated with sexual and financial appetites. Gluttony for *char, viande,* and *vin* are connected to lechery and sins of the flesh, while some fruits are viewed as aphrodisiacs. Oats and porridge are likened to bodily fluids in vulgar metaphors. Pork, bacon, lard, and larders come to represent corrupt members of the clergy—as symbols of gluttony, greed, lust, with the suggestion of corporeal resemblance to meat. Attempts at stealing cabbages or mutton, both common staples in the peasant diet, poke fun at *vilain* poverty and ignorance. Rotten foods, cooked foods, and fresh foods alike are employed as projectile weapons, allowing narrators to laugh in the face of famine and to mock warfare at the same time as foodstuffs are wasted in nonfatal battles. Spices are apt to be derided for their strong somatic effects, medicinal properties, high prices, and elite consumers; furthermore, just as spices transform the flavor of a dish, they may also be used to alter the narrative, providing a ridiculous twist. Poorly cooked or poor quality fatty foods, along with overripe fruit, provide comic relief in scenes of indigestion. Foods that are associated with heat, humidity, and flatulence become comic ingredients because of their sexual, aphrodisiac, and scatological associations. Round or phallic shapes of foods (in particular during this period, nuts, radishes, eggs, onions, roots, asparagus, carrots, cucumbers, sausages, etc.) also convey humorous sexual connotations, so that the mere presence or consumption of such objects, because of the resemblance to male genitalia, may signal comic intention.

It is useful to review for a moment approaches to humor, laughter, and the comic. Aristotle put forth the idea that humor is one of the defining characteristics of humanity, yet comprehensive or definitive accounts of terms such as humor, laughter, and comedy have eluded scholars for centuries, beginning with Plato and Quintilian. The universality and broad nature of the phenomena of laughter and humor make an all-inclusive definition impossible. Humor and reactions to comedy may be subjective, culturally specific, and often based on diverse societal and personal factors.

In the *Poetics* Aristotle defines comedy in part as:

> . . . an imitation of men worse than the average; worse, however, not as regards any and every sort of fault, but only as regards one particular kind, the Ridiculous, which is a species of the Ugly. The Ridiculous may be defined as a mistake or deformity not productive of pain or harm to others; the mask, for instance, that excites laughter, is something ugly and distorted without causing pain.

In addition to this Aristotelian quality of the below-average ridiculous action or individual fault, harmless amusement is a key aspect of the comic. Marcel Gutwirth has provided a general definition of the term *comic*, denoting ". . . the range of events, willed or unwilled, aimed at bringing amusement (or simply having that effect)" (6). No attempt at an all-encompassing

Introduction

explanation of these social phenomena of comedy is made here; rather a concise review of existing theories and a synthesis of certain elements and terminology applicable to the present discussion of medieval literary and culinary humor are offered.

Three major modern theories help to explain human humor and laughter, all three of which have been challenged, modified, and qualified over the course of the twentieth and twenty-first centuries. Elements of these broad approaches may be combined and related to different types and forms of humor, more specifically to food humor. Remaining the most accepted of the three approaches today, the Incongruity Theory of humor and laughter was developed by Kant, Schopenhauer, Kierkegaard, and many others. Inappropriate juxtapositions were comic for Aristotle too, particularly in the context of expectations surrounding socio-economic classes. Henri Bergson's well-known treatise on humor, *Le rire,* highlighted the juxtaposition of the mechanical on the human, the "mécanique plaqué sur du vivant," as the essential comic incongruity. The Incongruity perspective dictates that for a situation to be humorous or laughable, it must involve incongruity, or an unexpected juxtaposition. It is therefore elements of absurdity, incoherence, unlikely combination, or strangeness that may provide comic distance and cause us to laugh. Furthermore, exaggeration, overturning of conventions, or the inappropriate use of realistic detail can be incongruously funny.

John Morreall gives a broad new definition for humor and laughter, based in part on the Incongruity Theory, seeing them as amusement that results from the enjoyment of a conceptual "shift." Amusement is an important qualifier for Morreall, who points out that not every incongruous situation is necessarily funny or laughable; some may in fact provoke fear, for example. In working toward a new general theory of laughter, Morreall sees a shift in what is perceived as the most important element: "Laughter results from a pleasant psychological shift" (133). Providing a critical corrective, Morreall adds a caveat to the Incongruity Theory: ". . . though humor always involves the enjoyment of a perceived or imagined incongruity, often this enjoyment is accompanied by and boosted by our simultaneous enjoyment of an affective shift" (135). Michael Clark underlines that it is the perception of incongruity that is amusing (146). The Incongruity Theory of humor and laughter raises the fewest number of theoretical objections of the three theories and involves the fewest number of possible exceptions. One notable exception is the amusement and laughter expressed at actions or images that are expected, that is, those instances that are funny because we expect them to happen—because the punch line is known in advance. For instance, a certain behavior of a well-known character provokes laughter because of its repetition, foreshadowing, and inevitability based on familiar character traits.

In addition, Victor Raskin's linguistic theory of joke scripts, related to the Incongruity Theory and to the General Theory of Verbal Humor, provides a useful perspective. Jokes, according to Raskin, involve an opposition to the "expected state of affairs" and are connected to the abnormal. This type of comic turn of events may be seen in possible or partially implausible situations, but usually it deviates from the appropriate linguistic, societal, or narrative norm. Though the analyses that follow do not adhere to a linguistic perspective, which has its limitations, reference will be made to the terminology proposed by Raskin, who provides a useful typology of these playful "scripts" that we may borrow to better address and classify comic motifs in Old French literature, particularly in the narrative fiction of the fabliaux and the *Roman de Renart* (such as the scripts of Cunningness, Craftiness, Stinginess, Sexual Ignorance, and Sexual Opposition, evident throughout these short texts).

In the second major theory, the Superior Theory, humor and comedy incite laughter through derision. The Superior Theory dictates that one will find amusing those situations in which one feels superior; in other words, we laugh at someone inferior—friend or foe—when we laugh. The humiliation of others is thus funny in the sense that it raises the amused person above the object of their laughter and amusement. This hypothesis, favored by Plato, Aristotle, and Hobbes, requires hostility and/or humiliation to be present in the intent or the reception of the humor and explains why some people laugh when they see another person fall down in the mud or receive a cream pie in the face.

Introduction

Finally, the Relief Theory, or Release of Restraint Theory, holds that laughter is a release of pent up emotional and physical tensions. More physiologically based than the other theoretical approaches, the Relief Theory is limited, far from addressing every instance of comedy or laughter. The Release Theory of humor and laughter was expounded for example by Herbert Spencer and in Freud's *Jokes and Their Relation to the Unconscious*. The Relief Theory sees laughter as almost a cathartic moment, a positive physical reaction that relieves negative emotions based on anxiety, anger, stress, sexual frustrations, or societal constraints. Bakhtin's notion of carnival shares some similarities with this perspective (though unfortunately limiting the exploration of the condoned liberation of laughter to primarily the Early Modern period).

We may draw on elements of all three major perspectives on humor and laughter, as well as classify some of their structures according to Raskin's scripts. Culinary narrative, when allied with comic narrative, becomes a multifaceted literary device of critical ridicule. No doubt, incongruity forms a basis for most medieval humor, especially in comic situations involving unexpected behavior and incongruous use of objects, such as food fighting. But the humorous in the Middle Ages is constituted by more than just the incongruous. The Superior Theory is applicable with ease to the amusing trickery and hostility of the fabliaux and the *Roman de Renart,* texts in which the punch line is based on the humiliation, suffering, and incompetence of others who are often of a lower status. Moreover, many instances of culinary comedy have a tone that is both didactic and amusing, involving a feeling of moral superiority among the audience members who evaluate the caricatures and burlesque actions of the fabliaux characters. The Release Theory is relevant to medieval French comic narrative, which treats explicit social and psychological tensions, often questioned, ridiculed, or overcome through laughter at otherwise taboo or unquestionable subjects. The composition and reception of the fabliaux may be addressed by the Release Theory. A combination of the three theories provides the most useful framework for the study of culinary comedy in the Middle Ages.

As for a brief typology of comic techniques, a distinction may be drawn between the basic types of comedy that occur in the selected texts: verbal comedy, physical comedy, and situational comedy. All of these types of comedy may be integrated into a culinary element; surprise and suspense surround the audience's anticipation of what will happen with a given food item, the formal object of amusement. The incongruity of exaggerations, complications, characters' reactions, and misunderstandings, in contrast to (or in tandem with) our expectations provoke our laughter in parody of highly conventional genres. Food may serve a satirical or parodic function when coupled with unconventional, inappropriate behavior. The power of culinary comedy is its ability to disrupt. Conversely, culinary comedy helps on occasion to reinforce the same conventions it ridicules.

The first chapter presents a discussion of the roles of food and of literary convention in the Middle Ages and the complex manner in which they intertwine, setting literary culinary comedy in its socio-historical context. Medieval attitudes toward food and the implications of codified consumption in the Middle Ages are explored, making reference to textual culinary convention in romance and epic and to extant written cooks' treatises. An overview of the functions of food in culture and medieval culinary narratives accompanies a discussion defining the functions and effects of this humorous device. A contrast is drawn between the ubiquitous image of the bountiful feast and the daily realities of hunger. The focus is on the conventions of feast hospitality and on the excesses of gluttony and food play, with examples of culinary comedy found in romance, chanson de geste, and *chantefable*. The *chantefable* of *Aucassin et Nicolette* serves as a primary illustration of literary food fighting in a mock-epic battle that presents a violent inversion of convention; that is to say, such actions transgress, or infringe upon and violate, accepted social codes and cross the boundaries and limits of appropriate behavior in a courtly setting. The humorously incongruous use of food and exaggerated hunger in epic is equally striking. Certain young epic heroes of the chanson de geste, in particular Guillaume and Rainouart, are portrayed as brutish gluttons whose offensive and sinful actions are dictated by their demanding bellies rather than any traditional sense of duty. The other three contemporary genres treated in subsequent chapters are illuminated by close analysis

Introduction

of culinary humor because they are characterized by irony and ambiguous meaning, all of which are enhanced by incongruous and out-of-the-ordinary consumption.

The French verse narrative texts selected for the present study are generally considered comic because they aim at entertainment, amusement, and happy or successful conclusions. Considering the comedy of eating that transgresses the acceptable and expected boundaries of the otherwise highly conventional world of Arthurian romance, Chapter 2 takes Chrétien de Troyes's *Perceval, ou le Conte du Graal*, the thirteenth-century verse *Perceval Continuations*, *Durmart le Gallois*, the *Roman de Fergus*, the *Roman d'Hunbaut*, the *Merveilles de Rigomer*, and the *Vengeance Raguidel* as examples. A portrait of the conventional feast is drawn and then ruptured through an exploration of incidents of unknightly culinary conduct. Feasts and hospitality are fundamental elements of courtly culture, ridiculed by these derivative texts that situate comico-realism in opposition to convention. Audience expectations are presented and compared to unconventional situations, as we consider incongruity, irony, and ambiguity in romance. The guest-host relations discussed in Chapter 1—consisting of sharing, giving, and receiving food and lodging—provide an opportunity for verbal and culinary exchange and thus offer an occasion for culinary comedy to advance the comic plot to its happy ending.

It is remarkable that in *richesse* of the romance genre, so typified by opulent feast and the generosity of courtly *largesse*, we discover images of hungry knights searching for nothing more than a good, solid meal in a bleak landscape. At the Grail castle in Chrétien's *Perceval* and the *Continuations*, the naïve Perceval keeps his mouth shut except to eat and drink. Excessive eating is linked to his excessive silence. He commits many other social and culinary *faux pas* representing moral failings. The later romance heroes who follow a derivative trajectory exhibit even less admirable table manners, resorting to food fights. We find that as appetite grows in cultural and literary references, respect for convention diminishes. For Perceval, the blind following of seemingly empty convention is punished from the start. Conversely, for the thirteenth-century verse character of Gauvain, eating is an impetus to deviate from chivalric perfection and courtly convention in the *Vengeance Raguidel*. The portrayal of the reputation and renown of the twelfth-century Arthurian court is made suspect by the poor table manners of its best knights in the thirteenth century. Even the formidable Lancelot is degraded when forced to become a lowly kitchen servant in the *Merveilles de Rigomer*. Thirteenth-century French romancers composed with a glance toward past written and oral traditions and a knowing wink to the audience; such imitative romances use food and laughter to evaluate and rewrite.

Chapter 3 turns to the essentially ludic genre of the Old French fabliaux in an investigation of the humorous use of food combined with other subjects, or scripts of comedy. The function of food in episodes involving alimentary, sexual, scatological, social, and religious topics is examined. All three theories of humor, as well as semantic joke scripts, illuminate the comic logic of the fabliaux. Unlike culinary descriptions in romance, limited for the most part to aristocratic consumption, the fabliaux treat food in great detail, from preparation to consumption and (in)digestion in all members of society. We also consider the contemporary dramatic text of the *Jeu de Robin et Marion* in this light. Culinary comedy in the fabliaux treats the status of *vilains,* bourgeois, knights, merchants, innkeepers, prostitutes, performers, students, members of the clergy, and others who populate a predominately urban world with comico-realism. Eating brings members of these groups together in a shift in focus from social classes presented in romance and epic. As familiar communal spaces in the fabliaux, the kitchen and dining table are the appropriate venue for blatant mocking of certain social classes and for the subtle derision of human shortcomings. Food may be an item of trade in a mercantile exchange, a form of hospitality, a means of seduction, or the coveted object of bumbling thieves.

Fabliau episodes of culinary comedy are far more concerned with gender and sexuality than are the romance culinary comedy episodes. Husbands and wives bicker over the menu and steal food from one another. Female sexual and gastronomic appetites are combined in a misogynistic perspective, with the criticism that the female appetite is uncontrollable and sinful, leading men to gluttony and lechery, or tricking husbands and

Introduction

lovers through devious ruses. Furthermore, human relations to food are often constituted as erotic. This relation may be either verbal or corporeal. Rampant female and male appetites are unleashed in unexpected ways as the fabliaux use eating and cooking to explore gender dynamics. In narratives where our disbelief is suspended for the sake of fabliau logic or fabliau humor, where female orifices are portrayed as hungry and male body parts are often mistaken for sausages and meat, food or food-talk may substitute for sexuality. Sexual activity, in particular adulterous activity, is linked to foodstuffs, occurring around food or food-related objects such as tables, pantries, and knives. Moreover, meals may serve as a means to hide or facilitate such activity. More than one fabliau lover hides from a jealous husband under the cover of the dinner table or in the pantry. Meat cleaving and castration are confused. Cheating with food items doubles for cheating in the domains of sexuality and finance. The didactic and moral aspects of culinary comedy are explored in relation to the fabliaux and contemporary *exempla*, as well as in the chapter on the *Roman de Renart*.

The final chapter investigates food humor as it functions in the verbal comedy and cunning ruses of the beast fables, a genre in which most of the anthropomorphic and human characters are driven by the hunger for pleasure, the hunger for revenge, and the hunger for food. Throughout the many branches of the *Roman de Renart* there is a union of human and animal nature, particularly in relation to food. One aspect of life that animals and humans have in common is the need for nourishment, though humans dine whereas animals feed. The characters' rapports with food and with each other reveal much about their qualities and flaws. In the *Roman de Renart,* hunger, food seeking and stealing, and consumption reveal a cynical perspective on human nature, from which few occupations or classes are spared an evaluation of their stereotypical weaknesses and corruption. As in the fabliaux, hunger is associated with violence and deception, here heightened by the urgency and brutality of the animal kingdom. The Superior Theory of humor, in particular, sheds light on the laughter Renart's hungry antics invite. The social injustices of *renardie* are ripe for the humor and societal criticism allowed by culinary comedy. Food and hunger are recurring elements in most branches of the *Roman de Renart* in text and image. An analysis of manuscript miniatures, as illustrations accompanying the literary text, further our understanding of contemporary interpretation because these telling images reveal an animalistic world obsessed by food, with the characters feeding on weakness and gullibility while surrounded by humor, hunger, playfulness, and ignorance.

Culinary comedy represents a significant ludic element of the means by which twelfth- and thirteenth-century poets read, imitated, and (re)interpreted their predecessors with a critical eye. Food humor and food play are both amusing and dangerous. Like other types of play in human culture, food play involves adherence to rules, as well as trickery and pretense. In all of the texts explored, playing with food and different forms of food humor serves to quash both alimentary and literary conventions, calling into question accepted practices and audience expectations.

Chapter One

Food Fight

Medieval Gastronomy and Literary Convention

> Grant fu la joie el paleis segnorez
> Quant ont mengie et beü a plentez.
> —*Aliscans*

Food has always been one of the most essential and revealing elements of material culture because it is necessary for subsistence and survival. Food is also central to daily practices and important rituals, involving necessity, spirituality, and pleasure.[1] Food habits and table manners still serve as a method of transmission of tradition, values, and cultural convention. We may witness both static and changing trends in societal values by looking at food habits.[2] Diverse diets and eating practices are manifestations of cultural norms and differences. Brillat-Savarin's perceptive view of the pleasures and necessities of food, that gastronomy rules the entirety of life because it has to do with all areas of life, is applicable to previous centuries of consumers and cooks. This chapter maps medieval alimentary codes and culinary narrative. Food, cooking, and eating are as crucial to the literary portrayal of medieval cultural codes as speech, dress, violence, and gestures.[3] Serious and humorous images of the edible, tied to pleasure and pain, disgust and appetite, appear across medieval genres enhancing meaning.

Though in the Middle Ages the human earthly body was perceived as transient and imperfect, and bodily concerns were considered ephemeral and less significant than spiritual devotion in this period, food was nonetheless extraordinarily significant and symbolic. Diet, appetite, and the conventions of consumption are indicators of identity. Despite the fact that *étiquette* was not yet a term in French courtly vocabulary, eating and table manners constituted inescapable social codes in this period. Table manners are social constructs that reveal much about societal roles, expectations, and socio-economic distinctions, especially in the European Middle Ages. Images of food, eating, and drinking are problematized by the realities of class differences and the havoc often caused by hunger in medieval European society. Food and drink served as spiritual sustenance and medicinal remedy as well. Special diets for fast days, lean days, pilgrimage, and feast days could mark spiritual devotion.[4] In romance and epic, heroes often vow to fast during a quest or absence until they succeed and return to their beloved ladies (as in the case of Guillaume's promise to Guiborc in *Aliscans*, where he confines himself to dry bread and water). Indeed, feast days were a measure of time for most, even if not everyone had rich meats available to them in times of celebration; "thus eating, in dividing the year and marking the calendar, gives form to otherwise amorphous time. Using food to mark out time is indeed one of the few cultural universals" (Mars and Mars 12). As it still does today, eating special foods also marked important cultural events such as weddings, celebrations, and rites of passage. In addition, we will see how representations of codified consumption and food objects are used to address societal and sexual tensions. Representations of food in the twelfth through fourteenth centuries are conventionalized, and as such, they are well positioned to question and attack other societal conventions.

At the intersection of medieval French material culture and literary production, the chapters to follow trace the diverse combinations of cuisine and wit in secular Old French literature across generic and temporal borders (c. 1150–1350). The human body, consumption, famine, and the possibilities for innovation in the art of cooking with the new food items being traded from other cultures were all growing concerns in this period. Literary codes and culinary codes alike are at stake in medieval narrative fiction. Paradoxically, the prolific twelfth- through early-fourteenth-century period of vernacular secular writing was a time of inventive cuisine and lavish feasts for the wealthy and the struggle of hunger and malnutrition for the less fortunate in real life. Exotic and bountiful feasts were status symbols for the aristocracy or the urban bourgeoisie that were beginning to flourish. Marketplace economies and trade routes were expanding and changing established foodways. Recipe books and didactic manners manuals began to appear, especially among these gastronomically privileged groups in thirteenth- and fourteenth-century urban France. Still, peasants' struggles for daily bread are included only rarely in the literary corpus of this period. There are, however, countless detailed realistic portrayals of fasting, ascetic hermetic diets, and *vilain* food hoarding. On occasion even the courtly world is shown in moments of famine or siege, or errant knights find themselves in wasteland landscapes, though for the most part scholars have neglected these unpleasant aspects of realistic knightly existence. Both overeating and undereating could be cause for laughter.

Food Fights and Feasts

The *chantefable* of *Aucassin et Nicolette* (c. 1195–1200), the only extant representative of a hybrid genre, is one recognized example of atypical treatment of alimentary codes in medieval French narrative. This text combines narrative and lyric forms and is composed in alternating prose and verse, providing unexpected or exaggerated twists on courtly convention on many different levels.[5] As Tony Hunt has shown, *Aucassin* is a pastiche of several courtly models. Its comic discourse carries on a dialogue with several contemporary genres. This unique text exaggerates the conventions and stereotypes of epic and romance to entertain and to make a critical point about the emptiness of convention in courtly culture and narrative. Aucassin is a stereotypical male character who appears to be an ideal hero, physically and morally, with a few humorous peculiarities. His beloved Nicolette's interior and exterior qualities follow courtly convention for the most part. Questioning the relation between appearance and reality, *Aucassin* surprises us by combining imitation and culinary comedy in a world upside-down, Torelore, where gender roles are reversed and societal norms are overturned.

Comically, in this unrealistic *monde à l'envers,* rotten fruit, eggs, mushrooms, and cheese are used as arms by male and female warriors alike. Aucassin and Nicolette arrive in this world-upside-down through the chaos of a tumultuous and unexpected storm in an otherworldly water crossing. What the couple finds in Torelore, a place name itself suggestive of reversal, is equally as chaotic, disruptive—and other. The storm is touted as "grande et mervelleuse" [great and marvelous],[6] and the unknown land of Torelore is described as simply "une tere estrange" [a strange land] (XXVIII, vv. 8–10).[7] The strangeness of the land, as the hero and heroine soon discover, consists of unexpected twists of convention, reversed gender roles, and food fighting. Torelore is the opposite of their home of Biaucaire, which does adhere to most audience expectations of courtly and chivalric norms. The conventional Aucassin cannot accept the gender transgressions of Torelore, so he beats the king until he convinces the overly female monarch to leave his child birthing bed and to rise to the occasion and help his queen, who is fighting inappropriately for her gender and status, in battle.[8] The confused hero does not find the battle he expects. Instead, the battle that the king calls a "grande guere" [a great war] (XVIII, v. 15) upon close visual inspection turns out to be a violent yet silly food fight:

> Il monte sor un ceval, et Aucassins monte sor le sien, et Nicolete remest es canbres la roine. Et li rois et Aucassin cevaucièrent tant qu'il vinrent la u la reine estoit et troverent la bataille de poms de bos waumonné et d'ueus et de fres fromages. Et Aucassins les commenca a regarder, se s'en esmevella molt durement. (*Aucassin* XXX, vv. 14–20)

> [He gets on a horse, and Aucassin gets on his, and Nicolette stays back in the Queen's chambers. And the king and Aucassin ride until they come to where the Queen is and they find the battle of rotten wild apples and eggs and fresh cheeses. And as Aucassin started to watch them, he was very much amazed.]

Aucassin too regards the food fight as a *merveille*, the peculiar sight of which attracts his curiosity as he is drawn into the spectacle. He perceives this activity as completely other, as would the audience. Later, he laughs at his incongruous experience in Torelore. This unconventional battle scene lacks all habitual chivalric arms. Because it is unfamiliar, the hero cannot take his eyes off the culinary spectacle. The conventions of the

Chapter One

battlefield and the rules of the kitchen are distorted in a twofold criticism of societal convention. The hero's reaction grows from astonished amazement in the above prose passage to vocalized laughter in the following sung verse:

> Aucassins est arestés
> Sor son arçon acoutés,
> Si coumence a regarder
> Ce pleinier estor canpel.
> Il[s] avoient aportés
> Des fromage[s] fres assés
> Et puns de bos waumonés
> Et grans canpegneus canpés.
> Cil qui mix torble les gués
> Est li plus sire clamés.
> Aucassins, li prex, li ber,
> Les coumence a regarder,
> S'en prist a rire. (*Aucassin* XXI, vv. 1–13)

> [Aucassin stopped
> And rested on his saddle horn
> So he started to watch
> The full-on battle.
> They had brought
> Many fresh cheeses
> And rotten wild apples
> And big country mushrooms.
> The one who disturbs the water the most
> Is proclaimed the best of the knights.
> The valiant and noble Aucassin
> Started to look at them
> And began to laugh.]

In the narrative structure, the sung reaction and laughter follow directly the list of the food objects used in the ridiculous food fight. The scene uses incongruity to provoke laughter, as a mockery of battle, and indeed of chanson de geste battle narrative formulae. Aucassin pauses for a moment, as does the reader or listener, to take in the unexpected nature of this shocking scene. His laughter is amplified by the repetition and augmentation of the list of the food fight ingredients in the verse description. Different food items are added in the latter passage for further amplification of the absurdity of the scene.

The images of thrown food and the troubled waters further signify disruption. All of the food items are silly in this context and since most are round, soft, and small, they are absurd replacements for epic swords and other weapons (these foods perhaps also carry some humorous sexual connotations). The inclusion of rotten and wild foods adds to the incongruity, as food that is either inedible or unusual. The actions involve battle and contest, in a comic scenario that resembles a game, though the players are quite serious in their ardent fighting. Aucassin's laughter in the sung verse could be echoed in the audience. *Aucassin* is the first text to state so explicitly any courtly spectators' astonished and pleasant reactions to a food fight, implying that the spectacle of the misuse of food is considered amazing, entertaining, and funny in this period because it is so unexpected.

Here culinary comedy questions expectations about chivalric activity and war while it also reevaluates gender roles. This improbable food fight lacks verisimilitude and amplifies the image of gender twisting found with the king in labor instead of battle. Imre Szabics notes that the portrayal of the hero is ironic in this pointless battle, "... la vaillance chevaleresque d'Aucassin qui se manifeste dans une bataille sans enjeu ... une réplique satirique de l'exhortation du père rigoureux des premières sections" (1348). Through Aucassin's fantastic excursion, the topsy-turvy Torelore kingdom is shown to be a typical realm that is not, in fact, typical when it comes to battle and feast time.[9] Likewise, though the characters do not change or develop by the end of their journey, in the end we may interpret Aucassin and Nicolette as typical courtly lovers who actually participate in deviation from the norm of romance.[10] The memorable Torelore food fight scene could not be more incongruous or contrary to the horizon of contemporary audience expectations of epic warfare. It is in the context of ambiguous, ironic, unexpected thirteenth-century texts like *Aucassin* and the fabliaux that we may consider culinary comedy in romance, where the serious historical matter of famine and poverty among errant knights is portrayed in jest. Anne Elizabeth Cobby demonstrates that Aucassin represents "... a character forever at odds with conventions to which he is yet closely linked; and through him we are kept in constant touch with our

Chapter One

literary experience and expectations, whilst being shown that they are far from reliable" (*Ambivalent Conventions* 63). By extension then, the food fight—along with the actions of the accident-prone Aucassin—is disruptive of narrative and societal conventions because of its violently subversive use of humorous, unanticipated ingredients. Neither the Torelore king nor the queen assumes a typical role, while the bizarre spectacle of the battle itself breaks every rule of epic and romance. The appropriation of epic battles and courtly discourse is destabilizing. Throwing food therefore throws the courtly world into an upside-down spin.

More than one fabliau narrative centers on a similarly transgressive food fight. *De Caresme et de Charnage* situates food as weapons and violent characters. Like *Aucassin*, it mocks epic violence and battle. The hero has a suit of armor made of fish, with a roast-eel helmet and fish-bone spurs. Men, fish, and eels are actors in the fight. Pastry ingredients such as butter and flour are thrown around. Charnage acts more as if he were arriving at a picnic than a war; he brings peppered sausages, *andouille,* and mustard to become actors in the fight. Similarly, in the legendary bountiful kingdom of Cocagne, dwellings are made of meats and fish. This intriguing mix of inanimate and animate food objects provides grotesquely absurd humor. This medieval fabliau narrative of transgressive eating and monstrous bodies inspired analogous elements in Rabelais centuries later, as discussed by Mikhaïl Bakhtin as well as Barbara Bowen, Samuel Kinser, and others.[11]

Culinary comedy is not limited to the physical slapstick action of food fights. It also entails verbal food humor, involving puns, innuendos, double entendres, repetition, wordplay, and misunderstanding. Fabliaux titles are indicative of the many forms of culinary comedy: *Le prestre au lardier* [The Priest in the Larder], *Le prestre qui manga des meures* [The Priest Who Ate Berries], *Les perdrix* [The Partridges], *Le bouchier d'Abeville* [The Butcher from Abeville], *Porcelet* [Piglet], *La crote* [The Excrement], and *L'oue au chapelain* [The Chaplain's Goose] and others suggest the centrality of consumption and food-related items. In Renaut de Beaujeu's *Lai d'Ignaure,* for instance, verbal culinary comedy is evident. Verbal comedy is apparent from the title *Ignaure,* in which we see a reference to others' ignorance of the main characters' actions. Concerning food, a servant is scolded because of the poor quality of the hors d'oeuvre course; one is reproached for laughing at the food, for mocking the dishes. Food is thus something not to be mocked in polite company. Therefore, in more than one way, when food does become a mockery it becomes a critical or comic transgression of societal limits and the boundaries set by social mores. It also cannot go without mentioning that the courtly yet bawdy *Lai d'Ignaure* also includes a shocking physical scene of castration and cannibalism, as unfaithful ladies are supposed to eat a meal made from their dead lovers' body parts as punishment for their lust and indiscretion; this morbid meal is ironic and critical of female desire. Cooking, sexuality, and justice become entangled here in a comic context. It is ironic indeed that the women feast on the lovers' heart and genitals literally, though this perverted form of cannibalistic justice drives the twelve women mad in the end.

Feast and Narrative Convention

The connections between food and narrative and food and laughter (or amusement) are strong in many *romans d'aventure* and fabliaux. Moreover, these genres are depicted as frequent after-dinner diversions in *Les merveilles de Rigomer,* for example:

> Et, quant ce vint après souper,
> Si commencierent à border
> Et contoient de lor aviaus,
> Lor aventures, lor fabliaus. (*Rigomer* vv. 3059–62)

> [And when after-dinnertime came,
> They began to talk about and recount their stories,
> Their adventures, their fabliaus. (Trans. Vesce)]

Furthermore, the opening lines of many fabliaux claim their purpose as amusement and laughter. In romance there are depictions of the mealtime recounting of stories either in court, as in *Yvain, le Chevalier au Lion,* or at rich *vilain* or bourgeois homes as in *Les merveilles de Rigomer*. Whether narratives featuring culinary comedy were actually most often read or performed in a mealtime setting must remain conjecture in most cases. While it is beyond the scope of this study to speculate on the very tentative identities of audiences, it seems probable, that many may well have been feast time entertainment, as textual evidence suggests. For instance, in *Le vilain au buffet* a competition is held during a courtly feast for *jongleurs* who recount fabliaux and other narrative and lyric forms. The connection between narrative and food hospitality is also evident in the *Sacristain moine* fabliau prologue, which reminds the character and the audience of the custom that a lodger must share a fabliau or tale with his host; this is usually done at mealtime.[12] In romance, the ashamed character of Calogrenant tells of his embarrassing defeat during a feast time exchange of stories at the Arthurian court in Chrétien de Troyes's *Yvain*, representing a traditional communicative exchange of storytelling in culture and recapitulation in narrative.

Scenes such as those cited in the upside-down *Aucassin et Nicolette*, the *Lai d'Ignaure*, and others we will explore only appear deviant in the face of the conventionally courtly kitchen and dining scenes that they tend to contravene. Elements of the feast were important social signifiers, forming the identity of the romance courtly community. Narrative conventions are linked to table manners. Courtly conventions are tested and reinforced at the feast table. Manners demonstrate many things about the nature of an unknown character's arrival at court. Newcomers are welcomed and eventually integrated into the court during this important public ritual. Weddings and tournaments, often turning points or endings in romance, are marked with culinary rituals and abundant food. In romance, feasts at court are more than a setting or commonplace. The menu and manners of Chrétien de Troyes's knights show their relationship to chivalry, their personal development, and their status of integration into the court. Culinary comedy pokes fun at prevailing notions of the ideal knight; even a knight with the courtly reputation of Gauvain is guilty of uncouth table manners and breach of custom on more than one occasion. Feasts have many narrative functions, as a milieu of action, conflict, recapitulation or foreshadowing, and characterization. Meals are a public occasion for action and narration within narrative structures. The figure of Arthur uses feasts to voice concerns about his society or about his knights. He calls for action, vows to redress wrongs or avenge insults, laments the lost golden days when love was real and traditions were upheld, and talks of absent knights he misses. Prisoners are sent back to court; their entrance at mealtime informs the court and the romance's audience of far-away important events and of the glory of the Arthurian heroes. In romance, mealtime is thus an occasion for the important structural and character development elements of exile and return.

Feast scenes have the utmost narrative importance in romance, both structurally and thematically, as discussed in further detail in Chapter 2. Romancers use food to tell their stories and characterize their heroes. In manuscript miniatures, scenes at table are among the most common subjects of illustration in courtly romance. Tables are depicted as attended by servers and filled with roasted meats, fish, poultry, and communal serving vessels or just covered with a somber and elegant clean white tablecloth. As these feast narratives and images show, eating has social, psychological, and spiritual significance in romance. William L. Boletta comments that "food is one of the accessories of communal entertainment in chivalric society" (384). Far beyond descriptions of ornamental trappings, food and feast enhance meaning and therefore represent much more than accessories. In romance the table is a fundamental courtly space used for: a meeting place for strangers, the dubbing of young knights, the invitation to adventure or quest, the return of questing knights, returning knights' or prisoners' recapitulations of adventure, the return to courtly social life, matchmaking, falling in love, the celebration of marriage, and conflict resolution. Because eating was a communal activity, feasts constituted displays of status—wealth, generosity, courtesy. Moreover, feasts are often served in conjunction with performance and spectacle. Religion also has a bearing on food, in secular as well as ecclesiastical texts in this period. The Fisher King's table is an important spiritual space; his first action in the thirteenth-century verse Mannessier *Continuation* is to invite Perceval to "Mangiez!" [Eat!] (v. 32599).[13] The Grail is a serving dish; the hero's most important quest is to find out "del graal cui on en servoit" [whom the Grail serves] (*Perceval* vv. 3245, 3293, and 3302)—a question repeated throughout the romance. As

Chapter One

evidenced by the Grail procession at the Fisher King's table in the Perceval tradition, food itself may be the center of the spectacle, both visually and symbolically.[14]

With the social and narrative importance of the feast, to which we will return, many a romance verse is devoted to cooking and serving. All of Chrétien's romances include several culinary scenes and table service, as do many other romances; for example, Béroul's *Tristan* has five such scenes, *Le Bel Inconnu* has at least five, and the thirteenth-century *La mule sans frein* has three. Cooks and servers not only figure as the creators of feasts. They are agents of the construction of convention, codifying courtly ideals and on occasion constructing characters' identities by what and how they serve them. Cooks and servers provide the food that binds the courtly romance community together. These figures offer the opportunity for the speech, narrative, adventure, conflict, and courtly ritual commonly associated with central feast scenes.

A representative feast in this tradition would begin as follows. The guests are invited, arrive, remove their arms, and change for dinner, while the venison or other game is brought in and the meal prepared. The narrator adds that dinner etiquette is observed and the service is worthy:

> Et la mesniee n'est pas coie,
> Que toz li menders s'aprestoit
> De feire ce qu'a feire estoit.
> Cil corent le mangier haster,
> Cil les chandoiles [alumer],
> Si les alument et espranent,
> La toaille et les bacins pranent,
> Si donent l'eve as mains laver. . .
> . . . .
> Tuit levent, si vont asseoir
> Riens qu'an poïst leanz veoir
> N'estoit charjable ne pesanz.
> (*Charrette* vv. 2554–61, 2563–65)

> [And the house was not dormant,
> Everyone readied themselves
> To do what was to be done.
> One ran to ready the meal
> Another to use and light the candles,
> To illuminate them and burn them.

> They take the tablecloth and the basins,
> And give water to wash hands . . .
> . . . .
> All rise and are seated.
> Nothing disagreeable or weighty
> Was to be seen or thought in this place.]

A conventional motif, that of the challenging intruder entering during the feast, cuts into the description of the first course of dishes.

Communal meals provide a setting for character interaction, in which the nuances of the table manners of the characters can be telling. The feast is a space of communication, where men and women could come together as equals at court. In romance and epic, the feast may also act as a contrast to other actions, such as quests or battles, because "le banquet instaure une plage spatiale et temporelle, plaisante et paisible qui contraste avec les angoisses et les violences de la narration épique" (Combarieu, "Bonnes" 288). Meals serve as a catalyst to action, or as the scene of central narrative episodes. In the fabliaux and the *Roman de Renart*, culinary space is also the space of play. The kitchen, the table, and the larder or pantry are *loci* of comedy and of conflict across genres. Culinary conflict in these texts represents for the most part class struggle and gender wars.

In general, it is the richness and the variety of the cuisine that are valorized by narratorial convention. For instance, in Chrétien's *Erec et Enide* a feast is reduced to "De mets divers don sont servi" [Diverse dishes are served] (v. 6875) by the narrator who excuses himself to turn to another task. Many typical eating scenes in twelfth- and thirteenth-century romance are truncated because audiences are familiar with their conventions. Narrators warn the audience of their purposeful trimming of gastronomic details. It is a commonplace for the poet to say that a given feast is rich and varied but that either the poet will spare us a detailed description of the dishes, or that we must turn to other important events. The rest is left to audience imagination for the sake of other plot elements, as the narrator explains of Lancelot's meal in Logres, "De ce ne quier je ja parler" [I don't want to talk about this now] (*Charrette* v. 2072). There are so many gastronomic scenes that some must be emphasized over others. With this rhetorical device of culinary *brevitas*, poets in effect highlight the importance of scenes where they do actually describe the intricacies of table setting and the ingredients of a meal. Or, they may highlight the events, dialogue with the host, or action surrounding a meal by downplaying the description of the food itself.

Hospitality and Custom

Complex customs and codes surround food, cooking, and serving in this period. Such codes are echoed in fictional and didactic narratives. Food customs are particularly important in epic and romance feast narratives. For communal eating, table manners and food service figure in culinary manuals and romance alike. Along with these customs and codes comes a complex system of religious and secular alimentary symbolism.[15] Just as one would dress to impress at court, one also was expected to supply food to impress and eat to impress. The notion of custom itself was respected and revered in the Middle Ages, and good table manners were no exception to this reverence for tradition and ritual.[16] From hunting and harvesting to salting meat and food preparation, complex sets of customs were followed. In literary depictions of eating, from generous menu choice to polite table manners, from nutrition and diet to digestion, every action has meaning. Strictly codified, gastronomical etiquette is just as significant as other verbal or physical courtly conventions and cues to status in the construction of identity in the courtly world.

The guest-host relation is fundamental in human society, and is an especially important ideal that defines courtly culture in this period. Hospitality and the keeping of a well-maintained household are a prerequisite of courtly behavior and social status. Hospitableness is the virtue of giving. Hospitality is the offering of food, drink, and shelter to outsiders. A form of ritualistic exchange between guest and host in medieval narrative, it is about welcoming strangers or outsiders—the other—into one's home. In romance, sharing a meal is not only a gesture of *courtoisie* toward traveling peers; sharing food also provides an opportunity for peaceful communication. An exchange of food and drink allows for an exchange of words. Hosts may demonstrate their status through the level of their hospitality.

Food Fight

Hosts who are receiving strangers may also gauge their bond with the guest in their reactions to the hospitality offered. Perhaps the most familiar examples of medieval hospitality today are Sir Gawain's host in the Middle English *Sir Gawain and the Green Knight,* who physically exchanges wild game against things his guest has obtained in the castle, or in the French tradition the Fisher King's hosting of Perceval. Romances such as these treat hospitality as a culinary-verbal exchange. A dutiful concern for the welfare of guests—most often strangers—and for courtly hospitality etiquette is a chief characteristic of Arthurian hosts, as discussed further regarding feasts and *hébergement* in the following chapter on romance. Hospitality is more than an obligation to feed and entertain a guest. Providing food, along with shelter and safety, not only addresses a guest's needs, it creates a connection between guest and host, facilitating their interaction on other levels.

Along with the quality and quantity of the food, emphasis is put on a host's generosity and observance of hospitality convention. In *Lancelot, Le Chevalier de la Charrette,* the hero is offered lodging by his hospitable host who has just returned from hunting venison. Hospitality for him is natural and sensible:

> Li vavasors molt tost errant
> Vient ancontre le chevalier,
> Si le prie de hebergier:
> "Sire, fet il, nuiz iert par tans,
> De herbergier est huimés tans,
> Sel devz feire par reison,
> Et j'ai une moie meison
> Ci pres ou ge vous manrai ja.
> Lonc mon pooir que je ferai,
> S'il vos plest et liez an serai." (*Charrette* vv. 2022–32)

> [The vassal very quickly
> Went to meet the knight
> And offer him hospitality:
> "Sire," he said, "it will be night soon.
> It is time now to find lodging,
> You should do this; it would be sensible,
> And I have a house
> Near here where I will take you.

Chapter One

> I'll do everything in my power,
> If you so desire it, and I'll be happy."]

Lancelot is quite happy and relieved to accept this conventional invitation. He is treated, as any knight of his status should be, with spontaneous grace and generosity by the local lord. The host's family provide an "ostel avenant" [welcoming lodging] (v. 2036) in the kingdom of Logres, where captive family members cater to Lancelot's every need (vv. 2057–76). Dutifully, they jump up to greet Lancelot when he enters the house, then they serve him, disarm him, dress him in a new cloak, and sit him down to dinner. This is typical treatment of a chivalric hero in Chrétien and elsewhere.

These ideals were emphasized even more in medieval courtly literature through a complex discourse focusing on food objects and character actions. Necessity, communication, and confidence are included in a host's offering of food. Hosts and guests together may be praised or condemned by their gracious or uncouth actions in relation to required appropriate behavior. In the Middle Ages, hospitality is both a necessity and a "gesture of friendliness." Therefore transgression, or offense and infringement of the rules, takes place when guests turn the tables on the host in episodes of food stealing and food fighting, as in Rainouart's rude treatment of his hosts at the abbey.[17]

Hospitality scenes constitute one of the most common topoi of romance. Matilda Tomaryn Bruckner's useful survey of the Hospitality motif in twelfth-century romance lists virtually countless hospitality scenes, many of which involve food and drink. If we consult Bruckner's concordance, we find romances with several such instances of gastronomical hospitality. From Bruckner's list of several possible variables of hospitality in a selection of romances, I count the following use of food-related hospitality scenes: *Floire et Blanchefleur* (3), *Erec et Enide* (7), *Yvain* (9), *Ile et Galeron* (1), *Partonepeu de Blois* (about 13), the Old French *Ipomedon* (6), *Florimont* (5), and *Le Bel Inconnu* (6). I would add here that inappropriate abuse of hospitality also occurs in romance, as in *Perceval, ou le Conte du Graal, Fergus, Hunbaut,* and the *Vengeance Raguidel.* Certainly hospitality is one of the most crucial elements of courtly convention observed by literary knights seeking adventure or following the *droit chemin* of a quest. Hospitality in lower classes also becomes an issue in the fabliaux, a genre less concerned with court scenes.

Let us consider two brief examples of hospitality outside the courtly realm. In contrast to the generous hospitality of the courtly communities of romance, some less than courtly fabliau characters find themselves at inns and taverns, where they are supposed to pay for less than hospitable service. In the fabliau of *Plantez*, the innkeeper becomes an object of ruse and laughter because of his position as hospitality giver in an exchange of food service.[18] The contemporary fabliau of *Le pauvre clerc* [The Poor Cleric] addresses hospitality conventions. This tale emphasizes *vilain* greediness and feminine trickery. It recounts the tale of an inhospitable wife who invites a poor student for bread upon return from work at the mill and then refuses to make anything, saying she has nothing. The student has left Paris because of poverty and has had nothing to eat or drink since his departure from the city; he calls on fairly wealthy peasants for their hospitality. Though the wife denies the young man's polite request for hospitality, later the husband returns and invites the student in. The student retells how he saw the rude wife buy pork and take delivery of wine and the servant make bread; this lavish shopping trip turns out to be unknown to the husband, as is the priest hiding in the cupboard (finally the reason for the deceit is revealed). The moral of the story is charitable and hospitable, that "one should never deny bread to anyone, even someone one expects never to see again."[19]

Since food has an intimate connection with identity, hosts are shown serving food appropriate to their guests' status. Civitello also suggests that attentive medieval hosts and cooks were aware of the body's humors and the power food has to alter them; "among the upper classes, the good host was cautious and served a variety of foods to restore the balance of all personality types. Hungry peasants bent the rules and ate a diet heavy in vegetables" (57). The link between food and the bodily humors further suggests that guests may be judged by what and how they eat, hosts by what they provide and how they serve.

The central figure of the Seneschal, or Cupbearer, is another type of host figure. This office has a duty to serve the court. In

Chrétien de Troyes's romances, seneschal Keu's dialogues and actions often take place at mealtime or at the fire.[20] Keu's snide remarks and cynical joking at table are familiar Arthurian staples. Characters' identities are constructed during mealtime in the context of such exchanges. The Arthurian feast is the venue for most of Keu's chiding of young unknowns and of respected members of the Arthurian court alike. Keu makes fun of young new heroes such as Perceval, saying he has no confidence that the newcomer will succeed. Moreover, the Seneschal-come-trickster's most remarkably uncourtly mealtime offenses include insulting damsels and newcomers, and throwing the *nain* into the fire during a feast.

From midday through evening, whether knights are traveling or celebrating, happy reunions at court, meals, campfires, and picnics add zest to romance and epic narratives.[21] Conventions of changing clothes, hand washing before and after meals, and sharing dishes and trenchers at table are part of courtly expectations. Manners and etiquette are usually observed, aside from the exceptions to be seen in the next chapter. Reversals of fortune based on food are another important source of laughter, moaning, or tears, as with Gauvain in the romances of *Hunbaut* and the *Vengeance Raguidel*, or the many *vilain* and bourgeois characters robbed of their food stores in the fabliaux and the *Roman de Renart*. Several romance episodes from the late-twelfth through thirteenth centuries show transgressions of convention at table; the transgression of acceptable limits may come from disruption of the meal by an outside force, or from the unconventional behavior of an insider. Members of a given court or community as well as intruders are guilty of mealtime violations of the rules.

Two different examples of such rule breakers will suffice here. The transgression of the space of the courtly meal is the cause of serious disruption and conflict in the Arthurian romance of *Jaufré*, in which strangers trespass into the dining hall and infringe upon Arthurian customs or offend members of the court.[22] The romance of *Jaufré* is unique as the only surviving Occitan Arthurian romance. This thirteenth-century southern French romance presents criticism of Arthurian power with the violent intrusion of the other at an otherwise conventional feast. Characters (such as Arthur and Gauvain) and values once thought static are distorted through such transgressions at mealtime. The culinary disruption may come from an outsider, as in the case of the *Jaufré* monster, or from within the Arthurian court, as with Keu's mealtime jokes in Chrétien or Gauvain's uncouth food stealing in *Hunbaut*. In the romance of *Jaufré*, Arthur and his court are insulted by an intruder. The monstrous Taulat physically assaults and verbally attacks the king. The fact that the challenger is also a knight, and an insider, suggests his criticism of the Arthurian world from within. Second, the thirteenth-century epigonous verse romance of the *Vengeance Raguidel* also includes the motif of the feast interrupted, among many other comic reversals of chivalric and courtly convention. Completely out of character, Gauvain is portrayed as imperfect throughout the romance of the *Vengeance Raguidel*, often acting against convention. In this less than perfect persona, he uses eating as an excuse not to fight, delaying a battle to chew a few more bites, as observed in the following chapter.

Gluttony and Epic Food Fights

Gluttony is associated with the Original Sin—with Eve's pleasure in consumption of the apple—and it is a sin that leads to other sins of lust, sloth, and envy. It is understood that apples were a sign of sin. In Adam de la Halle's thirteenth-century pastoral *Jeu de Robin et Marion,* Robin gives his beloved some apples, which she stores in her bodice with bread and cheese, thereby associating the apple and other food with the female body, the pleasures of eating with the pleasures of sexual activity. The apples are a sign of his love and lust, while the picnic that they share together from her bodice shows they succumb to gluttony. Even Robin seems to find this food storage unusual when he exclaims that she should put the remaining food back in her basket instead of her bosom. Consumption then becomes a metaphor for sexual activity as Robin sings songs of culinary seduction to Marion, promising they will share a capon, and a pie, eating in a romantic way "Bec a Bec moi et vous" [Mouth to mouth, you and I] (vv. 660, 668).

Gluttony, indicative of immorality and lack of self-control, had to be avoided in order to achieve penitence, purity, and

Chapter One

devotion as indicated in religious and secular texts of the period.[23] All classes were confined to diets that were both available to and acceptable for them; for example, the priestly class was supposed to adhere to a strict ascetic diet, bordering on deprivation in some cases. Furthermore, laughter was seen to be as dangerous as gluttony in monastic life; in some monastic rulebooks both overeating and the laughter of *risus monasticus* were forbidden as sinful. Humorous overindulgence and even deadly gluttony occur in fictional narrative when characters overstep the bounds of acceptable consumption. Gluttons often suffer public humiliation and punishment in medieval French literature, as in one *exempla*-like fabliau, *Les trois dames de Paris,* about gluttonous women who become overly intoxicated at the inn by partaking of too much food and wine and merriment. They fall down drunk in the road, become covered in mud like mere excrement, then are mistaken for dead and buried. The moral of *Les trois dames de Paris* cautions against feminine intemperance outside of the court; these three bourgeois women get stumbling drunk while celebrating a feast day and a wedding. Falling down in the street leads to their accidental death. In an unexpected comic twist, the women return from the dead, following fabliau logic and lack of verisimilitude, to wreak havoc in the streets and promote extravagance, drunkenness, and sin to others.

The behaviors associated with drunkenness and gluttony were considered sinful and excessive.[24] Eating or drinking too much or too zealously to the detriment of convention was considered sinful. Medical and moral treatises alike warn against gluttony. Morality is tied to medieval culinary convention, and sinful behavior is not viewed in a positive light. Though Chrétien's Yvain and the other famished knights-errant we see in a new light in the following chapter survive with scarce meals on occasion, some gluttonous heroes of the chanson de geste could eat their fill from plentiful kitchens. The avoidance of the vice of gluttony was a central preoccupation in these texts. Ménard points out that

> ... tout au long du XIIe siècle, les mots de *felon, culvert, glouton,* sont des injures "classiques" dans l'épopée et se rencontrent indifféremment dans le dialogue et dans le

> récit[25] . . . ainsi l'auteur du *Roland* qualifie de *glouton* les païens et met la même apostrophe sur les lèvres de ses héros. (130)

By this time, *glouton* is a pejorative insult and can be a synonym for *felon*. Just as many actions that did not follow societal expectations were viewed as negative, from a religious perspective, gluttony and all associated forms of excess were seen as dangerous in this period. Gluttony, rules against gluttony, and perceptions of gluttony are all mocked in the comic short fiction of the thirteenth-century fabliaux and beast fable genres. Excess and *démesure* are seen as anything but virtuous for heroes and heroines from Roland on. Gluttons are also those who exhibit uncontrollable hunger and take pleasure in eating, as we will see in the cases of Rainouart, Perceval, Fergus, and Renart, who are never satisfied. Any excessive action may be interpreted as a character's moral flaw, an Aristotelian ugly and ridiculous comic mistake, in epic, romance, or fabliau. Excessive drinking and eating were looked upon with scorn (or forbidden) by the church in general and seen in a pejorative light by poets and didactic writers across insular and continental literature. For example, Ramon Llull's thirteenth-century Spanish treatise on the order of chivalry, and Caxton's translation of it even more so, denounces drunkenness and gluttony, saying that such behaviors pave the way for other antichivalric vices. Eating more than one's share or exhibiting poor table manners were thus perceived as dangerous and immoral. As such, inappropriate alimentary behaviors are popular subjects for didactic manuals and fictional narratives. Gluttony also substitutes for other types of excess, greed, and avarice in medieval French narrative, where characters that overeat or accumulate foodstuffs are equally greedy with money and goods. In the fabliaux, thieves are depicted as gluttonous as well as being stereotyped as greedy and sneaky. Similarly, gluttony often has a strong link to lechery. Priests who overeat often combine this excessive behavior with immoral sexual acts. Yves Roguet also shows gluttony as disruptive of order, concluding:

> La gloutonnerie semble donc s'établir au-delà de la simple politesse sur un dépassement anti-naturel autant que (ou

Chapter One

> donc) immoral d'un ordre du monde selon lequel l'homme respire avec le monde dans une correspondance qualitative et quantitative. (264)

Gluttony is thus disharmonious, causing havoc in the kitchen and rupture of religious and chivalric order. Gluttony is often considered funny or ridiculous in part because its excesses were so severely condemned as a cardinal sin and in part because these excesses are so physically evident.

In fictional narrative and at real tables, big mouths cause big disruption. For Roguet, any *débordement* at the table—that is to say any excess involving the mouth, be it consumption or speech—constitutes reproachable gluttony. The connection is evident between eating and orality; speaking or consuming too much was unacceptable in court. Roguet's study also therefore by extension links gluttony to loquaciousness:

> La mauvaise manière de table qu'est la gloutonnerie consiste aussi en l'excès de parole, qui va de la prise de parole pour qui n'a droit, l'enfant\, le serviteur, la femme, au débordement par celui qui y a accès. Certes il ne convient jamais d'être "trop parlanz" ni "trop parliers" car le trop parler est déplaisant et les exemples abondent de personnages qui savent être discrets, signes que le Moyen Age savait ce que parler signifiait. (264)

In addition to gluttonous speech, it will become evident from the following textual analyses that the Middle Ages also attached signification to the opposition between codified consumption and transgressive consumption. Gluttony in medieval narrative constitutes therefore more than overeating, so for this period at least we may address the philosophical question:

> Is a glutton simply a person who eats and drinks too much (leaving aside ... the question of how much "too much" is to be measured)? It is true that one typical type of glutton eats or drinks too much, not just on one occasion but quite often. But a tendency to eat or drink too much is not sufficient to make someone a glutton. ... it is the person who eats too much because of the pleasures of food and drink who is thought of as a glutton. (Telfer 104)

Indeed, other excessive behaviors that bring pleasure are associated with gluttony in the Perceval tradition and elsewhere.

Gluttony is thus attached to many behaviors of excess and to the physical and psychological desire for pleasure. At table, order must be respected and overeating or overspeaking constitutes overstepping courtly bounds. Table manners apply to everyone; manners must be followed, irrespective of rank, age, or gender. Talkativeness is indicative of poor table manners in this period, as Perceval's mother warns him on departure from the homestead in Chrétien de Troyes. Overindulgent excess and gluttony or related vices are not rewarded. These deadly sins are, however, the frequent target of humor in courtly literature.

The flawed heroes of epic may be evaluated by their alimentary actions, as with the heroes of romance in Chapter 2. In the chanson de geste *Aliscans*, the hero approaches the king's kitchen as he would the battlefield; Rainouart's gluttonous behavior ruptures the narrative and disturbs courtly order. He carries out a food raid and a food fight, his impolite, hurried actions in conflict with audience expectations of a typical epic hero. The excess in his behavior, coupled with the narrator's detailed account of his overindulgent consumption, reveals much critical humor. Here the epic kitchen is plentiful, with prepared meat, fish, and fowl. Humorously, with his characteristic brash and excessive behavior, the insatiable and impolite Rainouart eats everything in sight before it may be properly served at the feast table:

> En la cuisine fu tot seul Renoart;
> Assez i trove grües et mallarz
> Et venoisons, poissons, saumons, et barz.
> Il en a pris a mengier des plus cras
> Et si huma de savor plain un vas;
> Le col d'un cisne a pris, qui estoit fars.
> Quant ot mengié des poissons et des chars.
> (*Aliscans* XCII, vv. 4828–34)

> [Rainouart enters the kitchen
> He finds enough cranes and ducks,
> And venison, fish, salmon, and perch
> He takes only the fattest ones to eat,
> And he takes one whole vessel of sauce
> The neck of a swan he ate, which was stuffed
> And ate fish and pieces of meat.]

Chapter One

So that the audience may be clear on the didactic nature of this particular gluttonous scene, the once generous king even comments on Rainouart's excessive and gluttonous actions. Such savage eating of courtly dishes helps to construct Rainouart's identity. The long, detailed, and varied menu he gobbles amplifies the humor of his actions. Guillaume finishes the family breakfast in haste, because he often thinks of eating before duty: "Li quens Guillelmes fet haster son mengier, / Car en l'Archant en voudra chevauchier" [Count Guillaume hurried his eating, because he wanted to ride on to Archant] (vv. 4641–42). In addition to his hunger, he is depicted as a violent drunkard, mostly in a comic or burlesque tone.[26] He is a rustic kitchen hand turned epic hero. This epic glutton has a burly unkempt beard and is large in stature and jocular in nature. Indeed, Rainouart is one of the comic epic heroes whose exaggerated behavior results in what, fittingly, Daniel Poirion has referred to as ". . . vantardises de rudes guerriers, grands buveurs" (211). His seven-year stint as a kitchen servant and water carrier may contribute to his comic uncouth behavior, and indeed constitutes his identity of Rainouart *au tinel*, the water carrier. Eventually he returns to the kitchen origins from whence he came. In another episode, he laments that he is stuck in the kitchen when his real desire is to join the battle. He talks of sauces and food preparation with the same ardent tone he uses to talk of battle (vv. 3334 ff.). A vulgar caricature of Rainouart's eating and drinking habits is an omnipresent comic element. The narrator says comically that Rainouart knew well how to cook and how to eat. He is known to swagger and fall down by the hearth or participate in drunken brawls, for instance:

> Cil chevalier l'acuillent a gaber
> Et de fort vin sovent a abrever
> Tant l'en donerent tot le font enivrer.
> (*Aliscans* vv. 4455–57)[27]

> [This knight met them, joking around
> And often drinking much strong wine
> They gave him so much that they got him completely drunk.]

Although wine is associated with laughter and joking without violence here, this is not always the case. Rainouart is also

Food Fight

drunk on wine several times in *Aliscans* and in the *Chanson de Guillaume*.[28] In addition to his shopping list above in the kitchen raid, the repetition and accumulation of this epic hero's actions and libations are also comic. In the *Aliscans* culinary comedy of errors, Rainouart knows no temperance and again raids the larder with the same overzealous fervor that motivates him in battle. Rainouart conducts a food fight in a kitchen, attacking the cook who fears him as a dangerous intruder. He throws the cook into the ovens and employs bread as a weapon. Informed by Bakhtin, Susan E. Farrier suggests that violence and hunger served to associate certain European epic heroes with the lower classes, the *vilain* (153). Gluttony does not necessarily lower social status to the *vilain*; rather it questions the conventionality of the portrayal of epic heroes. Rainouart even sleeps in the kitchen after eating too much in *Aliscans*. Elsewhere in the Rainouart tradition, we have a parodic version of other *moniages,* marked by culinary comedy. In an abbey well stocked with meat, fish, and pâté, Rainouart eats his fill without invitation; he enters hungry (as usual), and feels revived by the aroma of garlic wafting in from the kitchen to continue on his way. He forces his way into the kitchen, knocking over the pious cook, serving himself with an ample portion of roast goose. He finishes off this brash eating frenzy with wine and claret in the refectory. His surprisingly uncourtly, excessive, and violent actions force the monks to flee. When the abbot later suggests that he become a vegetarian, Rainouart says that he intends to continue eating all the roast poultry he desires; indeed he awakens from his full-bellied slumber before monks go to pray to partake of a rather hearty midnight snack. He disturbs their pious thoughts, yelling for them to bring more wine and cursing. His actions here are inappropriate for nobles, *vilains*, and warriors alike. With good intentions, he steals and redistributes the wealth of the monks' bakery by handing out bread loaves to the poor. In a series of humorous mishaps and *faux pas*, Rainouart learns that monastic life is not for him. These infringements upon the limits set by monastic society are both anticlerical and antiepic in a sense. The drunken, gluttonous ravaging of the monastery is comic in its unexpected exaggeration of excessive, offensive, and nearly blasphemous actions.

Chapter One

Gluttony is about more than just the quantity consumed. Eating may be a sign of victory, generosity, and wealth in epic, but certain heroes go too far. And their infractions consist of more than just eating too much. In pertinent observation that can apply to the lessons Rainouart learns in the monastery, P. T. Geach points out that it was considered gluttony to eat in any exaggerated or excessive manner; he delineates five of these,

> Eating your food too quickly (*praepropere*), in excess (*nimis*), or too eagerly (*ardenter*), is prejudicial to your health, and may be gravely so; eating too expensively (*laute*) or making a fuss about having everything you eat just right (*studiose*) may lead to a seriously vicious way of living, with the neglect of justice ... or of charity ... too much attention of any sort to the belly diverts vital energies from what is worthier ... (Geach 133).

Heroes such as Rainouart, Guillaume, Fergus, and Perceval, are too keen in many respects, falling victim to gluttony and gluttonous viciousness while succumbing to appetite rather than heeding the call of chivalric duty and spiritual devotion. Similar comic hunger and gluttony appear in *Aliscans* and the *Chanson de Guillaume*. In one episode the young hero Guiot (little Guillaume) becomes distraught and cries over having missed his favorite Aunt Guiborc's breakfast spread, a *studiose* eating ritual that he has long cherished and respected. The older Guillaume remembers an enemy Saracen meal he has seen outside the previous day, counseling the hungry Guiot to feed himself and return calm and sated to the battlefield like his enemies. Indeed, epic thirst or hunger is conventional, but not comic. In contrast, the exaggerated infantile reaction is comical and the reference to his aunt's cooking seems out of place. Guiot even promises to defend his aunt in the event of his uncle Guillaume's death. He says he would pledge to serve his aunt, as she has so generously nourished him. His awkward compliment to his aunt is seen by his uncle as an insult. In the end, Guillaume leaves his nephew behind (forcing him back to his aunt's apron strings as it were) when he refuses to take him to into battle. There are echoes of this with another character in the *Enfances Guillaume*. In the *Moniage Guillaume,* the eponymous hero Guillaume is portrayed as a ridiculous glutton. He is more uncouth than any *païen* enemy confronted by his army. He becomes an obese glutton who is driven to attack if someone interrupts his meal. Guillaume also encourages the monks with whom he lives to eat more often and more heartily than they normally would. Comically, the hero is described as too fat for his clothes. In laisses IX–XI, Guillaume is the object of much jealousy because of his excessive and conspicuous consumption (what Geach would call *nimis* or *laute*). He eats three loaves of bread every day for every one and a half the monks eat; and he is a fussy eater (*studiose*). When they have beans, he requests beetroot, fish, and an entire barrel of wine for himself, not fully accepting their frugal, ascetic food habits. He is shamefully ungrateful, "chasing" his hosts away when he has finished his meal. In a satire of monastic-aristocratic inequality, the monks begin to worry they will starve in his presence and are afraid of his great physical stature. In one instance of physical comedy, when a monk refuses to give Guillaume the wine he demands, the monk is attacked and forced to hobble around on crutches after the violent outburst. They consider his gluttony "folly" and an "outrage" because he is never satisfied. Moreover, to clothe him takes more than double the fabric the monks have for their robes. Unlike the monks, he is unable to fast until *nones*. He is similarly concerned with food in the *Charroi de Nîmes*, where Guillaume hunts for himself and for King Louis and later honors the king by cooking venison for him while on the road. Comparable youthful obsession with food and drink to the detriment of duty or politeness occurs elsewhere, as in the epic *Huon de Bordeaux* and in the romance genre treated shortly.[29] The Old French subgenre of epic *enfances*, in particular, shows elements of comic origins and flaws.

That hunger, a symbol of *démesure*, is these heroes' most notable character flaw invites laughter when it disrupts the serious mood of other chanson de geste narratives.[30] It even leads Guillaume to the unlikely epic space of a fish market in the *Moniage*. *Huon de Bordeaux, Garin et Loherain,* and *Gerbert de Metz* are chansons de geste that include short scenes of culinary comedy. In these texts, it is a comedy of situation and of circumstance, as the characters must fight their battles in the kitchen rather than on the battlefield. In *Gerbert de Metz*, King

Chapter One

Pépin resorts to throwing knives. In *Garin et Loherain*, Begues engages in a food fight in the kitchen, throwing utensils, with an army of cooks by his side. He attacks his enemies with a roasting spit and roasts. Begues's attack has a more serious result than the food fight in *Aucassin*, breaking necks and skulls in a graphic description of epic injuries and bloodshed worthy of the *Roland*.

With a growing number of hungry heroes, food fights become less rare than one might expect in courtly literature. Along with bread, poultry is a weapon of choice in culinary comedy episodes across genres.[31] In the *Roman de Fergus* poultry is food for the hungry hero, a rustic brute with little training in Arthurian table manners. Roast chickens on a spit serve double duty as a weapon against his enemies. Comic plots that center on poultry in the fabliaux are to be found, for example, in *L'oue au Chapelain*, *Les perdrix*, and *Le prestre et la dame*. Partridges also appear along with quail and other birds in Chrétien's *Cligés* (v. 6345) and *Yvain* (v. 1267). The familiar image of the hungry hunter Renart salivating over Chantecler and several other birds entertained audiences of the beast epic. Furthermore, numerous manuscript illustrations of Renart or Isengrin show them attacking, eating, and enjoying poultry.[32]

Medieval Diet, Cookbooks, and Culinary Narrative

A brief look at food in its socio-historical context will help contextualize fictional culinary narratives.[33] Consumption and material culture in literature are beginning to receive the critical attention they merit today, but it is beyond the current focus to give an exhaustive cultural history surrounding medieval food and diet; studies in this area are offered by Terence Scully, Bridget Anne Henisch, and C. Anne Wilson, and the volume edited by Melitta Weiss Adamson. Food was a central preoccupation of the medieval mind. The opposites of scarcity and abundance of food are both portrayed throughout vernacular secular literature of this period. Failing crops or incompliant sailing winds could prove devastating. In thirteenth-century France both rampant hunger and inevitable religious fast days made gluttony a subject of serious sermons and entertaining fictional narratives alike. Medieval cuisine was dependent on the seasons and the success of crops, and bound by the constraints of the church during fast days (most often Wednesday, Friday, and Saturday) and the sparse menus of Lent. The very real and ever-present dichotomy of malnutrition and gluttony invited a critical literary response. In courtly or bourgeois literature, the economy of food becomes representative of other economies and societal institutions.

There is no doubt that food practices are culturally, socially, and geographically defined; in the later Middle Ages they become codified in literature and in didactic texts such as cookbooks and etiquette manuals.[34] Unfortunately, we have no extant cookbooks precisely contemporary with the romances and other fictional works in the present study, though some are contemporary with extant manuscript copies of some of the literary texts. Turning to slightly later culinary manuals can still give us some idea of traditions and conventions surrounding food that were already accepted practice decades earlier. Following the growing number of culinary allusions and descriptions in narrative literature in the twelfth and thirteenth centuries in France, culinary discourse began to flourish in other forms in late-thirteenth- and fourteenth-century France, often as part of didactic manuals. The following chapters reveal a corresponding moral culinary discourse in romance and short fiction. Beyond stock descriptions of Arthurian feasts, or short humorous food episodes, culinary arts narratives grew more frequent among late-thirteenth- through fifteenth-century patrons, some written with a primary audience of both young women and young men mind. Fourteenth-century France began to see cookbook production, codifying consumptive practices and showing pride in the refined manners and habits of the elite at the time.[35] The vernacular dominated in cooking manuals, and vernacular culinary texts, though few in number, became more accessible and more often distributed than Latin cookbooks in aristocratic households from the fourteenth century on. At the same time that the growing marketplace economy was providing more and more food choices and accessibility to different types of foods for the wealthy, more cookbooks and household treatises were also written, though still unavailable to the general public. That which was only hinted at in twelfth- and thirteenth-century fictional narratives

Chapter One

became codified about a century later in how-to manuals such as the cook's guide the *Viandier de Taillevent* (extant in both scroll and codex form) and the homemaker's instruction manual the *Mesnagier de Paris*.[36] These two texts, and several similar manuals, claim to be nonfictional accounts of the craft and art of cookery and housekeeping.

The *Mesnagier* is a didactic and moralizing culinary text dating from c. 1393 written for a youthful bride learning to manage her new household in a well-to-do urban setting. The *Mesnagier* was oriented more toward an urban bourgeois audience than the *Viandier* and other more aristocratic cookbooks, though it is based on the *Viandier*. This fourteenth-century didactic housekeeping treatise warns against gluttony and second helpings, heavy drinking, and snacking between meals, especially for young women. In addition to what may be assumed to be the author's favorite home-cooked recipes, the text gives moral advice on how to keep a first or second husband happy in his home. Parts are based on thirteenth-century source material from which advice and recipes are adapted. The dominant themes are domestic hygiene and marital bliss, both tied to proper food preparation. Instruction for meat preparation, roasting, and stewing is prevalent in this upper-middle-class cookbook, which includes simple, inexpensive dishes and celebratory fare alike. The manual shows several different ways of preparing meats, eggs, and other ingredients. The refined use of spices and sauces showing exotic influences are emphasized; however, the housewife is warned not to attempt elaborate courtly dishes that are too complicated, nor to invite guests who are too high on the social ladder.

Terence Scully calls Chiquart's *Du fait de cuisine* c. 1420 "Europe's first cookbook."[37] This mostly nonfictional account includes instruction for the activities of food purchasing, preparation, and serving. Banquet preparation, planning, and execution are detailed along with French and Mediterranean recipes. The text is in part structured on the daily life of a cook and is focused more on recipes than are previous texts. There are several extant cooking manuals from this period. Four folios of cooking tips are included in the larger encyclopedic work of the roughly contemporary *Recueil de Riom*. Along with a fervent production of other types of manuals (lapidaries, medical and botanical treatises) Anglo-Norman authors also produced a number of culinary texts in this period, usually assembled in anthologies.[38]

In the mid-fifteenth-century romance *Jean de Saintré*, a courtly hero's life is marked by meals and culinary conversations.[39] Jean follows his mother's advice on good nutrition and the avoidance of deadly sins such as gluttony. As a youth, he is a table servant, *un valet de table*.[40] As a knight-errant, Jean often breaks bread with his gracious hosts. Later, he must defend chivalry and does so by throwing an elaborate feast. Elements of this didactic narrative are reminiscent of the twelfth- and thirteenth-century Perceval tradition. Though these first alimentary manuals are somewhat later than the works investigated by the present study, they give us some idea of menus and table manners that endured over time. In addition, such later texts show the continued development of the functions of food.

Manuscript anthologies may reveal much about audience reception of kitchen and mealtime conventions and transgressions of these rules. Manuscript codices BNF f.fr. 1370 and BNF f.fr.1181 contain the *Manière de se Contenir à Table*, or the *Contenances de table*. Let us take MS BNF f.fr. 1181 as an example, a codex dating from the early fifteenth century, which includes: *Les Contenances de table, Autres contenances de table, Régime pour tous serviteurs* and *Les Enseignements de Saint Bernard, le régime de toutes manières* ... , as well as other similar texts such as Christine de Pizan's didactic manual *Introduction et regime que Christine de Pise donna a son filz* ... , and penitential psalms. The short verse poems of the *Contenances* give suggestions for table manners and behavior at public meals and feasts, showing the medieval equivalent of table etiquette, which echoes romance culinary narrative.[41] In the *Regime pour tous serviteurs*, we discover a veritable hospitality manual in which household servants and waiters are instructed on politeness, cleanliness, presentation, and manners. The other texts give advice on manners in all areas of life. To give an idea of the codified nature of medieval consumption, some of the countless manners demanded by these didactic manuals are, for example: one must share certain dishes and cups with one's neighbor, one must not pick one's teeth or nose

Chapter One

at the table, one must wash one's hands and wipe fingers only on the table cloth, one must not put finished bones back into serving dishes, one must engage in pleasant conversation. Some of these etiquette examples, though codified in later texts, appear in earlier romance, where the rules of table manners prove difficult for hungry epic and romance heroes to follow.

A general overview of diet, menus, and typical foodstuffs will be useful in discerning and contextualizing the roles such items are given in fictional narrative. Game and livestock were rare commodities for the *vilain*, with hunting and quality meats frequently reserved for local lords who often infringed on *vilain* land and rich forest resources.[42] Whereas large celebratory feasts remain the stuff of courtly romance, the frugal *bouillie* or frumenty (types of thick soup or porridge typically made of vegetables and grain and served with trenchers of coarse bread) were on the more modest menu du jour at this time for the less wealthy. Aristocrats had more access to protein sources, game meat, and preserved food than did poor communities. Bakeshops and cookshops offered prepared food in cities for the convenience of the wealthy or for travelers who could afford it.[43]

In the *Roman de Renart*, case in point, culinary details are rich in the description of Renart's and Ysengrin's pantries. Hersent reveals the contents of the well-stocked thirteenth-century French pantry: bread, salt, salted meat, cheese, eggs, and beer (VIII, vv. 304–07). In branch IX, Ysengrin demands that Dame Hersent cook capons and roast lamb, an aristocratic feast indeed. Elsewhere, the otherwise carnivorous Renart fills up on peas with lard (a well-known favorite peasant dish in the twelfth and thirteenth centuries) while a knight in branch XIII enjoys roast wild boar and capons, pâté, bread, and salt.[44] When the question of sharing arises in the *Roman de Renart*, the king usually has more than his fair share. In one episode of the *Renart*, the beef, veal, and mutton are all reserved for the royal family, while Renart is left to fend for himself.

As will be illustrated in the succeeding chapters, *li bacons* (any type of preserved pork, usually salted and quartered) figures as a staple in the diet of this period and as a comic device rich in significance in the Old French fabliaux and *Roman de Renart*. In the thirteenth-century *Jeu de Robin et Marion*, a central comic dialogue shows that bacon was very desirable and not always available. Robin has just eaten rich cheese and bread, but this is not enough before noon, because he has a craving for Marion's family bacon:

> ROBINS:
> > Diex, qui ore eüst du bacon
> > Te taiien, bien venist a point!
> MARIONS:
> > Robinet, nous n'en arons point,
> > Car trop haut pent as quieverons.
> > Faisons de che que nous avons;
> > Ch'est assés pour le matinee.
> ROBINS:
> > Diex, que j'ai le panche lasse. (vv. 148–54)

> [ROBIN:
> > Lord, how good it would be to have
> > Some of your gramma's bacon right now!
> MARION:
> > Dear Robin, we won't have any,
> > For it's hung high on the rafters.
> > Let us make do with what we have;
> > It is enough for the morning.
> ROBIN:
> > Heavens, how sore my belly is . . .][45]

Contrasting with the usual courtly diet of venison and poultry found in romance or the salty bacon of the fabliaux, in Chrétien de Troyes's *Yvain, le Chevalier au Lion* the hermit's diet is minimal; until Yvain brings fresh game meat he has only bread and water for sustenance. In *Perceval, ou le Conte du Graal*, the last Chrétien romance, we witness the stark contrast between upper-class secular meals and the more ascetic, pious alternative. The young Perceval's first gluttonous feast, consisting of meat and wine, is stolen from another knight. Later, when he discovers God, he enjoys the simple vegetarian fare of the enlightened and the penitent:

> Mes il n'ot se herbes non,
> Cerfuel, leitues et cresson
> Et pain i ot d'orge et d'avainne
> Et eve clere de fontainne (*Perceval* vv. 6501–04)

Chapter One

> [But he had nothing but greens,
> Chervil,[46] lettuce, and watercress
> And bread made of coarse wheat and oats
> And the clear water of the fountain.]

This new frugal diet helps to construct his identity and spiritual development. Purity is emphasized and the pious man eats for necessity rather than pleasure. The excessive uninvited drinking of wine that occurs earlier in the romance is replaced by pure water. Coarse-grained bread and vegetables show a striking contrast to Perceval's previous unchecked devouring of stolen pasties. As spiritual devotion takes the place of chivalric duty, so are Perceval's hungers altered. Gluttony and the needs, desires, and pleasures of the body have been surpassed as the earthly youth becomes a spiritual champion; we will consider his development further in the next chapter. Similarly, the pious hosts in the *Second Perceval Continuation* abstain from the flesh of meat, but have a bountiful feast of fish including salmon. The hermits are vegetarian, depending on grains, greens, bread, and water for penitential nourishment as in Chrétien as well as in nonfictional ecclesiastical works. Such spiritual diets are significant in verse and prose Grail romances.

Kitchens and dining tables are common scenes across generic lines. Whether the meal consists of a meager *bouillie* or of an elaborate selection of roast game and fowl, it follows a certain order and most diners comply with certain rules and table manners. Aside from those held on non-flesh days, courtly feasts of this period included two to three main courses of various roasted and stuffed meats and birds, accompanied by bread, wine, sauces, and very often pies. Roasting was the favorite technique of court cooks, as evinced in visual and textual manuscript evidence of both romance and cookbooks. Certain days demanded abstinence from meat for all, in which case feasts would provide an equally varied menu of fish and vegetables; the *Mesnagier,* for example, includes several different recipe options for different types of fish. Even more important than the dishes that are served are the events that occur in the kitchen or larder and at the banquet table in the highly conventionalized setting of the romance world.

Literary Implications of Historical Realities

Culinary comedy expresses shifting attitudes toward social and literary convention and serves as complex criticism of conventions and constructed identities, recasting social stereotypes of knights in romance and the movements of *vilains,* bourgeois, merchants, and priests in the fabliaux and the *Roman de Renart.* Changes in social behavior in the private sphere and changing balances of power in the political sphere led to response in literary production, particularly in thirteenth-century fable and verse romance. The different genres that were explored toy with the subversive possibilities of the juxtaposition of food and sex, food and religion, food and human flaws, food and class struggles.

When used and misused, food has a story to tell about the social position of those consuming it. Table settings, cookbooks, and menus distinguished classes. Feasts, with their large number of guests and elaborate, varied dishes, were expensive, and a mark of a higher socio-economic status. In literary representations, namely, romance scenes of weddings or feast days, kings and lords are often measured by their culinary generosity. Their mealtime largesse is a mark of their wealth. For upper and lower classes alike, consumption of food in these narratives is a form of verbal and physical exchange, be it in the mercantile, domestic, political, or even romantic sphere.[47]

The ravenous knights of romance, the gluttonous heroes of epic, and the famished *vilain* of the fabliaux were depicted as suffering from hunger for a reason. Environmental elements affected medieval diet and economy. Detailed accounts of famine (or of the unfair excessive consumption by a privileged few) are to be found in the short fictional narratives of the fabliau and the *Roman de Renart,* though allusions to hunger are made in the chanson de geste and elsewhere. In the twelfth and thirteenth centuries food was not necessarily plentiful or diverse for everyone. Many lower-class people suffered from hunger, malnutrition, and poverty.[48] This is one explanation for habitually hungry, and sometimes *vilain* heroes such as Perceval, Fergus, Renart, Rainouart, and Guillaume. The *Jeu de Robin et Marion* gives an indication of what lower-class people might eat for a celebration; for the group in the play a meager meal of *froment* bread, cheese, and clean water constitutes a good meal, while a potluck of all leftovers (sheep's milk cheese, bread, roasted peas, baked old apples, salty bacon, watercress, a pie, a capon, and salt) constitutes a "feste trop grande" for several people, who all contribute something to the meal (vv. 640–80). The animals in the *Roman de Renart* suffer from the same poverty and famine as the humans, residing in a veritable wasteland where only the privileged or the cunning obtain proper nutrition when it is not a feast day. Indulgence in gluttony or food fights using excess or rotten food were means to address such pressing issues through humor as I have suggested.

Later while these texts were still in circulation and being copied, real conditions became worse. For example, with the drop in temperature in Europe around 1300, climate factors had a great effect on agriculture and the marketplace. Though minor, the temperature change was nonetheless catastrophic for farmers. Then about half a century later (when many of the texts in question were still circulating), the plague caused dietary changes and disrupted the economy; as population and production diminished, prices of food went up. At the same time cookbooks and manners manuals were beginning to be written and copied, with such adverse environmental influences, food became harder to grow and to find, especially for the *vilain* class. Such difficulties are reflected in later texts.[49] Earlier texts too allude to similar catastrophes of failing crops and failing health. Culinary comedy could thus have brought about laughter with a sense of release or relief from the social and physical strains of famine for decades to come.[50]

It emerges as no coincidence that when food supply diminished, gluttony grew less acceptable and more apt to be ridiculed, while manners became more constraining and food humor became more prevalent and more appreciated as a response to these constraints. Looking at the narrative exploits of incongruous hungry heroes and clever *vilains* in this sociohistorical context will prove a valuable approach to the literature of this period. Culinary comedy, with its inherent inversion of expectation, provides a corrective and, as such, is fundamental to the imitative, derivative, and parodic texts we examine next. Observing culinary comedy—with its lasting humorous appeal and potent critical effects—in chanson de geste, theater, romance, fabliau, and beast epic not only gives us a taste of medieval literary and visual humor and medieval diet, it also lessens the distance between medieval compositional strategies and our readings and it addresses the complexity of medieval audience reception.

Chapter Two

Uncourtly Table Manners in Arthurian Romance

> C'a tous mengiers est sausse fains
> Bien destenpree et bien confite.
> —Chrétien de Troyes
> *Yvain, le Chevalier au Lion*

Excessive eating and inappropriate manners in late twelfth- through mid-thirteenth-century French Arthurian verse romance represent a striking departure from the genre's most essential conventions.[1] In the romance genre, culinary comedy serves a significant function as an incongruous element, an unexpected treatment of convention. Conventionality and feast customs are the foundation on which the portrait of the Arthurian court and its ideals are constructed. First to consider is the nature of the chivalric and courtly conventions that we will later see as being questioned by culinary comedy in order to better understand how the misuse of food disrupts courtly norms. The ambiguity in the portrayal of the Arthurian court and the structural and thematic function of the Arthurian feast are explored and then contrasted with the unexpected role of food in Chrétien de Troyes's *Perceval, ou Le Conte du Graal* and the multi-author French Continuations of the thirteenth century. Second, we turn to a comparison of Perceval's alimentary misconduct with imitative comic episodes in four roughly contemporary mid- to late-thirteenth-century verse romances: Guillaume le Clerc's *Roman de Fergus,* the incomplete and anonymous *Roman d'Hunbaut,* Jehan's *Merveilles de Rigomer,* and Raoul's *Vengeance Raguidel*.[2] There is a significant progression in the portrayal of the court that coincides with an evolution in the use of culinary comedy from Chrétien through these epigones. A shift toward comic realism becomes apparent. In a consideration of transgressive meaning, imitation, and literary parody, scenes portraying hunger, cooking, eating, stealing food, and food fighting will be explored. Food and hunger are significant images in these romances; they may be signs used to reinforce the status quo or to question order and convention. Culinary comedy plays with the innate expectations and ambiguities of romance.

The twelfth-century French verse romances of Chrétien de Troyes are at once highly conventional models of the genre and ambiguous narratives that question or mock with subtlety these same conventions. Chrétien's romances contain familiar themes, stock characters, and rhymes that were an inspiration for centuries to come. The conventionality of Arthurian romance invited ironic and critical response from Chrétien's own time on.[3] Conventionality, with the repetition or modification of conventions, creates meaning in the romance genre. When conventions and traditions begin to lose their meaning, imitators and parodists may twist, reform, or attack them to fit their projects. We are caught off guard by humorous incongruities. Though Chrétien's romances have remained the models of the genre for centuries of audiences and critics, it is clear that the romance audience's "horizon of expectations" becomes blurred in Chrétien's world. For the characters, the balance of chivalric duty and amorous obligations is at stake in Chrétien. *Le Conte du Graal* later combines religious devotion with this problematic balance. Knights must prove their worth to the Arthurian court through courtly and brave behavior. Erec, Yvain, Lancelot, and Perceval are characters depicted with flaws and failings in this quest for acceptance and balance. Yvain forgets his promise to his wife when he goes off to seek adventure with Gauvain. Erec forces his beloved into silence when she voices other peoples' critical views of his *recreantise* and loss of reputation; he must redress the wrong of forgetting chivalric glory in favor of marital bliss. Chrétien's Lancelot shows several deficiencies, and offends Guenièvre from the beginning of the romance when he hesitates to jump on the shameful cart to rescue her. As explored further below, the young, unknown Perceval shows his ignorance of courtly expectations from his first day in court, embarrassed by faux pas.

Chapter Two

There is an implication of changing ideals and decaying conventions in such ambiguous portrayals of knighthood.

Though in the French romance tradition the reputation of the figure of King Arthur extends far and wide as the magnificent model ruler, as we see through the eyes of the admiring hopeful young heroes in *Cligés* and *Perceval,* conversely Arthur is portrayed as early as Chrétien de Troyes as a figure often sleeping, forgetful, brooding, and melancholy, hinting at images of an impotent *roi fainéant*. From the Latin tradition and Wace on, Arthur is depicted as the maker of knights, a strong and inspirational figure who attracts men of exceptional prowess and courtesy to his entourage. In romance, Arthur is more of a central figurehead—around which the heroes rally—as opposed to earlier genres, such as the Latin chronicle, where he is shown as more active. Political and military difficulties of the time, as well as changes in narrative genre, contributed to these changes in the depiction of the king and his idealized court. In the beginning of the tradition, the strong and benevolent Arthur holds court, the court that is the model of chivalry for all others. Many romance heroes are Arthurian knights, holding a title and reputation that are beyond reproach because of their association with the formidable King Arthur. Young unknowns flock to the court to prove their worth and join the most respected order of knighthood.

In Chrétien de Troyes's romances, subtle suspicions of imperfection in the Arthurian court appear. Ambiguity creeps into character and narrator perceptions of the Arthurian court. *La Charrette* and *Perceval* begin a tradition of subtle irony and satire of Arthurian institutions. Arthur begins to be an ambiguous figure, wielding power but lost in thought and depression, in Chrétien's later romances and in imitations and adaptations for many decades, even centuries, to follow. In Chrétien, Arthur is shown on occasion as sad, confused, pensive, and melancholic. In some incidents he is not present, is late to arrive, or dallies in bed with the queen. There is a hint at the same *recreantise* that threatens to diminish the stature of other great Arthurian knights such as Erec and Yvain in Chrétien. In *Erec et Enide,* the king laments that his entourage of nobles has been reduced to five hundred. Arthur seems at times unable to live up to his reputation or carry out ceremonial duties. In Chrétien's *Conte du Graal,* when he arrives as a young unknown at court to be knighted during an Arthurian feast, Perceval wonders how Arthur can really be the "maker of knights" if he never speaks:

> Li rois pensa, qu'il ne dit mot,
> Et cil autre foiz l'araisone,
> Li rois pansa et mot ne sone.
> "Par foi," fait li vallez adonques,
> "Cist rois ne fist chevaliers onques.
> Qant on parole n'en puet traire,
> Comant porroit chevalier faire"
> ....
> Li vallez ne prise une cive
> Quant que li rois li dit et conte,
> Ne de son doel ne de la honte
> La raïne ne li chaut il.
> "Faites moi chevalier," fait il,
> "Sire rois, car aler m'en voil." (vv. 882–88, 926–31)

> [The King was thinking, so he did not say a word,
> And the other reasoned with him again,
> The King was thinking and did not sound a word,
> "By my faith," said the youth then,
> "This king never did make knights!
> When you cannot even get a word out of him,
> How can he make knights?"
> ....
> The youth didn't give a chive
> What the king said or told him,
> Nor of the pain or shame
> Of the Queen did he give a care.
> "Make me a knight," he said,
> "Sir king, because I want to leave."]

The comedy of the departure from Arthurian ideals begins here. Perceval doubts Arthur's reputation and begins to question the notion of Arthurian reputation as soon as he arrives at court and believes that Arthur never made knights because the king seems motionless, as well as powerless, not living up to expectations. Though he once revered Arthur's knights, idealizing them and admiring them upon first meeting in the opening of the romance, young Perceval's frustration indicates problems in this otherwise ideal court, where the king does not speak a word and the queen has been insulted. The repetition amplifies

Chapter Two

his frustration and disappointment. Moreover, by remarking that Perceval "does not give a chive," *une cive*, a small, inexpensive, and common culinary herb, Chrétien indicates that the court is beginning to be devalued and questioned in romance at this time. Like some romancers, the character Perceval is disenchanted with Arthurian reputations and ideals, wishing to depart from them. The audience may detect an inkling of narratorial disapproval of empty court reputation and convention, commonplaces that are so familiar at this point as to begin to diminish in significance.

Another subtle criticism found in Chrétien hints at the role of laughter in court. The haunting image of the humorless Pucelle in *Perceval, ou le Conte du Graal* who has not laughed for over ten years points to a need for humor, to a need for the constraints of conventions and curses to be lifted, and to a need for a new type of chivalric hero (vv. 990–1018). We are told that the court fool, whom Keu kicks into the fire, prophesies that the silent maiden will not laugh until the day she sees the one who will have chivalric glory and renown throughout the realm (vv. 1015–18). Her laughter is thus a prediction of Perceval's unprecedented future success and reputation. Though members of the court narrate their stories of valor and victory, defeat and derision, around her, she cannot laugh. When the young Perceval arrives at court to be knighted during a feast, she is saved from this solemn fate. The young unknown gazes upon her beauty and in return she laughs when she sees him (the repeated verb *rire* can mean both to smile and to laugh in this period). Her laughter and speech in front of the entire court feast predicts that he will become the best knight in the world:

> Et li vallez qui s'an aloit
> A une pucele veüe
> Bele et gente, si la salue
> Et cele lui et si li rist
> Et en rient itant li dist:
> "Vallez, se tu viz par aaige,
> Je pans et cuit en mon coraige
> Q'an trestot lo monde n'avra
> N'il iert ne l'an ni savra
> Nul chevalier meillor de toi,
> Ensin lo pans et cuit et croi."

Uncourtly Table Manners

> Et la pucele n'avoit ris
> Anz avoit passé plus de dis,
> Et ce dit ele si en haut
> Que tuit l'oïrent. . . . (vv. 990–1004)
>
> [And the young man, who was leaving,
> Saw a young woman,
> Beautiful and gentle; he greeted her
> And she, him. And she laughed in front of him,
> And while laughing, she said to him:
> "Young man, if you see the end of your days
> By my courage I think and know
> That in the whole world there will not be,
> We will not see, and we will not know,
> Any better knight than you,
> So I know and believe."
> And the young woman had not laughed
> For over ten years,
> And she said this in such a loud voice
> That everyone heard it. . . .]

Just as Perceval brings laughter and a different model of chivalry to the Arthurian court, so do later protagonists in thirteenth-century Arthurian romances such as *Fergus, Hunbaut, Rigomer,* and the *Vengeance Raguidel*. Thirteenth-century romancers used laughter to confront the extensive influence of Chrétien de Troyes's late twelfth-century innovation and refinement in the romance genre. Elements of parody and satire crop up in the imperfect portrayal of King Arthur, the status quo of the Arthurian court, and the best Arthurian knights in these later verse romances. Imitation and adaptation of Chrétien is widespread (no fewer than twelve Old French texts mention him by name), with countless adaptations and intertextual references in several languages. In response to twelfth-century questions and ambiguities, thirteenth-century romancers criticize and transgress conventional portrayals of familiar Arthurian heroes. Thwarted expectations invite laughter and a critical gaze from an audience familiar with prior romances, their idealism, conventions, and ambiguities. The focus of this criticism in later verse romances is usually on heroes' rapports with women, courtly behavior, and table manners. Gauvain and other thirteenth-century heroes of French verse romance become victims of their uncouth gastronomic appetites as new

Chapter Two

models of chivalry are explored. Gauvain, the best worldly knight and model lover of the Arthurian tradition, is depicted in a pejorative light by thirteenth-century verse romances, as in the *Vengeance Raguidel* in which he steals food, and his beloved and his own dogs abandon him for a better man.[4] In *Rigomer,* Lancelot surprisingly becomes an overweight kitchen servant. Bumbling unknown knights such as Fergus are introduced and mocked. Food stealing, food fighting, and weakness due to hunger become indicators of imperfections in knightly conduct and the moral, social, and aesthetic value of the tenets of Arthurian chivalry.

Hunger becomes both a serious and a comic motivation for the famished heroes of romance in this period. The historical threats to courtly society created by gluttony on the one hand, and famine on the other, precipitate scenes of comico-realism that transgress courtly expectations and criticize the idealism so prevalent in twelfth-century romance. Thirteenth-century vernacular verse romances depict realistic physical challenges faced by the real-life knight-errant who occasionally was obliged to fight, steal, work, and even beg in order to combat starvation and poverty while traveling. Many real knights depended on gifts, hospitality, and marriage for their welfare. However, the numerous generous hosts welcoming Chrétien de Troyes's heroes on a nightly basis were not the reality. Such hospitality was not always available, or if provided by rich bourgeois, had to be paid for. In the *Roman de la rose, ou Guillaume de Dole,* Guillaume de Dole is a knight so poor that his lands can barely support his six squires. Later, when he is robbed he actually has to go to work for a bourgeois innkeeper to earn money in order to pay for food and lodging and rejoin his beloved. In an episode rich in culinary comedy, Guillaume de Dole is hired by hostels for pilgrims to work in the kitchen, hunt, and carry out other menial tasks. Out of desperate necessity, Guillaume is shown making bread, waiting tables, making beds, and hunting for a small wage and tips over a period of a few months in each hostel. Only the hunting would have been an acceptable pursuit for a knight; his other duties are inappropriate, demeaning, and therefore comical, but he completes his tasks for the cash he receives. Even more ridiculous, Lancelot too is forced to work in the kitchen under different circumstances in the *Rigomer*. Historically, other poor knights turned to stealing as will be seen with Fergus and Gauvain in fictional narrative. Moreover, for the romancers Guillaume le Clerc, Raoul, Jehan, the *Hunbaut* poet, and certain contemporaries, the importance of eating equals the importance of the occupation of tournaments and valiant deeds so revered in earlier romances.

The Feast in Arthurian Verse Romance

In order to reflect on the manner in which culinary comedy exploits romance convention, we recall the narrative function of conventions surrounding meals and celebratory feasts in courtly literature. In art and literature, banquet scenes evoke the Last Supper or the bounty of heaven; on another level the Grail, the central Arthurian object, brings spiritually plentiful bread and wine to the feast table of thirteenth-century romance and sustains the Fisher King.[5] Communal feasts serve as a sort of pretext or prologue to most Arthurian romances. Weddings, coronations, dubbings, and victories are celebrated by formal feasts. Many romances begin with a highly formulaic description of a grand feast at Arthur's court, as Beate Schmolke-Hasselmann and others have shown. This gastronomic opening scene is more than the simple recounting of a meal. The setting, the lavish dishes, and the guest list have all become a standard in the thirteenth-century. Characterized by ceremony and spectacle, the Arthurian feast is also a milieu of exchange and action. At mealtime knights recount their successes and failures, while unknowns arrive with news, quests, prisoners, or adventure. Meals at court demonstrate the virtue of Arthurian largesse. Such communal occasions also bring the Arthurian fellowship together at the beginning of the narrative and are echoed in feast-day, tournament, and wedding episodes in which narration is combined with consumption.[6]

In the romance universe, many codes and taboos apply to eating and fasting. It should be remembered that "the Arthurian court as represented in medieval romance is, as we all know, much given to feasting and little to fasting" (Sturm-Maddox 119). Keeping in mind that culinary comedy works in romance as a contrast chiefly to conventions such as the opening feast in

Chapter Two

the Arthurian court when knights are subjected to hunger or unusual situations, mealtimes are normally an opportunity for display, entertainment, and testing. Indeed, one of the most commonplace elements of Arthurian romance is the customary refusal to eat until adventure (or news of adventure) comes to court. In *Perceval, ou le Conte du Graal* this topos occurs twice, for instance:

> Que ja par les iax de ma teste
> Ne mangerai a si grant feste,
> Que je cort esforciee taigne,
> Tant que novele a ma cort vaingne. (vv. 2765–69)

> [I swear on the eyes in my head that never
> Will I eat at such a great feast,
> That I will hold court by force,
> Until news comes to my court.]

Arthur's declaration makes clear the important connection between food, adventure, and storytelling. At the very moment that Arthur makes this noble decree, in the next verse, a messenger enters the hall. Comparable vows not to eat while awaiting adventure occur more than once in the *First Perceval Continuation* (vv. 6936–7136 and 12271–12506) and in *Rigomer* (vv. 18–272 and 14827–15530), as well as other contemporary romances, frequently at the beginning of the narrative. Adventure, challenges, and intruders are thus a conventional and expected form of transgression during the Arthurian feast.

Similarly, the *Vengeance Raguidel* opens with a lengthy version of this motif (vv. 1–105), with recourse to Arthur's will to uphold tradition in Carlion, ". . . car maintenir / Vout li rois la costume lors" (vv. 6–7). Though in other romances adventure usually arrives in a timely manner, here Arthur allows the dinner hour to pass when nothing happens:

> Li rois Artus ert costumiers
> Que ja à feste ne mangast,
> Devant ce qu'en sa cort entrast
> Novele daraine aventure.
> Tel fu lors la mesaventure,
> Que li jors passe et la nuit vint,

C'onques nule rien i avint.
S'en fu la cors torble et oscure.
Tant atendirent l'aventure,
Que l'ore del mangier passa.
Le rois fu mus et si pensa
A ce qu'aventure ne vint.
Dedens son cuer cest corols tint,
Que peu s'en faut qu'il ne muert d'ire. (vv. 18–31)

[King Arthur had a custom
That he would never eat at a feast
Until some new adventure entered his court.
This was now the unfortunate situation
That the day passed and night fell
And nothing at all happened.
The court was troubled and dark.
So long they waited for adventure,
That the dinner hour passed,
The King was silent and thought
That adventure would never come there.
He held this anger in his heart,
So that he almost died of fury.]

This passage is ripe with meaning, suggesting the demise of Arthurian, courtly, and romance ideals of tradition, custom, and convention. The long wait is indicative of the difficulty in maintaining tradition and of attaining audience expectations. Arthur is shown as melancholic at this recent state of affairs, so tied is his identity to the enforcement of custom and convention, especially the convention of holding court during feast time and providing entertainment or adventure. The court waits in vain for adventure, for many more lines and a much longer period than in earlier romances. The wait seems interminable, the court empty. When convention is not upheld, or is shown to be empty or unattainable, the principles of the Arthurian court begin to crumble, as we can see in the eyes of the hopeless sovereign and the literal darkening of the court.[7] There are numerous related feast conventions. In addition to not eating before adventure happens, other rules apply, such as not leaving before the meal is finished, as for example in the opening lines of *L'Atre Perilleux* or the *Vengeance Raguidel*.

It is against this idealized and conventional backdrop of the familiar Arthurian feast that humorous treatment of everyday

Chapter Two

life and bodily functions begins to appear. Later thirteenth-century poets reevaluate the traditional Arthurian dining scene and guest-host relations, setting them against less courtly, less traditional episodes involving eating. Because feasts and hospitality scenes are so frequent and formulaic, the audience would be familiar with the conventional scenes of other texts; we may posit that to a certain extent they also would have been able to compare them to unusual treatments of eating customs. In the present study, comic scenes of eating and food fighting are read in contrast to conventional portrayals of the Arthurian feast, revealing that food served not only as a humorous weapon in a thirteenth-century hero's arsenal, but also as a powerful means for poets to call into question literary and social convention.

The literary representation of the feast entails an intricate etiquette of preparation, hand washing, service, table manners, consumption, and social interaction. Elements such as seating arrangements, the menu, strange and *merveilleux* happenings, and verbal or physical exchanges between guest and host are important.[8] Chrétien shows model hosts with: Arthur in all of his romances, Guivret and Evrain in *Erec*, and Gornemant and the Fisher King in *Perceval*. The sharing of a meal between guest and host entails the sharing of food and stories; there may be many hosts along a knight's quest who provide food and reinforce courtly codes. Scenes depicting courtly conventions of eating are not limited to the beginning of a romance, however. In Chrétien's early *Erec et Enide*, a central Arthurian feast shows Arthur is not frugal, ordering his cooks and servers to supply guests with as much bread, wine, and venison as their courtly appetites can consume. All guests, rich and poor, were welcome, Chrétien tells us, and Arthur's spread is the model of generosity, featuring aristocratic game meat and flowing with wine:

> N'en fu tornez povres ne riches.
> Li rois Artus ne fu pas chiches:
> Bien commanda es panetiers
> Et as qeus et as botoilliers
> Qu'il livrassent a grant planté
> A chascun a sa volenté
> Et pain et vin et venoison.
> Nuns n'I demandoit livroison
> De rien nule, quelx qu'ele fust,

Qu'il a sa volonté n'eüst.
Mout fu granz la joie ou pales,
Mais tot le soreplus vos les. (*Erec* vv. 2055–66)

[Neither poor nor rich was turned away.
King Arthur was not frugal:
He ordered the cooks and servers
To bring in great abundance,
According to each guest's desires,
Bread and wine and venison.
Nobody asked for anything at all, whatever it was,
Without receiving as much as they wanted.
It was with great joy that he reigned in the palace
But I'll leave you without the details.]

A similar feast shows Arthur's generosity—how he honors and retains the best knights—in the celebration of Erec's coronation held at Christmas in Nantes in conjunction with the dubbing of new knights and somewhat extravagant gift giving (vv. 6488–6878).

Social graces and the virtue of largesse are important in any courtly setting, particularly when it comes to eating. Erec and Enide are shown conventional courtesy outside the setting of the Arthurian court when they meet a youth in the forest who prepares an impromptu meal of bread, cake, wine, and rich cheese for them with clean white napkins and handsome goblets (*Erec* vv. 3170–80). Erec is so grateful for this spontaneous courtly hospitality that he offers the squire/cook a horse in exchange for the impromptu meal. Later in *Erec et Enide*, even at a hasty meatless meal at the Arthurian court, appropriate table etiquette is followed and guests eat their fill of various fish and fruit on a properly set table (vv. 4237–42). Fish is also an important Christian spiritual symbol in Chrétien's *Perceval* (vv. 3007–10) and in later French verse and prose Grail romances; perhaps in eating fish the court is observing lean-day practices or preparing for Christian holy days, while the narrator is using fish to signal that a significant spiritual moment in the plot is imminent. More than just showing the generosity and spirituality of a given host, serving fish can therefore be a symbol of preparation and of spiritual purification.

In an exploration of class and wealth in this romance that features nobles both rich and poor, we see the kind invitation

Chapter Two

of a poor lord who is unable to clothe his daughter properly or pay for domestic help. Meals remain conventional throughout romance, while only the dishes vary according to the means of the host. The courtly etiquette of hospitality is observed by even the poorest noble host. Even Enide's poor vavasor father, who only has one servant, provides the hero with an admirable feast and a generous, hospitable welcome. Enide takes Erec by the hand and leads him to dine. This dinner invitation represents a crucial point in their relationship. As they sit by the fire, the servant prepares a rather extensive meal considering his lord's modest resources:

> Erec et ses ostes lez soi
> Et la pucele d'autre part.
> Li feus mout cler devant aus art.
> Li vavasors serjant n'avoit,
> Fors un tot seul qui le servoit,
> Ne chamberiere ne meschine.
> Cil atornoit en la cuisine
> Por le soper char et oiseax.
> De l'atorner fu mout isneax:
> Bien sot aparoillier et tost
> Char en broet, oiseax en rost.
> Quant le soper ot atorné
> Itel c'on li ot commandé,
> L'eve lor done en dues bacins.
> Tables et napes, pains et vins,
> Tost fu aparoilliez et mis
> Si se sont au maingier assis.
> Trestot quanque mestier lor fu
> Ont a lor volenté eü. (*Erec* vv. 488–92)

> [Erec sat with his host on one side
> and the damsel on the other.
> The fire burned bright before them.
> The vavasor only had but one servant
> He had no chambermaid or attendant.
> This servant prepared in the kitchen
> For the supper, meat and birds
> The servant was very adept;
> He knew how to prepare with care
> Meat bouillon and roast poultry.
> When the supper was ready
> Just as one had asked of him,

> He brought them two basins of water.
> Tables and tablecloths, breads and wines,
> Everything was ready and set
> They sat down for their meal.
> They had everything they needed
> And had as much as they wanted.]

The order of the feast and accessory rituals, the quality of the service, and the seating arrangements are highlighted here, as they are in most descriptions of feasts in the Arthurian court itself. Manuscript illuminations of Chrétien's romances also reflect the material culture of courtly table rituals. Moreover, Odile Redon, Françoise Sabban, and Silvano Serventi, in *The Medieval Kitchen,* address the conventional order of meals and feasts followed in the thirteenth and fourteenth centuries in France and Italy. The order of the dishes and structure of the feast are important, they show. Hospitality conventions are respected for the most part in narrative because this ritual welcoming feast provides the opportunity for dialogue, as the host and hero converse over the dinner table after they have enjoyed the meal.[9] In *Erec*, the narrator makes a point of saying they were able to talk after dinner. In *Yvain,* the romance is framed by Calogrenant's dinnertime storytelling of his adventures. In the Gerbert *Perceval Continuation,* it is the stated custom that a dinner guest must tell a story (vv. 12996–13263). Though not always an explicit stated rule, customarily guests are fed by their hosts before they are invited into discussion. In *Durmart* (vv. 3737–4148), *Rigomer* (vv. 273–408), and *Fergus* (vv. 1495–2044), guests eat before they are questioned by the host.

In most romance descriptions of courtly feasts, guests are invited to eat and drink *à volonté*. In this period, partaking in a copious all-you-can-eat buffet table was not considered gluttonous, since it was understood that guests would exercise reasonable polite restraint and share with fellow diners. In numerous romance descriptions of hospitality at mealtime, generous hosts, whether rich or poor, do their utmost to provide everything possible for the comfort and dining pleasure of their guests. In a typically courtly royal feast in Chrétien, the rich King Evrain gladly serves a variety of meat, fruit, and wine, providing a fine and proper welcome with ample service (*Erec* vv. 5572–85 ff.). Any deviation from this generous offering of food

Chapter Two

would be noticeable and provide opportunity for comment or comedy. Throughout the romance world, there are traditional and often unspoken duties, rights, privileges, and expectations that the knight-errant must respect when he sits down to sup with the local lord or fellow traveler in the course of his quest. When the guest is a knight of King Arthur, we assume the expectations are higher.[10]

Chrétien is not the only romancer who depicts lavish Arthurian table scenes. The thirteenth-century verse romance *Durmart le Gallois* includes even more culinary details and alimentary conventions.[11] There are many meal scenes, mostly conventional and not comic. In general, we may contrast the images of transgressive eating we will examine to these more predictable scenes that meet culinary expectations. After learning his genealogy, we are introduced to Durmart, who falls in love with a beautiful and courtly woman at a lavish feast of dear and unlimited clear, flavorful wine. The court enjoys a well-dressed, well-attended table with first-rate servants and musical entertainment. In another key scene, Durmart is depicted celebrating a victory meal at a long table before a large fire. Hand and face washing and other manners are observed. The meal is praised for being a mark of generosity and courtesy as Durmart rewards his men. Even squires have plentiful roasted meat and amuse themselves with entertainment at dinner. Arthur too is seen rewarding his men later in the romance; his ally Nogant finds the Arthurian entourage already well-fed and strong when he calls upon their help. It is thus rare for Arthurian knights to go hungry. Likewise, when Arthur is lodged by his cousin Jozefent, he is well served at a brightly lit table around which the guests discuss many subjects and recap adventures. Glory thus grows more at table than on the battlefield. Different classes are present at this feast, but all share the same polite manners, such as the Chapelain, seated at the head table, described as neither foolish, *sot*, nor ruffian. The narrator notes that Durmart le Gallois is seated at the table properly next to the Chapelain, while the youths sit on the floor around them. His first gesture as a maker of knights is to have the squires set the tables, before proceeding with the chivalric ritual. The *Durmart* table is a place of laughter and of narrative. The young Gallois hero, a Welshman like Perceval, laughs and recounts his story of glory. At another feast, Durmart and Le Félon de la Garde share the same *escuele* [dish], giving them the opportunity for verbal exchange. The self-proclaimed "royal" romance of *Durmart le Gallois* thus reinforces courtly ideals and conventions through food and eating at courtly feasts and aristocratic marriage celebrations.[12]

Eating in the Perceval Tradition: A Comedy of Manners

As we saw in the discussion of food habits in the preceding chapter, what one ate was a mark of one's class, while how much one ate or how much one enjoyed it was a mark of morality.[13] Identity is associated with consumption. Diet and behavior indicate status. Furthermore in the Middle Ages

> The type of food, the amount that was eaten, and the way in which it was prepared—these three factors together symbolized the social class or, as was said at the time, "quality" of the person. This expression had already been used in classical texts to indicate the individual character of the consumer and his or her subjective dietary needs, influenced at different times by the environment, the climate, the season, and the task performed, not to mention age, gender, and physical constitution. . . . Dietetics thus began to acquire, alongside its traditional character of health and hygiene precepts, a new role—that of establishing social norms and codes of behavior. These codes became increasingly rigid as time passed, reflecting a similar process in the social order. (Montanari, "Peasants" 182)

Distinctions between town, country, and court were most visible on the dining table, which was an indicator of quality, whether courtly or spiritual. Courtly feast offerings and behaviors could indicate a cultivated, noble background, while *vilains* and clergy had much more limited diets. The pastoral young Perceval is astonished at the Fisher King's feast in Chrétien (vv. 3192–3272), for he has never experienced candles so bright, tablecloths so white, or food so rich. The meal is characteristically aristocratic food such as the well-prepared fatty venison in pepper sauce served on a silver platter and the pure wine served in golden cups (both the meat and the wine would be reserved for rich nobility, in particular the rich game meat unavailable to the *vilain*). He observes the hand-washing ritual using clear, warm water and enjoys his hearty, refined meal. After dinner, they have the opportunity to talk while the servants prepare their beds and costly fruits and spices that would have been unavailable to less luxurious households: dates, figs, pomegranates, nutmeg, cloves, digestive remedies (in this case, pastes made of powdered pearls, herbs, and honey), Alexandrian ginger paste, pure aromatic wine (the wine is prepared without honey or pepper, common flavorings for lower quality wine), and blackberry wine with clear syrup. Chrétien tells us that Perceval "de tot ce se merveilloit trop" [he marveled at all of this] because he was unfamiliar with it (vv. 3272–73); however, elements of this meal would be familiar to an affluent noble household on a feast day. It is humorous that, based on the narrator's comments, the naïve Perceval seems as astonished by the opulent meal as by the mysterious Grail procession. We will return to Perceval's relationship to food momentarily.

Following courtly table etiquette establishes a knight's acceptance within Arthurian courtly and chivalric conventions. In several twelfth- and thirteenth-century Arthurian verse romances, good manners are rewarded. Customs are not merely stated, they are shown in practice. Adherence to custom is of central importance for the characters of romance. Deviance from custom usually has adverse results. This reverence for the principles of courtesy and chivalry is made clear in dining scenes where proper etiquette is contrasted with poor manners. Dining scenes are nearly as common as battle narratives. In romance occasionally, courteous knights receive food whereas rude knights are denied a warm welcome. It is also considered impolite to refuse an offer of hospitality, as when Erec tries to refuse Arthurian generosity to return to his duty but Keu scolds him (*Erec* vv. 4005–17). *Perceval, le Conte du Graal* (vv. 4151–4583) includes similar scenes of return and recognition in the Arthurian court where the hero tries at first to turn down hospitality. Again in the *First Perceval Continuation,* good manners are rewarded by food and bad manners result in refusal. In the most striking instance of refusal, found in the *Merveilles de Rigomer,* Lancelot declines the hospitality of a strange elderly man; the knight's rudeness makes his would-be host cry. Lancelot is punished, in a sense, later in the romance for unconventional impoliteness, so unbecoming of an Arthurian hero. In such episodes, laughable inappropriate actions function both as didactic *exempla*, and as a contrast to heroes who act with tact.

Culinary comedy in romance begins with a departure from the model of the Arthurian courtly feast. The subtle comic criticism that originates in the young, inexperienced Perceval's first lesson in proper and improper table manners in the twelfth century develops, through the operations of literary imitation and adaptation, into full-scale food fights and elaborate quests for food in later romance and other genres. One comic food episode in Chrétien de Troyes's *Perceval* is elaborated and adapted in thirteenth-century verse romances.[14] The intertextually related group of *Continuations* and derivative romances spans nearly two centuries, in a continued exploration of identity and identity tied to consumption. The ambiguity of the unfinished *Perceval, ou le Conte du Graal* invited response and continuation, building off episodes of Perceval's ignorance and poor manners as he debuts in the unfamiliar courtly domain. Much reinvention and repetition with variation appears in the romances that take their inspiration from the culinary comedy in Chrétien's *Perceval*, with an evolution in the episodes involving food, hunger, hospitality, and humor.

Perceval may be interpreted as a *bildungsroman* or as an innovation on the quest formula so prominent in earlier romances. The didactic nature of Chrétien's unfinished *Perceval* has been studied from many angles. It is useful to consider his adherence to etiquette and table manners as well. Perceval's quest is a journey for growth and understanding. Throughout his spiritual journey of self-discovery and apprenticeship in the courtly and chivalric world, the as yet uninitiated Perceval commits both serious mistakes and comic blunders. When the wide-eyed young Perceval first sets out from his family's remote abode to join the ranks of Arthur's knights, he is oblivious to anything other than his mother's teaching. The narrator remarks on his below-average knowledge of the world, "Mais il ne savoit nule rien / D'amor ne de nule autre rien" [He knew nothing, not of love nor of anything else] (*Perceval* vv. 1941–42).

Perceval then shows this naïveté through his actions and errors. The unknown, untrained young hero follows maternal instructions literally. Misunderstanding based on his mother's teachings results in awkwardly humorous situations.[15] For example, his well-meaning yet overly zealous greeting and kissing of La Demoiselle de la Tente during his second adventure shows how Perceval's home schooling often provokes dire consequences. Though he later learns more about the courtly world from his mentor Gornemant, Perceval's tendency to follow advice to the letter has an even graver effect in one familiar instance; in heeding Gornemant's warning against impolite loquaciousness he fails to ask the requisite questions that would illumine the Grail mystery at the Grail feast. It is left to the audience to determine that by extension any blind following of convention does not necessarily produce the desired reactions in the courtly universe. Transgressive actions with food, here the consequences of taking advice and convention too literally, further criticize the conventions themselves.

Perceval begins the romance as a stranger to the court and a stranger to convention. Food is at the center of Chrétien's exploration of the nature/nurture dialectic, an opposition treated by several Old French romances. Perceval's relation to food forms his identity, through inclusion and exclusion. Numerous gaffes season the first part of the romance, designed to demonstrate Perceval's raw background. Meanwhile, his true aristocratic nature is revealed slowly, and he becomes indoctrinated with the precepts and trappings of chivalric and courtly convention. Food is part of this development from the beginning. Hunger is one of Perceval's characteristics from the outset of the romance, where Perceval demands that his mother, who tries desperately to keep him at home, feed him before his departure for Arthur's court,[16] "'A mangier,' fait il, 'me donez! / Ne sai de coi m'arraissonez'" ["Give me something to eat!" he said. / "I don't know what you're trying to reason with me about"] (vv. 455–56). The last meal with his mother is not insignificant, considering the ramifications of his departure for her. From the beginning, Perceval prefers eating to reasoning or speaking. He is concerned with his body and the physical trappings of knighthood, rather than with meaning and convention. Scenes of cooking, serving, and eating food occur

Uncourtly Table Manners

throughout the romance (*Perceval* vv. 2571–73, 2582–84, 915–19, 3284–89, and 8236–44). Undeniably, in a narrative so colored by culinary detail, table manners serve as a gauge of the knight's worth because in Chrétien's era, table manners were an evolving part of flourishing court and city cultures:

> The development of table manners, which occurred at the height of the Middle Ages in both cities and courts, played a part in the cultural establishment of privilege, defining its style as much as its content. Courtly and urban manners were defined, first and foremost, by exclusion—a rejection of anything rustic—and nowhere was this more evident than at table. Tableware, and the way the table was laid, also distinguished one class from another, as did the art of cooking itself. (Montanari, Introduction 250)

"Anything rustic" was therefore considered other in the world of courtly romance, and any rustic behavior, such as poor manners, was also the butt of many narrative jokes. Chrétien's comic Demoiselle de la Tente episode functions as the primary illustration of Perceval's uncouth table manners and therefore of his uncourtly upbringing, sheltered from the tenets of knighthood and court behavior. The inexperienced Perceval, sure to follow his mother's advice once again but remaining ignorant of the details and precise nuances of appropriate etiquette, helps himself to another man's pasties. The hungry and fatigued young knight enters an unknown young woman's tent in the absence of her knight. The narrator emphasizes his hunger,

> Li vallez a son cuer ne met
> Rien nule de ce que il ot,
> Mais de ce que geüné ot
> Moroit de faim a male fin. (vv. 696–99)

> [The young man took nothing to heart
> Of what he heard.
> But because he had fasted;
> He was dying of hunger in misery.]

Thus "Por la fain qui formant l'angoisse" [Because of the hunger that greatly distresses him] (v. 707), he is attracted by the sight and smell of freshly cooked victuals. In another

Chapter Two

departure from knightly behavior, he advances and serves himself with little hesitation. He does not listen to the woman's plea. The Demoiselle thinks mistakenly he has come to rob her of her ring. On the contrary, the narrator tells us that Perceval is interested only in the full wineskin and the three fresh meat pies he finds under fine white linen. His hunger motivates him to steal and consume these meat pies and wine (vv. 700–11). Perceval takes pleasure in drinking a good portion of the wine,[17]

> Et verse an la cope d'argent
> Do vin qui n'estoit mie liez
> Si en boit sovent et granz traiz. (vv. 710–12)
>
> [He pours into the silver goblet
> The wine that had not one bit of sediment
> And drinks frequent and large gulps of it.]

The gluttonous portrayal of Perceval recalls the brutish young heroes of epic discussed above, and identifies him as rustic and noncourtly. Here Perceval is portrayed humorously as a bumbling fool with no manners rather than as a malicious thief. The narrator exclaims that "Ne li anuia pas cist mes!" [Nothing displeases him in these offerings!] (v. 705). The quality of the linen, the wine, and the food indicates that he perhaps would have received pleasant and generous hospitality from a very wealthy host had he followed convention. Comically, Perceval is unable to finish all the stolen pies and invites the astonished maiden to join him. Though he makes this (conventionally medieval) polite attempt at sharing and then carefully covers the leftovers, he gets into trouble, not with the Demoiselle, but with her knight. The unwitting host returns to discover that his dinner has been gobbled up by an impolite stranger who neglected to ask permission. In tears, the traumatized Demoiselle describes the hungry intruder to her knight:

> Mais un valet gualois i ot,
> Enïeus et vilein et sot,
> Qui de vostre vin a beü
> Tant con li plot et bon li fu,
> Et manja de vos .III. pastez. (vv. 751–55)

[A Welsh youth, disagreeable, *vilain*, stupid,
Who drank his fill and more of your wine
And ate your three pies.]

The comedy resides in the fact that the audience is aware of his mistake and his origins, but that Perceval himself remains ironically ignorant of his breach of codes of consumption. The references to Wales and to *vilains* are meant to amplify the description of "rustic" origins and manners. The humorous and somewhat shocking pie-stealing episode, as an example of hospitality rituals gone awry, provides more than just a few gastronomic giggles for the audience. The episode underlines the principal themes of the romance and marks a significant milestone in Perceval's journey and inner quest. This memorable and influential scene is also given comic significance in light of the serious mistakes Perceval makes later at the Fisher King's table. Furthermore, the pie-stealing episode in the tent does more than serve a didactic purpose, inviting imitation and reinterpretation from later romancers. There are three other major meals in *Perceval*, all of major significance. The mysterious meal at the Grail castle and the mostly serious meal with Gornemant are equally significant.[18]

The *Perceval Continuations* and several other thirteenth-century French romances are influenced by this central episode of culinary comedy. Food is central to the portrayal of Perceval's development in the prose romance *La Queste del Saint Graal* because when the young knight takes food without asking he is still an earthly knight; and when he refuses it he has developed into a more spiritual character who seeks spiritual sustenance. Looking at the serious spiritual allegory of the Bread of Life in the prose romance tradition, Boletta notes that Perceval's ". . . abstinence from food and loyalty to Christ are related" (386). In addition, food shows both character development and generic evolution in the verse romances, where it is a central comic device in the *Continuations*. For instance, in the Wauchier *Continuation*, Perceval becomes even more hungry and food-obsessed than in Chrétien's romances, especially on two occasions in the forest when he is frustrated by the lack of food in the wild yet bleak setting.[19] In the Mannessier *Continuation* the first thing Perceval does when meeting the Fisher

Chapter Two

King is to eat as soon as the Fisher King bids him to do so, "Mangiez, biau sire" (v. 32599). Food is at the very center of the Mannessier text and its spiritual journey, including the creation of food by magic (vv. 42469–638). Just as the emphasis on the Grail as an object providing sustenance is underlined, in the Mannessier *Continuation,* Perceval is now in a sense a glutton of food and of speech, who is not afraid to speak at table or ask questions; he waits until his host offers food to partake of the meal. The *Continuations* show him as sometimes sad or confused, frustrated or desperate. The analogous character of Fergus is cast in similar light decades after Chrétien. The food-stealing episode and the central alimentary passages inspire imitators or epigones of Chrétien on three levels. First, food and consumption may be used as a test of a knight's experience and courtesy. Second, through such comical errors, the romancer may begin to question conventional courtly behavior. Finally, gastronomic transgressions invite audience interpretation and criticism of narrative constructs.

The *Roman de Fergus:* Imitation and Culinary Comedy

Awareness of strategies of imitation and reinterpretation in this period may inform the exploration of the comic and parodic use of food in thirteenth-century romance. Arthurian verse romance, with its stock characters, well-known quests, codes, and the values of King Arthur's court, attracted an especially significant amount of adaptation and imitation. Widely disseminated for many years following their composition, Chrétien's romances present an Arthurian universe that is at the same time steeped in ideal chivalric and courtly tradition and permeated with comedy and irony, inviting comic and parodic response from successors. Familiar Arthurian paragons of chivalry are replaced by rustic unknowns, and courtly behavior is distorted in times of desperation. From Chrétien through some of the later prose romances, audiences are presented with subtle hints of changing ideals and decaying conventions.[20] The power of such criticism is enhanced by culinary comedy.

Compositions following in the footsteps of Chrétien's five successful romances show his influence, with varying degrees of parody, pastiche, and illusion. A vogue of imitation of the Arthurian verse romance marked early- through mid-thirteenth-century French and Insular literary production. As Beate Schmolke-Hasselmann and the contributors to the collection of *The Legacy of Chrétien de Troyes* (ed. Lacy, Kelly, and Busby) have shown, not many romancers escaped the influence (indeed the anxiety of influence) of Chrétien. Often, medieval romancers imitated to create. Creation was a form of renovation. The fact that he was a reference in the century following his work leads one to conclude that his successors, his *pasticheurs*, were often trying to come to terms with Chrétien's work and perhaps paying homage to him. Thirteenth-century authors had to deal with the presence of Chrétien's reputation and influence. Beate Müller notes that, "parodists have also been suspected of simply being envious of the success of others and resorting to parody as a means of revenge" (5). Though perhaps not completely a form of revenge, in a sense, thirteenth-century romance imitation can act as confrontation. Through imitation, the poet could address his models face to face, accepting certain elements and rejecting others. Biting humor or world-upside-down critical inversion represented one stance taken by imitators in this period. The *Fergus* treats themes similar to those found especially in Chrétien and the early-thirteenth-century *Continuations* of Chrétien's *Perceval*, such as the balance between love and chivalry, the importance of reputation, male friendship, and the rules of *courtoisie*, as well as the importance of custom, tradition, and convention.

The thirteenth-century reader of *Fergus* would almost certainly be familiar with some of Chrétien's oeuvre, and any thirteenth-century reader of Chrétien would have noticed to some extent that romancer Guillaume le Clerc has imitated, unashamedly borrowed from, and cunningly responded to this target material, these "hypotexts," to use Gérard Genette's term.[21] Reducing this romance to the essentials, Guillaume le Clerc takes *Perceval* and the *Continuations*, which feature the story of discovering one's innate nobility while searching for the Grail, imitates them, reworks them, and rearranges them with new material, in order to tell the story of an uncouth youth's search for sufficient food, a decent suit of armor, love, and a seat at the Round Table.

Chapter Two

By focusing on examples from the thirteenth-century French verse romances of *Fergus* and *Hunbaut*, it is evident that such poets chose lesser-known Arthurian heroes and a series of minor quests. Though these romances have been seen by some scholars as somewhat parodic, while others have dismissed them as mere (or poor) imitations of Chrétien, they have much to reveal about thirteenth-century compositional strategies and the use of humor. Let us now consider in detail two romances bound together in the thirteenth- to fourteenth-century anthology of Chantilly MS Musée Condé 472, a rich codex that also includes romances of Chrétien, the prose *Perlesvaus*, and four branches of the *Roman de Renart. Fergus, Hunbaut,* and the *Merveilles de Rigomer* are colored by comic vision. The *Roman de Fergus* is a highly imitative romance, a pastiche that recombines material from all of Chrétien's romances and from the later *Perceval Continuations* with new material and humor.[22]

Guillaume le Clerc, composing *Fergus* around 1225–30, relies heavily upon episodes from the Perceval tradition. From the opening lines of the *Fergus*, Guillaume le Clerc consistently imitates aspects of the Arthurian universe as presented by Chrétien de Troyes and the *Continuations*. In *Fergus*, the eponymous hero is modeled on Perceval, but he seeks a hearty meal and a satisfying nap rather than the Grail.[23] Fergus takes what John L. Grigsby termed Perceval's "avid eating" ("Heroes" 49) to a new level. The later romancer's use of Fergus, as an unfamiliar hero who fights with roast chicken on a spit rather than employing more chivalrous arms, indicates a critical view of knightly codes and conduct in earlier texts. Whereas in earlier romance Arthur's knights have a reputation for nimble swordplay, the ravenous Fergus becomes known for his prowess in food fighting. This is a comic and amusing text that often mocks its hero; Guillaume le Clerc alludes to the entertainment value of the romance, "Grans joie viegne as escoutans!" [May great joy come to those who listen to it!] (*Fergus* v. 7012).

Fergus undergoes a similar journey to Perceval's during which he obtains knowledge of the courtly world, though the thirteenth-century romance does not address the same serious spiritual issues. Akin to Perceval's courtly and chivalric training, the youthful Fergus too shows development as he both takes advice and learns from his mistakes. The transformation of the hero is a comic element in *Fergus* and its hypotext. From beginning to end, the romance shows Fergus's development and integration into Arthurian society. Depiction of his carnal appetites for food and sleep takes over the depiction of a young hero of aristocratic heritage. This draws attention away from the nature/nurture dialectic first presented by the character of Chrétien's Perceval toward a more realistic and physical emphasis. Fergus's gastronomical infractions introduce incongruous and transgressive elements into the burgeoning comico-realist tradition in romance. From the beginning, his *vilain* nature is highlighted by impolite and violent actions motivated by hunger. This comedy of action has a different effect from that in the chanson de geste where the heroes' violent actions are sometimes motivated by hunger or excessive eating; though hunger and thirst try the stamina of Old French epic heroes, in the *Fergus* the realistic portrayal of bodily needs mixed with comedy shows the fallibility of romance society and the imperfect hero's place within it. Because of his body and its needs, Fergus suffers; as Grigsby wrote so aptly of Chrétien de Troyes, "Chrétien knew how to make his heroes suffer" ("Heroes" 42). For Fergus, the suffering from hunger is as intense as other heroes' painful suffering from lovesickness or from battle wounds.

The earthly human body is explored further in these later texts.[24] The noteworthy amount of sleeping, eating, food fights, and other noncourtly pursuits gives the work a less courtly or idealistic tone than the texts it imitates. Though clearly Fergus's adventures of the quests for the wimple and the magical shining shield have been inspired by the serious and meaningful quests led by earlier heroes of Arthurian romance, there is a lighter, more comic tone to them than in Chrétien or the *Continuations*.[25] Fergus seems overly preoccupied with his body, and the following examples show how this concern for the body is used to comic ends, transforming ordinary knightly encounters into hysterically incongruous jesting. Subsistence and survival are valorized throughout the romance over adventure and glory. Fasting is emphasized over feasting in the comic replay of this perennial dialectic. Fergus is always hungry and shown getting into trouble because of his insatiable appetite. The

Chapter Two

thirteenth-century hero of verse romance is in search of food nearly as often as he is in search of the object of his quest.²⁶

Contrary to Arthurian values as laid out by Chrétien, Fergus turns to villainy and lawlessness. Guillaume le Clerc mentions several times that both Fergus and his horse are thin and famished (e.g., vv. 3671–72).²⁷ Some of Guillaume le Clerc's comic perspective is adapted from the *Second Perceval Continuation*. In one scene, Keu the sarcastic Seneschal, or cupbearer, and Arthur and their hungry traveling entourage attempt to invite themselves to an impromptu dinner. Keu in his usual impolite manner threatens to take by force the roast bird he craves.²⁸ In the analogous episode, Fergus has not eaten for days, is riding along, and suddenly glimpses smoke rising from a fire. Fire would be easily recognized by the hero and the audience as a sign of the kitchen and cooking, as travelers of all ranks often cooked over fires in the open and kitchen chimney smoke could be visible from afar (as in one branch of the *Roman de Renart*, where the smoke attracts the hungry Isengrin). Upon close investigation, he smells chickens cooking on a spit, and rides up to a group of robber knights who are preparing to sit down for a meal. Brashly, Fergus jumps down off his horse and throws down his arms, intending to share their meal. Without a polite greeting or conventional request for hospitality, the uninvited Fergus grabs a rare large loaf of freshly baked uncut bread and spiced wine all for himself.²⁹ Comically, he is so determined to fill his aching stomach that he grabs the hot cooking utensil, "not caring if he burns his hands." In picking up this utensil and burning himself, he shows that he is not only uninitiated into the ways of courtesy and chivalry, but that he has no training in the kitchen and little knowledge of food, cooking, or proper manners. Then he eats and drinks until his appetite is sated without uttering a word. In a humorous and parodic reflection of epic battle, he attacks the chicken and the wine, consuming it in one *coup*, just as he downs his human adversaries with ease in one forceful *coup*. The swiftness of his desperate actions and the lack of reflection or courtesy on his part represent a departure from culinary and hospitality norms, inviting laughter from an audience who is ironically aware of his buffoonery and insolence, and who may laugh because of feelings of superiority, if we apply the Superior

Theory of humor here. Rudely, Fergus steals food from fifteen robbers, with such a disregard for courtesy that even the outlaws' villainous leader comments on how offensive and uncultured he is. Hence, as the outlaw's statement indicates, Fergus's mode of consumption disrupts an already corrupt and marginal model of chivalry. His manners identify him as somehow lower than the *vilain* outlaw knights from whom he steals. Moreover, the comic twist is that the Arthurian knight intrudes on someone else's feast for once, contrary to the convention that anticipates challengers arriving to interrupt the typical Arthurian feast day. In contrast to Fergus, the narrator indicates that the leader of the robbers possesses a unique perverse sort of courtesy. He declares that the group will permit the intruder to eat his fill and only afterwards request he pay for what he has consumed. Fergus hears them, but comically continues to chew and takes another whole loaf of bread. This excessively impolite action provokes his estranged hosts to react (vv. 3338 ff.). The head robber reminds the intruder of the code of the time, saying that the rude stranger was never invited, never called when the meal was served. Accusing him not only of improper manners but of sin, they call Fergus a *glouton* and remind him that one just does not do that without asking, and particularly without paying. The interaction with these comical robber knights represents a displacement of convention and a realistic image of knights who were forced to turn to stealing and criminal acts to survive their travels or fulfill their duties.[30] In *Rigomer*, Lancelot is also confronted by robber knights who attempt to take his arms and horse; this is a commentary, using physical comedy, on the growing number of outlaws and bandits in France at the time, as reflected in legal texts, sermons, and several fictional narratives. As will be seen shortly with the *Roman d'Hunbaut,* it is humorous here that the courtly and normally well-fed, well-provisioned Arthurian knight is robbing the robbers themselves. Furthermore, the comedy resides in the critical diatribe against Fergus's failure to observe conventions of consumption or honor among criminals. The narrator invites us to imagine the surprise and disgust of even these robber knights who are themselves on the margin of society. They are marginal in that they live in the forest and steal, outside the influence of the Arthurian court and the constraints of courtly

Chapter Two

etiquette. Fergus disrupts and ignores the most *vilain* of common courtesies as he continues to ruin the meal.

In this episode marked by physical humor, the enraged robber knights retaliate once they realize Fergus has consumed their meal without compensation. Comically making excuses and amends, Fergus attempts to explain the custom of his country, claiming that one normally eats one's fill before discussing the details of the bill. Fergus offers them his new silk tunic as payment, but the robbers intend to take his horse and arms instead. Overcoming great odds, Fergus then instigates a food fight and risibly defends himself by throwing roasting chickens and burning skewers or bits of wood from the cooking fire (*Fergus* vv. 3243–3406). For a knight who is considered by reputation in this text to be "the best except for Gauvain," this is surely astonishing behavior. He vanquishes thirteen of the fifteen unwitting outlaw hosts, and Guillaume comically remarks that they were thus paid what they deserved.[31] Two hungry survivors beg for mercy, so Fergus sends them back to Arthur to be reformed. He then falls asleep with a full belly, drawing a close to the episode. In a juxtaposition of *vilain* behavior and courtly convention, the food fight episode amplifies the text's perspective on the nature/nurture dialectic, demonstrating that no matter how much chivalric training, courtly indoctrination, or hereditary nobility one has, it is still possible to return to one's roots, even to the point of animal savagery. Here Fergus's expectations of quests and hosts are dispelled. Nothing remains of the lifestyle he imagines when as a youth, just like Perceval, he is impressed by the spectacle of Arthur's awe-inspiring entourage come out of the forest. His hunger for Arthurian status and noble chivalric life is supplanted by his physical appetite.

This episode from the *Roman de Fergus* also recalls Chrétien's Demoiselle de La Tente episode, in that they are both scenes where a young knight turns to food stealing, showing his lack of manners. Earlier allusions to Perceval in the text make the connection clear. The purpose of these food-related incidents in the narratives is not merely as comic relief. Comic heroes develop over the course of the narrative. The food scenes show the characters develop from country brutes with no proper manners into courteous Arthurian knights in part because of their aristocratic blood, though they do not realize their own noble identities. In the end, both become reinscribed into Arthurian order, learning to control the body and its appetites. Fergus assumes he is owed food by his unwitting hosts, making a similar error to that made by Perceval with the Demoiselle de la Tente. Guillaume le Clerc is thus continuing to highlight the questions of courtliness and identity raised in Chrétien de Troyes's romances. He adds to this imitation a further note of comedy, thus amplifying the humorous and critical implications found in the original. The sharing of a meal between guest and host is one of the most important Arthurian customs, as we have seen, as it provides the opportunity for communication and exchange. Here, however, is a twisted portrayal of the custom and no expected guest-host relation or customary dialogue is possible. Therefore, in this instance, Guillaume responds to Chrétien and the *Continuations* in demonstrating that the Arthurian ideal is a false construction and does not hold up under all circumstances. The unmistakable inappropriate actions destabilize expected romance ideals.

The body and hunger are presented in a more realistic fashion in the *Roman de Fergus* and *Hunbaut* than in twelfth-century *romans courtois* or *romans d'antiquité*. Fergus's unacceptable eating habits become evident when, after some successful fights, Fergus is riding along in a stupor, mocking the memorable passage of Perceval's love-trance provoked by the image of drops of blood on the snow that remind the young lover of his lady's complexion in Chrétien. In commonplace fashion, Fergus declares his love for the lady Galiene. He swears not to enjoy a night of food and lodging until he is reunited with her and she is unharmed (*Fergus* vv. 2546–2808). Foreshadowing hunger that will bring about an episode of culinary comedy, the narrator remarks that it has not occurred to Fergus to eat for two whole days, so persistent is he in his amorous quest. In a common romance vow that is later proven impossible, Fergus has sworn not to let food or lodging delay his quest for his *bien aimée*. The determined lover thinks only of his beloved, but soon his hunger overcomes him. Guillaume le Clerc uses repetition, until we can almost hear the growling of hunger pangs in his stomach in this realistic detail concerning the body and its appetites. They plague and torture the young

Chapter Two

knight, to such an extent he thinks to himself that if he had buckets of silver he would relinquish them for a piece of bread. Bread, and especially good or pure bread, being a rare commodity at the time of composition, Fergus is unable to find any.[32] He becomes obsessed by his ever-growing hunger until bread replaces the female object of his quest. Such vows are mocked in a similar manner in the fabliau of *Guillaume au Faucon*, in which the hero goes on an exaggerated hunger strike until adventure leads him back to his lady; like Fergus, the fabliau protagonist turns weak, pale, and hallucinates, not from lovesickness but from his insufferable hunger—an inappropriate cause of these symptoms for a courtly lover. The moral value of this type of conventional vow is questioned through humor.

In the occasionally didactic tone of this romance, Fergus's absurd or uncouth actions are explained with a proverb: "Par besoign fait on maint desroi: / On dist que besoigne n'a loi" [Necessity is the cause of much wrongdoing; they say need knows no law] (*Fergus* vv. 3287–88). Fergus often turns to inappropriate violence in times of need or confusion. Hunger and neglect of the body had already arisen as a problem in Chrétien; they are the cause of much humorous and uncourtly behavior. For instance, when Chrétien's Yvain has been driven mad to live as a deranged Wildman in the forest (*Yvain* vv. 2785–9954), he turns to eating raw meat and sharing a hermit's hard, dry, moldy bread baked thriftily with barley and straw. Eating raw meat shows that he has lost touch with his court culture and indeed with human society. In a similar proverbial tone, Chrétien explains that the food seemed fine to Yvain, "C'a tous mengiers est sausse fains / Bien destenpree et bien confite" [Since hunger is a well prepared and well mixed sauce for any meal] (*Yvain* vv. 2854–55).[33] Both proverbial narratorial interventions underscore the idea that even Arthurian knights are driven to ignore courtly conventions to survive.[34]

In contrast to the beginning of *Fergus,* where food was scarce and had to be stolen and eaten quickly, the narrative ends with an appropriate resolution, marked by food and plenty. This time gluttony rather than desperate hunger is portrayed in a different light. As expected, the conventional wedding is celebrated by a plentiful feast, but with three times as much food as was needed for the guests. There are realistic culinary details such as the clouds of smoke rising from the kitchen (vv. 6942–81). Despite Fergus's frequent hunger, here the romancer underlines the abundance of food in the romance, intervening to say that the Arthurian entourage stuffed themselves to their hearts' content. Guillaume le Clerc then assures the audience that he is more than capable of describing the meal and the manner in which it was served and consumed, though he sometimes chooses to omit the details. Guillaume is responding with *brevitas* to the prevalent descriptions of culinary scenes and menus present in contemporary texts.

Le Roman d'Hunbaut: Gauvain's Good Reputation and Bad Manners

Other romances, such as the slightly later thirteenth-century French verse *Roman d'Hunbaut*,[35] expand the corpus of food narrative and culinary comedy. Hunbaut was composed in the third quarter of the thirteenth century during a climate of fervent narrative imitation and parody. Despite some unfavorable twentieth-century scholarly reviews, *Hunbaut* is interesting as part of a wave of thirteenth-century parodic and transgressive comedy, where food fighting and food stealing become prominent comic motifs. Before three hundred lines of this critical and humorous romance have passed, both Gauvain and Arthur remark upon failings in the king's power and the stature of his court. Schmolke-Hasselmann noted that in *Hunbaut*, even "Arthur, who is universally held to be wise, often behaves stupidly in practice" (64). Like criticisms appear in Chrétien, as we have seen, where Arthur is portrayed as both the powerful "roi qui les chevaliers fait" [king who makes knights] and a silent melancholy figure who does not participate in the action.[36] The simply suggestive and ambiguous twelfth-century portrayal of Arthur as pensive, inactive, or defenseless is magnified further in *Hunbaut*.

Culinary comedy in the romance of *Hunbaut* is marked by situational comedy and irony. It is not the particular foods that the protagonists eat, but the circumstances of their hunger and how they eat the food when they obtain it that is funny. In *Hunbaut*, the failing Arthurian court is mocked further when

Chapter Two

the traditionally central character of Gauvain forsakes Arthurian and chivalric conventions in order to sate his voracious appetite. It is atypical that not only Perceval and Fergus—who come from an unsophisticated background—but also Arthur's renowned and refined nephew Gauvain, are driven to impolite and silly behavior by their grumbling bellies. A *vilain* emerges in Gauvain when his self-discipline and conventional behavior succumb to human needs and desires. As with Fergus, hunger reduces Gauvain to just a man or nearly an animal. In one focal incident, Gauvain and Hunbaut set out for an adventure that is marred by mishap and the challenges of realistic travel and survival in mid-thirteenth-century Europe. Their journey as companions follows courtly conventions and borrows many commonplaces. However, Gauvain ignores several stern warnings about the scarcity of food for the duration of their intended itinerary. Bakeries and cook shops in tents were widely available to travelers in the mid-thirteenth century, selling loaves of bread, roast fowl, and pies outside of cities, as illustrations detail in contemporary *Roman d'Alexandre* manuscript images. However, the adventuring knights' realistic journey leads them to a land devoid of merchants or wild game. This type of wasteland is not incongruous in and of itself in the French Arthurian corpus, but Gauvain's behavior in the landscape of this particular narrative is incongruously humorous.

Moreover, it is clear from several such instances of incompetent behavior that by this point in the Old French romance tradition Gauvain's character is no longer immune to human weaknesses. Here he leaves aside his habitually eloquent courtly discourse that audiences have come to expect, complaining direly that he is absolutely famished.[37] Usually known for eloquence in court and finesse on the battlefield, the once model knight has a humorous confrontation with hunger rather than conventional jousts and witty repartees. Through Gauvain's hunger, attention is drawn to the body and realistic details (*Hunbaut* vv. 847–1277). Hunbaut retorts with remarks in the tone of "I told you so," for he is more familiar with the terrain and knows that chances of finding game to hunt, food to buy, or even a crumb of bread are slim. The expected retort, as a punch line, is humorous because with Hunbaut we have antici-

Uncourtly Table Manners

pated the outcome of Gauvain's actions, and it is even more ridiculous because it is about food, which is normally not an insurmountable problem for the Arthurian knights. With comical, friendly banter, Hunbaut questions Gauvain's preparedness for adventure, in an implied sarcastic criticism of Arthurian knights in general.

When motivated by hunger, Gauvain is no longer the model of courtesy he once was. He is ridiculed by situational culinary comedy. His loss of his typical courtly speech and status as the paragon of Arthurian chivalry and courtesy when he is faced with realistic everyday physical challenges is a source of comedy. In a comedy of manners episode reminiscent of Fergus's chicken-stealing, Gauvain spots a smoking fire with juicy, tantalizing poultry roasting on a spit.[38] Gauvain declares that with a little courtesy, he will succeed in getting them something to eat. Hunbaut approves but warns ironically against the use of violence, and the comedy of action ensues. Gauvain asks the knight tending to the feast if he may partake in their delicious meal. When he hears the rude response and refusal of hospitality, Gauvain fights him with ferocity, stirred by hunger, until the inhospitable hosts abandon their meal. Then the victorious Gauvain gorges himself on this bountiful stolen feast. After Gauvain's comic disregard for his warnings, Hunbaut reluctantly joins him in the uncourtly feeding-frenzy. The description of their actions is comic in its excess and exaggeration. With the humorous incongruity of this culinary episode, the romancer is critiquing the false nature of Arthurian courtesy as only suggested by Chrétien de Troyes. Flaws are revealed through the actions of culinary comedy, playing on fallibility hinted at by Chrétien.

In the *Roman d'Hunbaut,* survival and subsistence overshadow convention with realistic details of food; scenes often involve descriptions of rustic cooking that provide comic realism. In courtly feast scenes, descriptions of food preparation are usually truncated because the emphasis is on the serving and enjoyment of the meal. In both *Hunbaut* and *Fergus*, there are realistic descriptions of roasting on a spit over a campfire, details of rustic cooking lacking in earlier texts. For such romance heroes, sustenance becomes more of a central

Chapter Two

occupation than table manners. As in the *Roman de Fergus*, the *Roman d'Hunbaut* shows the heroes' return to the norm and reintegration into courtly life, also represented by a copious and celebratory feast. This community banquet contrasts with their nearly solitary and savage meals on the road. In addition, courtly feasts, though often excessively prepared, are without urgency, violence, or physical comedy. In *Hunbaut*, once Gauvain's hunger is sated and he resumes his normal chivalric activities, he saves his sister and sends her back to the court with Gorvain, who then recounts the heroes' adventures over dinner (*Hunbaut* vv. 3415–3618).[39] The audience would no doubt be familiar with this commonplace setting, and ritual feasting is thus linked once again to conventional narrative in the end. As in the other romances discussed above, these characters must participate in this conventional courtly feast to show their good conduct, to recapitulate their stories, and to be reinscribed into the Arthurian status quo.

In addition to providing entertaining criticism of convention, episodes of culinary comedy such as those in the examples selected here serve an essential purpose in the structure of the narrative. A final illustration from the satirical *Hunbaut* demonstrates the structural importance and relevance of culinary comedy. Other episodes are tied to the central episode of Gauvain's pilfered meal. Gauvain and his companion Hunbaut are pursued later by the very knight whose meal they interrupted. Coincidentally, he turns out to be a forgiving prior acquaintance of Gauvain's. This second meeting presents another guest-host situation and an opportunity to demonstrate sophisticated and polite table manners this time. This character, with his connection to food, becomes crucial to the heroes' development and to the plot, since this host's castle controls the only port from which they can provision themselves and embark to reach their intended destination, the abode of the king of the Isles. Thus the injury to the host caused by the stolen food and the subsequent reconciliation suggests that the heroes are allowed to rectify their actions and eventually to achieve their quest and become reintegrated into the court. In this sense, culinary comedy is tied to narrative structure.

Knightly Kitchen Duty

Gauvain is not the only model Arthurian knight who is mocked through culinary comedy. Several other romances are heavily influenced by Chrétien yet deviate from and question his conventions through culinary comedy, building on the ambiguities in the portrayals of all of the ideal Arthurian knights. The *Merveilles de Rigomer* is one of the lengthier examples of a sustained pastiche and occasional parody of earlier romance convention. Many familiar characters, such as Yvain, Cligés, and Keu, as well as scores of common motifs are reused and reinterpreted. Structurally, it presents narrative formula, themes, and episodes reminiscent of Chrétien's conventions, as it alternates the adventures of Lancelot with those of the foil Gauvain. In addition, *Rigomer* recalls prose and verse Grail romances in the mysterious otherworldly destination that is the object of the Round Table knights' quests as well as a measure of their worth. One of many indications that something is wrong with the system is the curious presence of the knight without weapons (who has no name and is referred to as unarmed), as well as numerous attempts made by outlaws to steal Lancelot's arms, in an endeavor to render him impuissant and to question his identity, with one episode literally removing every chivalric and courtly element from his identity through the device of culinary comedy.

In this mid- to late-twelfth-century verse romance, Lancelot finds himself prisoner and defenseless after losing his magical lance. Disarmed and dismayed, he succumbs to a cunning woman who gives him a ring that makes him forget everything. Lancelot tumbles into a downward spiral and is in a sense punished for his failures as a knight and lover that have accumulated in this text as well as intertextually. He forgets his identity and reputation as a knight of Arthur's court. In losing his identity and connection to the Arthurian community, he essentially loses everything. A conniving woman leads him to the kitchen to torture and humiliate him. As a kitchen servant and unwitting cook, Lancelot is forced to do embarrassing kitchen labor. The incongruity of a knight in the kitchen is even more striking here than in the case of the epic hero Rainouart, whom we saw earlier in his familiar role of kitchen help and glutton. These

Chapter Two

manual tasks are demeaning for any knight, approaching punishment or penance. The fact that his captor is female adds further insult to his changed identity. She leads him around like an animal, forcing him to chop wood for the kitchen fires and to cook meals. Because the behavior of these heroes of two different literary genres, epic and romance, warrants shame and embarrassment, they must suffer, as Grigsby demonstrated regarding Chrétien's characters. However, Lancelot's suffering here is of an unusual nature, as it is not battle, lovesickness, or exile that tortures him mentally and physically, but rather household chores and food preparation. This episode of Lancelot's time in the kitchen recalls the shame and public humiliation he experiences in *La Charrette,* but with an implication for class hierarchies. It is demonstrated that there is little difference between knights and servants or craftspeople, two groups that appear often in a positive light throughout the text. The other victims of the rings' transformative powers are forced to become blacksmiths, masons, weavers, carpenters, and farm hands while extended descriptions of these activities suggest sympathies with such less than courtly mundane activities normally reserved for members of a lower socio-economic status. These unknightly tasks would have been perceived as funny and transgressive, as suggested by the narratorial intervention in which the audience is asked to promise not to laugh if the narrator recounts the specifics of the ex-knights' weaving and serving activities. It is evident that the women's task of weaving and the servants' kitchen duties when performed by knights would have been construed as incongruous, inappropriate, and therefore amusing by the audience.

Kitchen duties clash with knightly duties. Lancelot's origins and noble nature could not be further from the culinary role he is expected to play. Much humor results from the incongruity of this situation, questioning both the construction of Lancelot's identity and the construction of chivalric precepts in society. This denigration continues over a period of an entire year of captivity. Adopting *vilain* eating habits, the knight soon grows fat and grotesque. The one-time model of chivalric prowess is thus lowered to the status of kitchen help. The narrator compares him to an animal after this humbling sojourn in the kitchen: "Mais tot i estoit bestïaus / Et ausi fols comme une bieste" [But soon he became an animal / And as foolish as a beast] (*Rigomer* 14002–03; trans. Vesce). The narrator also notes that the knight behaves like a crazy and ignorant creature that does not know the difference between right and wrong; in behaving like an animal around food, eating too much and not caring about morality or the dangers of gluttony, Lancelot's incongruous actions provoke laughter. In this case the culinary comedy is situational. It is not the food itself that is inherently silly, but rather what Lancelot is forced to do with it. Anything other than hunting or enjoying a feast would be beneath his status. In contrast to his irreproachable reputation for strength, courtesy, and noble origins repeated throughout the text, in the kitchen the audience witnesses the ridiculing of one of the most respected Arthurian knights in a comically absurd situation. Other members of this world-upside-down court full of no-name amnesiac servant knights laugh at Lancelot. The narrator repeats the distinction between his former knightly deeds and feats of prowess contrasted to the demeaning tasks set for him in the household. His typical behavior is so transformed by this wearisome experience as a servant that the audience wonders if he can be reintegrated into his former position at the top of Arthurian courtly society.

Though far more humorous, this episode has a similar function to Yvain's madness in the forest in Chrétien's *Yvain, le Chevalier au Lion*. Both knights fail and must suffer humiliation and eventual madness. They both live like animals, consuming a diet that is inappropriate to someone of their social status, in Lancelot's case too much food, and in Yvain's, raw ascetic hermit's fare. The comically monstrous transformation of Lancelot's body from human to animal in the *Rigomer* is even more noticeable than the unwilling change in his demeanor. He becomes a fat, grotesque figure, losing his stature as a model of male beauty and strength in the grease and grime of the kitchen labor.

The narrator concludes this episode of culinary comedy by underlining that Lancelot's life is like a prison and his kitchen duty is difficult. The captive knight is found in a later recognition scene that is poignant but not conventional. When Gauvain discovers him in this sorry state, he is brought to tears by the shocking distress and gluttonous *vilainie* of his long-time

Chapter Two

companion. Lancelot does not recognize Gauvain, reacting like a scared and confused animal because of his new role and new environment. He does not even recognize armor, believing that Gauvain is a stranger in a diabolical metal suit; tellingly, he tries to convince Gauvain to learn a new trade, then he threatens him, saying he will roast or drown him alive, and banishing him from the kitchen. He has become fat and gluttonous as well as stronger; the narrator amplifies this uncharacteristic description by saying Lancelot carried an oxen yolk all by himself, likening him to a horse or camel. Here the ridicule of Lancelot is contrasted to Gauvain's chivalric and courtly perception. The difference between them is striking. Gauvain remains poised, well dressed, and soft-spoken, while Lancelot has become a grunting beast. Before the amnesiac Lancelot is found, he is subjected to manual labor in the kitchen and becomes a talented cook after much suffering and retraining. In fact, he rises to the rank of head cook. He excels in everything he does by nature, as the audience might expect, but the idea that he has become the best cook in the land is an achievement ridiculously below his social status and reputation. Since Lancelot has lost his memory through enchantment, he thinks nothing of bragging about his new culinary talents. In this temporary persona, he invites Gauvain to try his bread and butter and cheese and a roast chicken *au poivre* recipe accompanied by fine wine, obviously some of the delicious reasons for his recent obesity. Gauvain finds this out of place, as would the audience, who would be equally shocked and amused; but Lancelot, comfortable in his new cook's garb, seems to have forgotten the duties once attached to his suit of armor. As Sir Lancelot is transformed comically into Chef Lancelot, his time in the kitchen mocks conventions of hierarchy and class. His transgressions and ignorance of traditional roles call into question the empty meaning of courtly status and behavior. Elsewhere in the romance, he experiences nontraditional fighting, such as fighting with a piece of wood from the cooking fire or fighting against cats.[40]

Gauvain makes haste to arm the delusional Lancelot, to give him back his identity, his knighthood, nobility, and masculinity, and to remove any possible doubt of the importance and necessity of knightly activity in society. The narrator devotes several lines to describing Gauvain's actions. He is reduced to tears at the demeaning spectacle of his former companion Lancelot, and this is significant because, to the best of the narrator's knowledge, Gauvain has never cried before for any reason. Gauvain comments that when King Arthur hears this news he will die of anguish and grief, since presumably it is understood that adherence to knightly behavior, convention, and pride is Arthur's primary concern. In a striking psychological portrait of his reactions to this spectacle of culinary comedy, Gauvain vacillates between laughing and crying, echoing precisely the narrator's view of the conventions of knighthood and of romance, with a dual tone of both humor and disappointment throughout the composition.

Moreover, drunken or unusual hosts, along with robber knights, are also present in *Rigomer,* a romance that plays with convention on nearly every page. Unusual forms of consumption also mark the texts, such as the falcon that only eats the heads of knights served in their own helmets. This foreboding image is only one of many formidable examples of monstrous consumption that the Arthurian heroes face in the quest for Rigomer. Spiced wine and claret flow for Yvain and Gauvain so that their hosts may take advantage of their gluttony when they are "drunk and unarmed," entertained by the enticing music accompanied by the flirtations of the resident maidens. Cligés too is treated to a lavish meal as the guest of honor before he must face a customarily lethal battle. But hunger is rampant in the land, and the knights must often go without meals to attain the quest of Rigomer, so far is the distance and so bleak is the wasteland geography they must traverse. With much repetition, the narrator indicates before each knight's arrival at Rigomer that each goes through a period of famine. The fact that Lancelot undergoes hunger and hardship, that he is often invited to accept strange types of hospitality, and that robbers are constantly trying to steal his arms implies that his identity and connection to convention are being questioned. To underline this reevaluation of the figure of the ideal knight, more references to feasts, drink, hunger, or famine occur in *Rigomer* than in most prior verse romances.

The figures of Perceval and Fergus come from rustic backgrounds to learn the conventions of courtly and chivalric society in Arthur's court, whereas Lancelot does the reverse. Lancelot falls from one of the highest positions in the Arthurian court to one of the lowest servant positions in an unknown court then rises again, in a different sphere of society, to become head cook. The *Rigomer* court depicts a world upside down, where nothing is as it should be and the validity of socially constructed identity is called into question. When the change in status is portrayed as so simple, it begs the question of readers, if a knight can become a kitchen servant, is not the reverse also an easy feat? The kitchen space is different from the typical setting or frame of the Arthurian dining hall; it presents a distorted image of this communal eating space. Once again, the kitchen is thus shown as the space of otherness in romance. The kitchen itself may be considered one of the *merveilles* in the *monde à l'envers* of Rigomer.

Hunger, Cowardice, and the *Vengeance Raguidel*

In the thirteenth-century Gauvain romance the *Vengeance Raguidel,* romance narrative conventions are parodied as the chivalric and amorous reputation of Gauvain becomes fuel for comedy. Culinary comedy fills one of the most telling episodes in Gauvain's career in this text. The culinary comedy here is based on the dichotomy of appearance and reality. Whereas in earlier romances Gauvain is a model of chivalry and an admired ladies' man, here he is ridiculed by his lover. Though he is known elsewhere for his physical prowess, here we see hints of cowardice and weakness. Food is employed as an attack on Gauvain's flaws. At least two eating scenes mock Gauvain's imperfections, which are only hinted at in earlier texts. Though imperfect, he is not misguided as was the case with Fergus and Hunbaut; rather he turns convention on its head for his own purposes. Similarities to this arise in *L'Atre Perilleux*.

The first of these uncommon Gauvain scenes in the *Vengeance Raguidel* is a nod to mysteriously significant processions and the solemn feasts of the Grail romances. The hungry Gauvain arrives at a mysterious empty castle. Much to his delight, the table has been set with a vast array of *mets* and *entremets,* including roast meats, peacock, fish, bread, and wine (vv. 730–41); up to this point the description of the feast is rather typical for an aristocratic household. Then Gauvain proceeds to gobble up his savory meat without speech or ceremony. Again, we see that as with Perceval the act of forsaking conversation for food is an error that implies moral imperfection. Instead of a scene full of rich religious significance, the famished Gauvain reduces the opening of this feast scene to a sort of knightly pit stop. Later when a Grail-like procession does pass by him in the castle, he, like the young Perceval of the *Conte du Graal* before him, neglects to speak. The humor here arises in his motivations for remaining tacit. Gauvain is not heeding a mother's warning against loquaciousness as was Perceval, nor is he astonished by the spectacle, or *merveille*, parading in front of him. Rather, he is hungry and continues to eat with urgency, "N'i a celui qui mot li die" [There is not a soul who speaks any word to him] (v. 771). Gauvain's lack of speech is unusual for him, since he is usually characterized by his social skills, his courtly and persuasive discourse. Instead, skipping a host's invitation and other conventions such as hand washing and small talk, Gauvain turns to gluttony, eating twice, and eating alone. Consumption continues to replace duty. That he goes for second helpings while he is alone and not scrutinized by the eye of the court amplifies suggestions of sinful *demésure* in his nature, because one was considered a glutton in this period when one ate too much or took too much personal pleasure in eating. Gluttony mirrors the impurity of the body that threatens Gauvain in the Grail romance tradition. Our intertextual expectations of this once great hero are thwarted, inviting a humorous and critical view of a character, who decades earlier was nearly irreproachable, who cares for eating more than for custom or meaning.

The only traditional element of this strange feast is, oddly enough, that it is later interrupted by an unknown intruder, as in *Jaufré,* for example. This intruder (who has come for revenge for his lost love, unbeknownst to the hero) threatens and challenges Gauvain, saying that it is the custom for him to kill all knights who dare trespass, thus entrapping him with the lure of such allusions and elegant feats. This revelation of a deadly custom would not itself seem out of place to contemporary audiences, since such intrusions, threats, or calls to adventure are quite common in Arthurian romance. However, Gauvain's response is not. He offers to pay for what he has eaten, therefore taking away a notion of polite generosity and transforming it into a mercantile exchange. When he learns he must pay through combat, Gauvain makes a very humorous and uncharacteristic plea to delay the challenge—until he has finished eating! Gauvain's relation to this food constructs his identity as a cowardly glutton who hesitates, which could not be more dissimilar from his typical portrayal in earlier texts. Taking up a cowardly yet cunning stance at the table, Gauvain takes his time nibbling and chewing on a few last bites, thereby using the respite granted to prepare for the impending fight:

> Gauvains respond: Issi otroi
> La bataille, mais laissiés moi
> Solement III morcials mangier
> Et puis au lever, sans targier,
> Conbatrons entre vos et moi.
> "Or mangiés, je les vos otroi,"
> Fait li chevaliers erranment.
> Atant Mesire Gauvains prent
> Del pain, en sa bouce l'a mis,
> Et après a son elme mis
> Qui sus la table ert devant lui;
> Ce torna à mult grant anui
> Au chevalier, quand il le vit. (*Vengeance* vv. 823–29)

> [Gauvain responded: "Here I agree
> To the battle, but let me
> Eat only three more pieces
> And when I get up, without delay,
> Let's fight, you and I."
> "So eat, I'll grant you them,"
> Said the knight.
> So Sir Gauvain took
> Some bread, and put it in his mouth,
> And afterwards he put on his helmet,
> Which was on the table in front of him;
> This really bothered
> The knight, when he saw it.]

The smooth-talking hero uses his meal as an excuse to prepare and arm himself. Gauvain answers with, therefore, false recourse to courtly politeness to be allowed to finish his meal in peace:

Uncourtly Table Manners

> "Vos feriés grant mes proïson
> Et je l'tendroie à traïson
> Se de rien me mesaissïés
> Devant ço que j'aie mangiés
> Les trios morcials tot à loisir;
> Et je doi faire mon plaisir,
> Tant con les trives dureront.
> Et saciés qu'eles ne fauront
> Ains erent li morciel mangié." (vv. 841–49)
>
> ["You would do me great wrong
> I would consider it treachery
> If you did anything to upset me
> Before I have eaten
> The three pieces at my leisure;
> As I must do for my pleasure,
> For as long as the truce lasts.
> And no fighting will be done
> Until I eat this morsel."]

Gauvain adheres to feast convention by not getting up from the table before he has finished the meal. The table is laid according to convention, with a nice tablecloth and an impressive spread of expensive dishes and accompaniments. Moreover, the length of description of the dishes, the fish, pork, venison, roast birds, plentiful bread, and good wine, and of his eating and chewing is exceptional, and exceptionally comic (vv. 730–876). Gauvain takes his time and the episode, including the description of the food and Gauvain's chewing, spans an unusually long number of lines. The challenger makes haste to fight, but yet does not deny Gauvain's observance of courtly culinary convention. If his actions are interpreted not as gluttony, but from a different perspective, Gauvain uses literal codes of conduct to his advantage, here to save himself from physical harm. They continue to argue:

> Si [Gauvain] est asise en tel manière
> La table, qu'il en fist castel.
> Encore avoit le tiers morcel
> Dedens sa bouce, qu'il mangoit. (vv. 872–76)
>
> [He (Gauvain) was sitting and the table was placed in such a way
> That he made a fortress out of it.

Chapter Two

> He still had the third morsel
> In his mouth that he was eating.]

The humor here is in the original approach to preparing for battle and in the mix of culinary and military references. His stomach takes precedence over challenge, duty, and glory, but he uses this moment of bodily need and pleasure to ready his arms. Gauvain at the same time follows convention and transgresses it. The scene of the intruder at Gauvain's lonely feast represents the presence of the other, of challengers to the empty courtly traditions of twelfth-century romance. The hero eating alone in silence, challenged while surrounded by the courtly trappings of an otherwise typical feast, shows that the hints at faults in Arthurian ideals in twelfth-century romance are extended in a further satire of their conventions and institutions. Gauvain and the challenger respect the boundaries of the feast, but Gauvain plays with convention by mixing eating and fighting.

In a sense comparable to the mishandling of food in the *Aucassin* food fight, a meal is used, if only momentarily, to replace battle, and food to replace arms. This is a double breach of convention, ignoring the social significance of courtly speech and chivalric conflict. Eating, and by extension, physical concerns, therefore, impede Gauvain's ability to speak with courtesy or to fight in both the romances of the *Vengeance Raguidel* and *Hunbaut*.

Conclusions

Several conclusions may be drawn about the use of culinary comedy in the Arthurian verse romance genre. A growing concern for the body, especially the masculine body, and its physical appetite is evinced in romance episodes concerning the search for food in the decades following Chrétien. Because they are culturally defined, representations of food and nourishment are in any period a manifestation of their social context, here a reflection of the status of the Arthurian knights. Normally, food and the expectations surrounding its consumption are related to and illustrative of the conventions of Arthurian society. Chrétien's *Perceval*, the *Continuations*, *Fergus*, the *Vengeance Raguidel*, the *Merveilles de Rigomer*, and *Hunbaut* provide an alternative gastronomical discourse, in which the real importance of famine and malnutrition is satirized and audience expectations are questioned. Acceptable guest-host relations are modeled then contrasted with the exaggerated and desperate actions of Gauvain and the eponymous heroes of romance. The episodes portraying food fighting are comically incongruous because they are in contrast to audience expectations. In these texts both unknown and familiar knights are depicted engaging in uncourtly behavior, hinting at past, present, and future faults in the Arthurian universe. Many thirteenth-century verse romances thereby challenge Arthurian ideals and literary convention in portraying moments of crisis through transgressive culinary comedy. These epigonous romances manipulate convention, deriving more meaning from food fights than from the all too familiar actions of the Arthurian courtly feast.

In the late-twelfth through mid-thirteenth centuries, French Arthurian verse romances created a climate of playful imitation of courtly and literary convention by exploiting culinary comedy in the form of transgression, exaggerated unexpected behavior, incongruity, and physical action with violence involving food. Culinary comedy has two essential amplifying effects in romance, concerning both individual characters and the conventions of the genre. As we have seen with examples of gluttonous epic heroes in the preliminary chapter, in the romance genre knights' identities become constructed in part by their proper or abnormal alimentary behavior. Normally models of chivalry and courtesy, in later romances Arthurian knights become frustrated, unnecessarily violent, distracted, and uncouth when deprived of food, the opposite of many Arthurian ideals. When hungry knights act in ways contrary to the ways of *courtoisie* and *chevalerie,* we witness adverse reactions to behavior that is typically not seen in courtly dining rooms. The culinary comedy that torments Lancelot in *Rigomer* suggests that cooks, farmers, and craftspeople are more important to society than questing knights-errant, and that knighthood is an empty phenomenon with identity being constituted by a name and a suit of armor.

In a consideration of culinary comedy, we gain insight into the means by which romancers read, imitated, and

Chapter Two

(re)interpreted their predecessors with a critical eye. In contrast to conventional feast scenes, representations of the rituals of eating are mocked, followed too literally, or subverted. As an investigation of the fabliaux and the *Roman de Renart* will demonstrate in the following chapters, culinary comedy is not limited to the Arthurian romances of Chrétien and his followers. Chrétien and the continuators introduce culinary comedy to romance and decades later the epigonal romances and other genres add to this ill-mannered and scornful laughter. A new frank, realistic, and entertaining discourse surrounding food, hunger, and comic violence in these texts arises in opposition to twelfth-century romances where the lavish feast, with all of its costly culinary trimmings and courtly behaviors, was the norm.

Chapter Three

Much Ado about Bacon
The Old French Fabliaux

> Mar fust il onques por bacons!
> —*De Haimet et Barat*

The funny side of the human body, male and female, is revealed in the Old French fabliaux.[1] Often scatological or erotic, these short verse narratives put a comic focus and an ironic twist on prominent human needs, desires, and fears. Fabliau humor, especially culinary fabliau humor, is a multifaceted tool, simultaneously entertaining, criticizing, and interpreting images of the human body's frailties and appetites. The humor of the fabliau genre is achieved through the juxtaposition of the preparation and consumption of food with criticism of certain aspects of social institutions and human nature. Real pressures of survival invited relief in fictional humor linking food to scatology, religion, and sexuality. The fabliaux, with a dismal, mistrustful view of the moral weakness of all walks of life, furnish the perfect platform on which to mock human nature through human interest in and need for food.

In the fabliaux, the representation of consumption is far from that of the elaborate public feasts attended by the noble characters of Arthurian romance and their entourage on the occasion of nuptial celebrations or tournaments. The fabliaux situate themselves within a specific cultural context and portray daily life, urban and country. Set in an urban environment characterized by growth and commercial activity, the narratives often center on private life and private activities inside the home or the inn with occasional forays into the marketplace. By the late twelfth century, town and country were increasingly separate in France, with a growing gap between rich and poor households

Chapter Three

within each sphere. The growth of a cash monetary economy had an important impact. Rural debt grew as did urban poverty; city-dwellers became increasingly dependant on rural agriculture in this period, and marketplaces grew in size. Elevated taxes were levied. Charity was commended and even codified. There was much upheaval and expansion in the time of the composition of the fabliaux. Upward mobility was common in town and country; soon there were more than three estates, and people struggled to climb the social ladder or gain fortune outside of their social status. People began to mistrust the new greedy, upwardly mobile urban merchant class that tried to imitate nobility and the secular clergy; these public opinions are reflected in the fabliaux. Humor often centers on survival in the urban bourgeois and *vilain* communities, as in *Le vilain ânier* [The Peasant Mule Driver], which takes place in the realistic setting of a busy thirteenth-century Montpellier urban marketplace.[2] The size and number of such public spaces were growing at this time. Rosanna Brusegan describes the setting of the fabliaux as a terrestrial universe (49). Because of this setting and the growth of the French comico-realist tradition at this time, these narratives give detailed accounts of aspects of everyday life. Crucial scenes occur in the bedroom, the barn, the pantry, and the kitchen. Cooking and eating are often depicted in more private settings than in romance; we see women alone in the kitchen cooking and eating and couples having intimate dinners. In addition, crimes such as adultery, burglary, and even murder are cast in a derisive light when related to food or mealtime. Crimes and ribaldry with food as an accessory are highly satirical. The fabliaux show a range of consequences with realistic punishment or comical escape. In fabliau logic, a constant battle between the haves and the have-nots, those characters who eat well have usually tricked someone to get their meal, or else they deserve to be tricked out of their gluttonous stockpiles of food.

The Fabliau Genre

Fabliau production began on a grand scale in France in the first quarter of the thirteenth century, contemporaneous with many courtly romances and some branches of the *Roman de Renart*, with production continuing into the fourteenth century.³ Fabliaux were composed in the midst of a climate of parodic and derivative literature. *Fableors* demonstrate their familiarity with Arthurian romance, as, for example, in *Le pescheor du pont sur seine* [The Fisherman of Pont-sur-Seine], where Gauvain is mentioned as the world's best knight. As is often the case when we consider medieval literary production in terms of genre, defining the fabliau genre proves problematic because it is not homogeneous. Over the history of fabliau scholarship, generalized taxonomies attempting to include the varied characteristics of from 120 to 160 narratives in the Old French fabliau genre have been suggested. In a late-nineteenth-century study, Joseph Bédier first reduced them to "un conte à rire en vers" [a laughable story in verse] (30). Of course, this definition has since been contested or augmented on countless levels for being at once too broad and too limiting. It is now widely accepted that many medieval texts resist strict generic classification. Norris J. Lacy, in *Reading Fabliaux,* and Simon Gaunt, in *Gender and Genre,* have warned against the futility of the task of considering these diverse texts as a homogenous group; they stress the ambiguity inherent in the fabliaux.⁴ Gaunt's study underlines the "fluidity" of gender, genre, and class in the fabliaux.

However, it is useful to make a few generalizations. First, fabliaux are brief texts, often using anonymous two-dimensional stock everyman and everywoman characters. The fabliaux provide little development of the context for their anecdotes. The general goal of the fabliaux is amusement, which is achieved often through situational comedy. Most frequently, fabliaux are humorous, though some are quite serious and many include an edifying moral or a general didactic tone. Plots are in general simplistic, though many involve convoluted deception and trickery. The topics may be courtly or *vilain*, bourgeois or subaltern, sparing no victims from their cunning ruses.⁵ They demonstrate a cynical worldview, critical of infidelity in love and dishonesty in commerce. The comedy of many of the texts we consider may be labeled as black humor. They show extremes of morality. Some of the texts involve crime and violence. Fabliaux range—with a certain level of subjectivity—from subtle to disgusting. They are indeed carnivalesque in the Bakhtinian sense, and may be erotic, vulgar, scatological, or downright silly. For example, the *fableor* or scribe who wrote down *Le prestre qui fu mis au lardier* [The Priest Who Was Put in the Larder][6] warns us of the vulgarity of the text, claiming that it is only meant for our entertainment and laughter. Suspension of disbelief, and perhaps suspension of moral or religious belief, is necessary on the part of the audience in order to be able to appreciate the humor and criticism involved, since such humor may be interpreted today as illogical and even obscene at first glance.

In the revered tradition of *auctoritas*, many fabliaux claim in their short prologues to be true stories or hearsay, tantamount to today's urban legends. Dozens of *fableors* refer to their narratives with some form of the terms *fabliau* or *fable*. Some of the many diverse terms to describe these compositions found in the texts themselves are, as written: *fables*, *dits*, *contes*, *essamples*. Over sixty of the one hundred fifty-odd compositions most commonly considered fabliaux refer to themselves as fabliaux, indicating an awareness of genre that can be rare elsewhere in medieval literature. The narrators thus may consider them as stories, fables, or as *exempla*, being proverbial or sentential in nature. Some of the fabliaux fit the Victor Raskin and Salvatore Attardo linguistic definitions of the General Theory of Verbal Humor in jokes or humorous short pieces. Fabliaux exhibit some of Attardo's prerequisites for the verbal humor found in jokes, including narrative strategy, the use of certain scripts, logical mechanisms, language, target, and situation. Many humorous fabliau plots do indeed involve two or more opposing agents, one targeted by the other, with the logical mechanism (often involving food or sexual activity) bringing them together in opposition. Often, the situational and verbal humor of the fabliau is akin to the joke genre, with a setup and a punch line.

The self-proclaimed goal of fabliau composition—and performance—is often joy and laughter on the part of the audience. The narrator of one fabliau that relates a plot to steal food speaks of his work as funny and offers this self-reflexive proverb:

> En petit d'eure Dieus labeure,
> Tels rit au main qui soir pleure

> Et tells est au soir corouciez
> Qui au main est joianz et liez. (*Estula* vv. 84–86)
>
> [God works in a short time
> He who laughs in the morning cries at night
> A man who was upset at night
> Is joyous and glad in the morning.]

The narrator shows that his efforts are for the audience's enjoyment and laughter. Even didactic and proverbial fabliaux aim to please.

Gender wars and the tense relationship between the secular and the religious are the problematic politics of the fabliau corpus. Mercantile and feudal relations come into play as well. Fabliaux are highly conventional narratives, often extremely predictable and full of negative stereotypes. Fabliau humor preys on the naïf, the gullible, and the *vilain*, regardless of gender or social status. We know that the less-than-diligent husband, the greedy bourgeois, or the lecherous priest will get their due in the end.[7] The unexpected manner in which we arrive at the inevitable end, the ruse, the vengeance, is of interest to the audience. Finally, as in medieval romance, it is not originality that counts, but the manner in which the story is told.

Comic narratorial intervention is frequent in the fabliaux. The bias of the *fableor* is often detectable. The narrator frequently sides with the most moral or the cleverest. The narrator sometimes sympathizes with a specific character (usually the underdog) or character type. For instance the cuckolded husband is normally preferred over the lecherous priest. There is a general mistrust of women and feminine wiles, but women are not necessarily the losers in the game, though some are mocked or even beaten by their male counterparts in certain texts.

Occasionally, narratorial sympathies support the poor *vilain* peasant instead of the rich bourgeois.[8] In any event, they usually present some sort of challenge to social order or status quo, where the hierarchy is reinforced in the end. Let us turn now to a quintessential tale of an upwardly mobile *vilain* who fails, in the narrative of Merlin Merlot. In the beginning the *vilain* is described as so poor that he cannot even put one meal on the table for his wife and children. His family laments that they are

Chapter Three

starving; he cannot keep his children from crying or his wife from giving him disapproving looks. He is discouraged about the harsh winter that is aggravating his hard life as a simple woodcutter who works with his own small mule, a realistic portrayal. As he is complaining aloud while walking in the forest, he hears the voice of Merlin promising to make him a rich man. With his family's help he finds the treasure Merlin has promised under his fruit tree. But the poor woodcutter only changes his lifestyle gradually, so as not to provoke the suspicions of his neighbors. He slowly reduces the time he spends working in the woods. He sells his mule and has enough to eat. The narrator says he lives like a bourgeois. Later, the poor peasant asks Merlin to make him provost of the town, to make his son the bishop, and to make his daughter the wife of a rich lord. He becomes greedy, serving the interests of the rich and forgetting the poor *vilains* who were once his peers, the narrator warns in a moralistic statement. Merlin is offended that the other becomes disrespectful; instead of "Sire Merlin" the woodcutter now uses the diminutive "Merlot" and thinks he has no need of the sorcerer's services. No longer meriting his riches because of his attitude, the former *vilain* has become arrogant, in Merlin's opinion. Though the woodcutter tries to change his lot in life, with short-term success, his luck changes when the narrative comes full circle and he finds himself once again hungry and penniless. Echoing a common fabliau moral about the consequences of greed and the ambitions of new wealth, money has turned him into a haughty fool. Once he has lost everything, his children, savings, and property, he becomes happy to go to the woods once again to provide food for his wife. Thus, attempts at a rags-to-riches transformation, whether comical or serious, often fail in the fabliau.

Though hunger often motivates upwardly mobile or criminal behavior, the fabliaux feature plenty of ample meals and copious feasts. As in the romance narratives discussed in the previous chapter, the *fableor* turn to the dining table to set the scene or bring characters together. Mealtimes and feasts serve this narrative purpose in part because they are highly conventional. Structural placement of meals in the narrative frequently marks beginning, middle, and end, as it can in romance. Eating in these scenes involves a highly ritualized description of the menu or a highly formulaic quantity of food. The fabliau feasts involve less pomp and ritual than the courtly meals of Arthurian romance, but they nonetheless serve an important narrative purpose. In addition, the fabliaux include realistic culinary scenes in pantries, cellars, and kitchens. Mealtime is often the scene of much action and narration in the fabliaux. Lavish feasts and modest suppers alike are the scene for many of the habitual fabliau crimes: ambushes, cruel trickery, adultery or rape, and stealing. Notable mealtime action occurs, for example, in the cannibalistic fabliau *Le Lai d'Ignaure* by Renaut de Beaujeu, where the serving of the hors d'oeuvres heralds a violent ambush; it is only when the meal is finished, the narrator tells us, that the character must promise never to speak of this affair. Kitchen knives are part of the plan for revenge, and someone is scolded for laughing at the appetizer. The exploitation of the culinary element escalates in the end, in a black-comedy scene in which the courtly ladies savor the refined flavors of the knight's heart.[9] *Le Lai du Lecheor* also begins with a contest, followed by a discussion of knighthood and narrative that turns bawdy, set during celebrations of the Breton feast of Saint Pantelion. These two "lais" fit most definitions of the fabliau genre. Both of these examples suggest the importance of the mealtime setting. Unlike romance meals, fabliau meals are often more than a formulaic occurrence; they become part of the action.

Consumption of food, food preparation, and food conservation appear at the center of a great number of extant fabliaux. Food may be crucial to the plot, or merely provide a mealtime setting for other intrigue. Sometimes it is the specific food item that is inherently funny, and sometimes it is a ridiculous action with food that renders a fabliau humorous. Below we consider select examples of culinary comedy; first of all, humor related to food and morality; secondly, culinary scatological comedy; and finally, culinary sexual comedy. Culinary comedy in the fabliaux often entails scheming and food stealing as part of the ruses that form the plots and subplots. One difference between romance and the fabliaux is that, in the fabliaux, food stealing often involves elaborate ruses, trickery, and clever schemes, whereas in romance or epic, knights' brute force and impolite table manners seem to suffice to entertain and criticize genre

Chapter Three

or society. The characters that steal food in the fabliaux are not generally knights, but known thieves, *vilains*, and gluttonous greedy women. The deceit and thievery in the fabliaux show a taste on the part of audiences, whomever they may have been over the years, for a more *vilain*—today one might deem more street-smart—tale with realism and cunning desperation; it is, however, unlikely that the contemporary audience included members of the illiterate, poverty-stricken *vilains* often portrayed on the pages of these texts.

Food-Based Humor and Morality

Fabliau characters are what they eat, morally and socially.[10] In the fabliaux, as in real life, food habits and food symbols can be an indication not only of identity but of morality. Moreover, a person's relation to food, or what one eats and how it is eaten, is an indication of character. This relationship between morality and food is the basis for most of the culinary comedy in the fabliaux. More specifically, many fabliaux explore variations on the binary opposites of temperance and gluttony, hospitableness and greed; these and many other social qualities relate often to food as well as to its sensual and criminal aspects. Overindulgence, avarice, and envy are the major themes that mark a large group of food-related fabliaux. Characters covet their neighbors' food stores, livestock, wealth, and spouses. Actions and speech involving food are frequently the only elements of characterization given in these concise texts. For instance, the wife in *Les perdrix* is shown to be greedy and selfish when she single-handedly eats a dinner meant for three. Elsewhere, in a brief but condemning portrait of their profession, the cowherds in *Aloul* are concerned only with their bellies, motivated to work and follow orders only by the promise of their next meal. From a depiction of coprophilia to an insatiable appetite for poultry, we investigate the manner in which narrators show the true nature of their characters through what and how they consume, often with a critical view toward bourgeois women and clergymen.

In *Jouglet*, culinary comedy is used as multilayered social criticism that is directed in general at the failings of human nature, and more specifically as an ally against the stereotype of the ignorant *vilain*. It also mocks courtly wedding conventions (of the common type seen in Arthurian romance) and attacks unscrupulous, greedy minstrels. This is no courtly wedding celebration. The protagonist, Robin, is a young shepherd whose father is also no stranger to hard manual labor in the fields. The narrator informs us that he is an only child, and that he has grown up physically, but not mentally,

> Molt estoit fol e estordiz
> De fol sens e de fole chiere
> . . . .
> Mes il croissoit devant son sens,
> Com font oncore tez i a! (*Jouglet* vv. 6–7, 12–13)
>
> [He was very foolish and giddy
> With foolish wits and a stupid face
> . . . .
> But he grew up physically before his intelligence grew,
> As does many another person!]

The psychological portrait embedded in the story of the immature young man's upbringing is the setup for the humorous twist. The narrator implies with subtlety that his feeble intelligence and meager mental capacities will result in his downfall.

More than just the exterior trappings of celebration, the institution and sacrament of marriage are at stake in this text. Young Robin's mother arranges a marriage for him with Mahaut, the innkeeper's daughter. His matchmaking mother succeeds in having him marry above his station in life; the comic wedding episode that follows calls into question this upwardly mobile practice in the contemporary portrayal of the constant *vilain* and bourgeois attempt to ascend the established hierarchy and question the status quo. When the wedding day comes, Robin invites the minstrel Jouglet (whose name recalls his profession) to enliven the festivities. Here we also see a comical portrayal of the *jongleur,* who seems even more concerned with causing and laughing at the pain and suffering of his patron than with any table scraps he might obtain. When he sees that Robin likes pears, he devises a ruse to convince him to overeat. Pears are generally understood as an aphrodisiac and to eat pears can be symbolic of lechery. The *jongleur* uses

Chapter Three

Robin's gluttony to feed his own greed and feelings of mental and social superiority. Jouglet requests he give him all of his finished pear cores in his glove, enough to fill it. The gluttonous groom, not reflecting on his inappropriate actions, eats more than his fill until his belly is distended and painful. At the time, pears were seen as healthy and instrumental in balancing one's humors, but they have the opposite effect here. The excessive consumption of pears does not act as a strong aphrodisiac here as one might expect, but rather as a powerful laxative.

In a comic appeal to the absurdity of etiquette, to add to the groom's digestive suffering, the minstrel tells him that one should not defecate on one's wedding day, because it is "trop grant ledure" [too revolting] (*Jouglet* v. 89). But, the narrator exclaims in a detail indicative of the comico-realist nature, the groom cannot endure, "Quer son ventre li douloit molt" [because his belly was in so much pain] (*Jouglet* v. 91). The suspense is finally broken when Robin relieves himself. Loss of self-control and bodily control through gluttony, ignorance, and gullibility are not often rewarded in the fabliaux. The groom's diarrhea causes embarrassment, and to add insult to gastric injury, he only soils himself further when he goes to wash his hands in an unclean bucket, mocking the courtly hand washing custom. In addition to the physical humor, dialogue is very important in this nearly dramatic text.

There are tangible links between the culinary comedy of the fabliaux and the culinary comedy in vernacular moral *exempla* of the same period. The fabliau of *Jouglet* appears in one extant contemporary thirteenth-century manuscript anthology, along with the didactic manual *Le chastoiement d'un père à son fils,* a moralizing text that is a fair indication of the audience's awareness of the importance of manners (in British Library MS Add. 10289). The co-presence of these texts in a thirteenth-century compilation invites our comparison of their content and functions. *Exemplum* XVII of this text also includes an analogue to *Jouglet.* Here the *Chastoiement* uses culinary comedy in another case of *jongleur's* revenge. Once again, an unsuspecting character is framed as a glutton. Gluttony is a humiliating insult in both *Jouglet* and this *exemplum.* Both occur in a public place and result in laughable embarrassment. "La Viande et les os" [The Meat and Bones] is one of many *exempla* concerning food. The father counsels his son to be generous with friends and servants and recounts the story of a jealous *jongleur* who gets revenge on someone who has received more recompense. The disgruntled performer collects all the bones at the feast, stacks them up in front of his rival, and publicly accuses him of gluttony. Instead of becoming the laughing stock of the court, the insulted *jongleur* retorts with verbal culinary comedy, saying that at least he has not eaten both the meat and the bones like an animal. The courtly crowd is amused at his wit, and they laugh at the other minstrel's thwarted attempt. This *exemplum* at the heart of the *Chastoiement* shows a similar concern for the degenerating scruples of minstrels. In addition, the *exemplum* "La Viande et les os" shares many structural and content similarities with the fabliaux. It also emphasizes the use of culinary comedy across generic lines to ridicule greediness and question social climbers. These food-jokes thus serve an edifying as well as entertaining purpose.

The comedy of action and food is present again in the *exemplum*-like fabliau of *Le prêtre qui manga des meures*.[11] This simple, short tale (directly following the *exemplum*-like fabliau *Le vilain ânier* in the one extant manuscript) is also a fabliau with at least one moral that may provoke audience laughter at their superiority to the humiliated priest. The stated moral at the end of the narrative is that it is prudent not to speak too soon, for the result may be unpleasant and humiliating. The implied morals are first of all that one should not count one's blessings too soon, lest they result in a self-fulfilling prophecy, and secondly that one should resist temptation and gluttony that detract from religious devotion. On his way to the market on his mule, a priest is distracted from his devotional reading by the sight of rich blackberry brambles. Patiently, his seemingly trusty mule waits for him while he gorges himself on the ripe berries. At the same instant that the unsuspecting priest declares it a good thing that nobody has startled the mule by crying out, he shouts aloud while thinking to himself in his own head. The animal bolts, leaving the priest stuck in thorny, painful brambles. This type of foreshadowing occurs in many fabliaux, especially those that include culinary comedy. It is funny because we know the punch line in advance, and are only waiting

Chapter Three

to hear the slapstick outcome of the protagonist's comic situation. Here the priest is duped and ridiculed by his own gluttony. Elsewhere more cunning characters get away with delicious crimes.

The comic tales of the fabliaux demonstrate no lack of plots involving sly culinary ruses that follow Raskin's Cunningness Scripts; for example, *Les perdrix* in which a wife resorts to verbal trickery to cover up her own gluttony. The ravenous wife cannot contain her desire to devour the two fat partridges her husband has hunted. She has freshly roasted the birds that are intended for dinner with the local priest as the guest of honor upon her husband's return. She greedily gobbles them up herself before her husband arrives. The members of the audience smile or laugh at the psychological portrait of a glutton as they watch her taste the meat with some hesitation and delight, finish the first bird with delight, then guiltily contemplate the second one. Desire overcomes her when she completely devours the second partridge down to the bones in a frenzied loss of self-control.[12] This fabliau implies a connection between uncontrolled female culinary appetite and female sexual desire. Considering the way her private pleasure and physical satisfaction are described, the scene in which she devours the birds is one of the most sensual scenes concentrating on the female body in the entire fabliau corpus. She reacts with deception, as if she were a true fabliau adulteress attempting to save herself with a lie.[13] She frames the house cats with the evidence of the carcass of the bird and regains her composure.

As he returns to the home, she innocently tells her gullible husband to go sharpen his knife in order to carve the birds. She blames the disappearance of the birds on the unsuspecting priest, and the husband pursues him. Roast partridge thus becomes an emblem of fabliau stereotypical deceitful women. She essentially lies to both men, doing them both a disservice, in order to literally serve herself.[14] She tells the priest that her husband is out to castrate him; when he runs away frightened, the hungry husband chases him with a knife yelling *double entendres* to the effect that he will "take them back warm," or "just abandon them on the spot if he gets caught." Here the comedy is physical and verbal. This is one instance of many in the fabliaux where food and sexual organs become interchangeable. Here the priest knows nothing of the missing dinner birds, thinking only of his own guilty genitals. First, the wife's overindulgence and spontaneous ruse to cover it up are physical and verbal. Second, the fleeing priest's misunderstanding the husband just as the wife has orchestrated masterfully is also a comedy of action and of words.

The choice of partridge for the meal is perhaps more than a reflection of good taste or coincidental food source availability. The bird is a sexual and moral symbol. In Pierre de Beauvais's *Bestiaire*, written in the first quarter of the thirteenth century, we find that the partridge is a diabolic and deceitful bird.[15] Based on a reference in a biblical prophecy, Pierre explains in this traditional bestiary that the female bird is dishonest and takes babies that do not belong to her. The mother bird of the bestiary steals eggs from other nests, raises and leads the baby birds as if they were her own for a time, then they return to their mother. The negative side of this image is twofold. First it shows females as deceitful robbers. Second, and more importantly, the female bird becomes the agent of the devil, literally leading the flock away from good under the influence of evil. The use of the culinary image is humorous, as it shows the wife in *Les perdrix* gobbling up the birds; at the same time, it constitutes her identity (indeed her gender) as deceitful and sinful in relation to the image of the partridge. Moreover, these negative aspects of the hungry fabliau wife's identity are amplified by the detail that she uncontrollably consumes two birds.

The battle of the sexes becomes a food fight in the culinary fabliaux that deal with gender but are not erotic in nature; we consider the culino-erotic tales below. Marital strife is the source of conflict and comedy in *Sire Hain et Dame Aineuse* [Sir Hate and Lady Hateful]. The author, Hue Piaucele, depicts the imperfections of the contemporary married household, with everyday squabbles and subsistence-based problems. It shines the same pejorative light on feminine wiles and female subversive behavior as *Les perdrix*. The hateful wife, Dame Aineuse, probably motivated by spousal abuse as we discover later, refuses to cook for her husband the dishes he desires. If he wants vegetable purée she serves him whole peas, or poorly cooked vegetable purée. If he asks for boiled meat, she roasts it instead and deliberately covers it in ashes to suffocate his gastronomic enjoyment. Choosing the technique of roasting over boiling is tantamount to choosing courtly over *vilain,* thus an affront to the husband's way of life and an indication of the wife's desire for upward mobility and change of her status. One day he provokes her ire by asking for a particularly difficult to prepare and bony ocean fish, so she poorly prepares some freshwater fish. In addition to their realistic discussion on the merits of the various ways of cooking meat and preparing vegetables, there are numerous references to fish and ray in their discussion, suggesting an audience familiar with specific types of dishes.

The couple's ongoing culinary dispute comes to blows, with the wife nearly as violent as the husband. Their fight is likened to *guere.* The war is on a private scale, however, limited to the confines of their interior courtyard. The subject of food begins the quarrel that grows into an intense argument about who literally wears the trousers in the family. Among other culinary insults the wife uses is the notable "you're not worth two whitings!" (*Hain* v. 229). Several fabliaux use culinary language in insults and descriptions, as in the proverbial saying at the heart of *L'oue au chapelain.*

Finally, a third party is called in to resolve the Hain's dispute. The tale is entertaining at first, but it ends with a justification for wife abuse, saying a wife must obey her husband, conform to his wishes, and cook what he desires. Good cases have been made for reading the fabliaux as showing varying levels of misogyny, feminism, and antifeminism. In this episode, the woman uses her culinary talents as a power play, expressing her distaste at the injustice of their household hierarchy. In the end, the masculine order is restored and the narrative, when read as a moral *exemplum,* suggests that women remain subordinate to their husbands. Culinary comedy and physical and mental cruelty are used to communicate this moralizing and misogynistic lesson.

Class-Based Culinary Comedy

Even more frequent than culinary marital household squabbles are humorous encounters treating mercantile and hospitality relationships. In Eustace d'Amiens's *Le Bouchier d'Abeville,* a normally scrupulous butcher is refused lodging by an uncharitable priest. The narrative attacks the merchant class and the clerical orders with equal verve and presents a parody of uncharitable clergy. The cleric is far less charitable than he pretends to be. *Le Bouchier* is an exploration of the moeurs of thirteenth-century urban commercial interactions. This tale provides further evidence that food is the sign of wealth and generosity, measuring a clerical innkeeper's worth as well as *largesse*. In the beginning of the narrative, we learn that the butcher is kind, generous, charitable, and not evil. The comico-realist treatment of social status is fairly transparent in this episode. We witness a disparaging view of the hypocritical and dishonest merchants of the time, selling livestock that is too expensive, being greedy and vicious. He considers them pigs, difficult negotiators, with whom he cannot do business (v. 20). He returns without replenishing his stock. The weary butcher's voyage home is long, and he stops for the night in a village, where the uncharitable cleric who has been recommended to him for lodging refuses to house a mere layperson, demonstrating an underlying elitism among clerics and clergy.

The narrative that follows adheres to Raskin's scripts of Stinginess and of Craftiness/Cunningness. The resourceful butcher pays the greedy, inhospitable holy man for lodging by cooking mutton stew with the innkeeper's very own sheep, which he has stolen. His host ironically accepts and enjoys the mutton dish as payment; laughter is invited by the ironic origin of the mutton since the audience knows the unwilling host is enjoying his own sheep that the butcher has just slaughtered. The butcher, whom the narrator says is charitable, courteous, and loyal, then continues to make the host pay for his uncharitable and lecherous nature; he then seduces his reluctant host's maid and mistress with the promise of a quality sheepskin. The host finally realizes he has been duped after buying back the sheepskin from the butcher and linking it to the mutton stew. The inattentive host comically gets more than what he deserves. The powerful irony of the tricked innkeeper satirizes a real-life quarrel between the butcher's social class and higher-up merchants or clerics. In the end, however, the narrator demonstrates little faith in either the butcher or his host; the butcher goes too far, contrary to his characterization in the beginning of the tale as kind and not evil.

Chapter Three

A similar parody of the greedy merchant class is presented in the fabliau often titled *La Plantez* [The Abundance].[16] Here again the innkeeper becomes the object of ruse and laughter. In a realistic portrait of class struggles and hunger, a poor Norman traveler goes to a tavern in another region to spend his last penny and enjoy his last crust of bread with a cup of wine. The snobby innkeeper intentionally spills half the wine while pouring it for the poor, hungry, thirsty man. For revenge, the dejected Norman sends the innkeeper for cheese and lets all the wine drain from the entire barrel in his absence. A bar brawl ensues upstairs in the tavern, kegs are spilled and mugs broken, so that in the cellar the narrator exclaims colorfully that one could even bathe in wine. The butcher is told earlier by a woman that he is the only one in town who has wine, and that his cellar is very well stocked. To settle the argument, the two go before the King, who declares all too logically that he who lost is the loser, evoking the tavern keeper's own proverb "He who spills the wine will profit by it." The ending mocks moral *exempla* in its comic ambiguity.

In a portrait of corruption in another echelon of society, prostitutes and pimps are also satirized through the ironic ruses of fabliau culinary comedy. These figures embody urban debauchery through their economic, sexual, and gastronomic practices. City eating in the fabliaux provides a strong contrast to the courtly feasting of romance. The supper table and the bedroom are the chief sites of ruses in the fabliaux, as will been seen below. Excessive eating and drinking often lead to fabliau characters' ultimate destruction. In this case the setting is a house of prostitution, further underlining the fabliau's demonstration that the body and its appetites often take precedence over reason, wisdom, and morality. However, in *Boivin de Provins*, the protagonist in this allegedly autobiographical piece outsmarts this formula in advance.[17] *Boivin* is a fabliau that mocks peasants, bourgeois, pimps, and prostitutes alike, sharing many formal similarities with the farce. It is set in a familiar public space of play and exchange, a *foire*.[18] In this ludic space, there is excessive eating and excessive obscenity. The unstated moral of *Boivin* finds fault with human excesses through the actions of a comic trickster. The comedy is verbal and physical, when a wily *vilain* concocts a ruse to convince prostitutes that he has more money than he really does. Through his cunning, feigned ignorance, and deception, he succeeds in having them prepare for free a feast of poultry and wine, for which he pays nothing. The lavish dishes and drink, accompanied by the free services of a prostitute, are intended to put Boivin in a vulnerable position where they may steal his purse. But his foresight directs him to cut his own purse strings in advance before their own attempt at treachery can be made, so that the prostitutes think his wealth has already been stolen. Female gluttony, drunkenness, and greed are mocked, as the women of this community consume in excess. Unlike the poor *vilain* woodcutter, who despite Merlin's gift returns to his *vilain* nature and activities, Boivin breaks away from the audience expectation of the fabliau rule once a *vilain*, always a *vilain*.

Culinary comedy in the fabliaux demonstrates common points and common faults shared by different socio-economic classes, also serving to highlight the corrupt nature of both urban and courtly society. Most characters in the fabliaux are caricatures of their socio-economic status (and usually two-dimensional or stereotypical). Rich and poor alike are mocked for their gluttony. Lower classes use cunning to obtain more copious fare. In the moral of *La vieille qui oint la paume au chevalier* [The Old Woman Who Greased the Knight's Palm], the narrator's lesson touches on the hypocrisy of the rich and the unfairness of class differences. This unfairness engenders deception and even physical violence. In the *Bourgeoise d'Orléans,* the household servants assault their master, leave him for dead on a dung heap, and enjoy a feast fit for a king with the wife. In the most explicit statement of disapproval of class inequality, he says the poor have no rights. The master also alludes to bribery as, ironically, a necessary and acceptable way for the poor to get what they want and need to survive.

Thieves and Food Robbers

Elaborate ruses to steal food are the stock intrigue in culinary fabliaux. *De Haimet et Barat,*[19] (bound in one ms. with *Les quatre larrons* [The Four Thieves]) is a tale of culinary thievery. The moral of the story suggests that one should be careful in one's choice of friends and expect the worst if one associates

Chapter Three

with thieves, "Mal conpeignon a en larron" [Thieves make bad companions] (v. 518). This lesson is learned when food is stolen in a comedy of errors. As in the *Bouchier* and *Boivin*, this thieves' fabliau also involves class humor and greedy characters; another similarity between these culinary fabliaux is the denigration of unscrupulous or criminal behavior. *De Haimet et Barat* is a story about three thieves who are ostensibly friends, two of whom are brothers. Travers—a thief, but an honest one, as the narrator claims—becomes the victim of the two brothers Haimet and Barat.

The narrative structure of this fabliau provides a setup for a humorous twist with a pretext that foreshadows the rest of the tale. The story begins with a game they invent to measure their skill and dexterity. The thieves send their finest on a challenge to climb a tree and steal a bird's eggs out of the nest. He successfully carries out the furtive task. A second challenge is given, to put them back. Here comedy ensues when the stealthy thief begins to climb the tree a second time and one of his companions follows to give him a nasty surprise; he steals his friend's underclothes as he concentrates on the challenge of not breaking the delicate stolen eggs.[20] This pretext establishes a tendency to rob even their friends, albeit in jest in this first instance. The brothers show how deceitful they can be, even with a fellow thief like Travers, again echoing the proverbial warning at the beginning of the text. Motivated by hunger, jealousy, and revenge, the brothers plot to steal Travers' ham. In the setup for an episode of situational culinary comedy, just before Christmas Travers has prepared a large ham and hung it from the main beam of his house. With the familiar technique of foreshadowing the treachery to come, the narrator tells us that it would have been wiser for him to have sold it and avoided any grief over the bacon.

Travers and his crafty wife hide the ham under some straw to foil any attempts at burglary. She goes to bed and Travers takes a walk in the garden, thinking to himself that perhaps he was wrong to think ill of his colleagues Haimet and Barat. Meanwhile, the devious Barat comes to the wife in the dark, pretending to be her husband. There is repetitive mistaken identity of people and objects in this text. Cases of mistaken identity are common in the fabliaux, where characters are gullible and unaware of individual differences, seeing only gender and class. Furthermore, with the suspension of disbelief in these short texts, family members frequently are unable to recognize one another. In *De Haimet et Barat*, the thief imitates the husband and feigns forgetfulness, asking his wife where he left the ham. As is typical in the fabliau genre, she is gullible and reveals the location, enabling the thieves to run off with the precious purloined meat. The struggle to carry home the stolen bacon is a slapstick sequence with physical humor including falling, stumbling, and mistaken identity.

Stealing the bacon in the Middle Ages has symbolic sexual significance and can represent sexual and adulterous acts in many fabliaux; as I have noted elsewhere pork products often stand in for genitalia and body parts. Here stealing the bacon is associated with a nighttime visit that imitates spousal relations in a comic cross-dressing, gender-bending incident in which details such as a nightgown and missing underwear are also highlighted. Later one of the robbers mistakes Travers for his brother, and Travers mistakes one of the disguised thieves in drag for his wife. The robber dons the wife's white nightgown and imitates her voice. Travers hears the voice and deviates from his pursuit. When he realizes his error Travers asserts his defeat and stupidity, declaring that he has learned his lesson where "Entrez sui en mout male escole" [I have entered a very evil school] (v. 376).

The thieves take the pilfered meat back to their camp. While they gather wood for the fire, Travers, still without underclothing, takes the pig down from the tree where they have hung it, and ties himself up there. The combination of the introduction of an incongruous body with the repetition of mistaken identities produces a comic effect here, as the deceived character attempts to catch the deceivers at their own muddled game. In the end of this lengthy fabliau, Travers and his wife decide to cook the ham rather than wait to eat it or to sell it and risk theft again. While the meat boils over the fire the thieves try to snag it out of the pot with a long utensil but they are thwarted once again. The honest, good-natured Travers resolves to share and invites the thieves to partake of the meal; of course they steal the best pieces for themselves, once again invading the marital space and disrupting the couple and their bodies.

Chapter Three

There is an implied "it takes a thief to catch a thief" moral in *De Haimet et Barat*. These shambling thieves are portrayed as *vilain* and most concerned with stealing foodstuffs. The comedy lies first in the fact that they are going to such extreme efforts to steal food, rather than something of more worth. Second, the repetition of their many failed attempts and incompetent *vilain* ruses adds to the comedy in the Aristotelian sense of the below-average character with faults and mistakes that are ugly and ridiculous.

As observed above regarding the *Roman de Fergus* and as will be seen below in consideration of the *Roman de Renart*, thievery is a major plot element of culinary comedy. The idea of a dimwitted criminal is compelling in the fabliaux. Similar to the *larrons* in *Haimet et Barat*, the two greedy brothers of *Estula* are comic figures, representative of poor, hungry peasants jealous of the richer classes. It is a tale of poverty and hunger. The *fableor* is biased against the growing riches of the bourgeois, framing the tale with a discussion of the injustice of societal repartition of wealth, and in particular, of food. Narratorial interventions on the subject of hunger are fervent, suggesting that hunger is: a companion, an advisor, a thing of suffering, an enemy. He declares there is nothing worse than hunger and that the two brothers are hungry, thirsty, and cold, and therefore defenseless against the power of poverty and what it can drive them to do. Here desperation leads to crime and humorous consequences. The target of the conspiracy becomes a nearby rich neighbor, with an appetizing field full of cabbages and barn full of sheep. Though cabbage was common fare for rich and poor alike in this period, the brothers are so poverty stricken that they must steal even this inexpensive, readily available, and easily grown staple to survive.[21] The stolen cabbage becomes an emblem, however meager and commonplace, of the unjust balance between rich and poor.

When the brothers arrive to partake of the neighbor's bounty, and before the comic action begins, the narrator reminds us that poverty makes many people commit foolish acts. Again, hunger motivates ridiculous actions. Situational comedy turns into verbal comedy as misunderstandings accumulate around the ham. The rich bourgeois hears a commotion as one brother attempts to steal the fattest of the sheep. He sends his son to call the guard dog, named Estula. When he calls the dog in the dark, the thief hears "Es-tu là?" and answers instead, thinking it to be his accomplice. In a comic scene requiring our suspension of disbelief and comprehension of fabliau logic, the bourgeois's son believes it is really the dog that spoke. The bewildered youth returns to the house to announce the strange and miraculous news to his father. The father, needing empirical proof, calls the dog, "Estula!" and hears a similar spoken response. With this evidence, he calls for a priest to bless the talking dog. When the priest arrives, there is a case of mistaken identity with the robbers. The priestly garb appears in the dark to one of the brothers to be the stolen sheep slung around his brother's neck; because of this misperception he calls to the figure he thinks in the obscurity and confusion is his brother in hasty anticipation of the meal, saying he will sharpen his knife and get ready to carve him up. Once again, a clergyman's body is mistaken for livestock (or food) and animal and human flesh become confounded. The priest is unaware of the plot to butcher a stolen sheep, and flees, fearing his own throat is about to be cut. Hence in *Estula* there is an element of comedy that echoes strongly the case of linguistic culinary comedy and mistaken intention found in *Les perdrix*.

In the confusion, the brothers flee the farm with cabbages and a stolen sheep, with which they hurry back to their nearby abode. They intend to carve up the meat, boil the cabbage, and prepare a feast to make them forget their hunger and poverty. The narrator recounts that when they returned to eat, laughter came back to them and they joked and laughed together. They laugh as they cook and eat because their hunger is sated and because they have fought famine with their own wit. The brothers' reaction of laughter at the end of the ruse signals the end of the narrative and may also echo amused audience response. The links between food and laughter, eating and narrative, are reinforced at the end of the day.

Food and Scatological Humor

The Incongruity Theory of humor holds that unexpected juxtapositions result in amusement. In a genre marked by vulgar jokes, obscene innuendos, unexpected twists of fate and

Chapter Three

surprising punch lines, culinary humor and scatological humor are often combined in the humorous thirteenth-century fabliaux, foreshadowing similar bodily comedy in late medieval French farce, in Rabelais, and in later centuries and other languages. The juxtaposition of food humor and scatological subjects addresses social and literary conventions. Culino-scatological humor is rich in possibilities for social criticism, since it is a mixture of humor, disgust, and morality. In mid-thirteenth-century France, this type of humor was present in other genres. For instance, in the *Jeu de Robin et Marion*, food, in the form of a pastoral picnic and a courtly feast, is at the center of the dramatic text, while digestion and the frailties of the human body are portrayed as derisory. In one scene from the play, the king asks one of his guests to comment on the food. His appreciation is unexpectedly graphic and uncouth:

> LI ROIS:
> > Or, di Huart, si t'aït Diex,
> > Quel viande tu aimes miex.
> > Je sai bien se voir me diras.
>
> HUARS:
> > Bon fons de porc pesant et cras
> > A le fort aillie de nois.
> > Certes, j'en mengai l'autre fois
> > Tant que j'en euch le menison.
>
> BAUDONS:
> > Hé, Diex, con faite venison!
> > Huars n'en diroit autre cose. (vv. 544–52)
>
> [THE KING:
> > Now tell us, Huart, so help you God,
> > Which food you like the best.
> > I'll know whether you're telling the truth.
>
> HUART:
> > A good thing of pork, heavy and fat,
> > With a strong garlic walnut sauce.
> > Truly, I ate so much of it the other day
> > That I had the runs from it.
>
> BAUDON:
> > Oh, My God, what a dainty dish!
> > Huart couldn't say anything more seemly.][22]

The same subject of humor, involving food that causes indigestion, flatulence, and defecation, appears in the fabliaux linked to descriptions of particular foods, as for example in the fabliaux *Jouglet* (in which eating pears excessively leads to indigestion, diarrhea, and embarrassment) and in *Le pet du vilain* (in which cooking and eating greasy meat with garlic is the catalyst for flatulence, causing humor and confusion). Such recipes and food critiques, along with vulgar details of unsettled stomachs accompanied by an unsettling sarcastic tone, make a mockery of recipes, cooking manuals, and the etiquette of the feast in courtly romance.

The stereotypical everyman and everywoman characters of the fabliaux typify, embody, and exaggerate the functions, powers, and needs of the human body. Case in point, *Le vilain ânier* is an *exemplum* as well as a "petit conte à rire en vers" that treats, with clarity in vibrant images and potent odors, the contemporary issue of increasingly fluid social classes and the rise in number of successful social climbers. The moral comes as no revelation after this unsubtle scrutiny of a *vilain* overstepping class borders and the boundaries of his situation in life. His below-average, and apparently tainted, worldview is also ridiculed.[23] Using particular foodstuffs as emblematic of the upper class and excrement as symbolic of the lower class, *Le vilain ânier* treats class difference and the threat to the upper classes posed by upwardly mobile peasants. In this simple tale, the *vilain* donkey driver accustomed to transporting loads of putrid manure finds himself on a perfumed street full of spice merchants with the refined odors of herbs and spices wafting in the air. Not familiar with such perfumes, the *vilain* faints, only to be revived by a *preudhome* with a scent of manure. The story is comic because we are told the protagonist is used to living with the odor of manure and therefore we are aware of his lowly station in life. In addition, spices are powerful comic ingredients because of their perceived effect on the body at the time. Medically, many spices were seen during this period to have curative powers, while others, such as pepper, cloves, cinnamon, cardamom, nutmeg, and anis, were also revered for their properties as aphrodisiacs. Because of their medical and psychosomatic qualities and their ability to affect the human body—unwittingly on occasion—spices are another of the medieval "funny" foods.

It is only when he steps outside his world of dung, that is to say, his station in life, that the *ânier* is made aware of his role and the impossibility of living differently. In his case it is not intentional, but a didactic element of the story warns against intentional attempts at changing one's lot in life. The moral of the story makes a strong statement on beliefs surrounding difference and the other. This lesson underlines the difference between *courtois* or bourgeois and *vilain*. Moreover, it suggests that one must stay in one's position within society or face harsh consequences, a common sentiment in the fabliau. He is even mocked by his own stubborn mules, who refuse to move and then do not react when he faints in the middle of the road. The poor *ânier* is thus physically held back by social borders. Pitiable, unrefined, and funny, he lies in the muck and mire instead of standing head-and-shoulders with the affluent bourgeois spice merchants of the marketplace. Here the sense of smell mixes with the sense of humor to produce critical identity construction. The sense of smell was an important part of medieval and early modern culture, as important as the sense of taste. Smell and odor are strong signifiers, particularly since perfumes, smells, and flavors (from heavy wood fire smoke to garlic to sweet spices like cinnamon) were so important in medieval cuisine. The food-related dichotomy of manure and spices allows an entertaining aspect to this strong social statement. The poor driver's sense of smell leads him to be sniffed out as someone who does not belong. Changing the status quo is out of the question in the fabliau, and the audience laughs at those who try through commerce to rise from lowly *excrement* to luxurious *épice*.

Rutebeuf likewise addresses the human body and the effects of food in relation to class in *Le pet du vilain* [The Peasant's Fart].[24] He touches on the scatological, the olfactory, and the religious. He plays with the limits of comic narrative and with Aristotelian comedy of the Ugly and the Ridiculous. The poor peasant's digestive troubles are caused by his poor diet that is fatty and seasoned with too much garlic. His fart is mistaken for his soul leaving his earthly body by the gullible devil. The damned "soul" is trapped in a bag and released in hell, where its odor is as unpleasant and poorly received as it would be on earth. The peasant unwittingly confuses the devil through his poor nutrition and uncontrollable intestines.[25] We may assume that poor diet and flatulence, combined with the naïveté of the *vilain,* provoked laughter or smirks on the part of some audience members, as it may have in the similar case of *Jouglet.* Confusion is the basis for many a fabliau anecdote; here it is merely poor nutrition and digestive troubles mistaken for a more spiritually significant phenomenon. This fabliau *exemplum* was circulated widely for centuries; an adaptation of it recurs in the sixteenth-century *Farce du Meunier,* giving us another indication that food and indigestion remained subjects of moral and social comedy in short fictional narrative for years to come.[26] Furthermore, narratives portraying flatulence are not rare in other genres at the time of the peak of fabliaux production, and were considered entertaining, as one uncouth character in the *Jeu de Robin et Marion* suggests:

> GAUTIER:
>   Faisons .i. pet pour nous esbatre;
>   Je n'i voi si bon. (vv. 466–67)
>
> [GAUTIER:
>   Let's fart to amuse ourselves.
>   I don't see anything better to do.][27]

Flatulence and indigestion become symbolic of *vilain* poor diet and poor manners in this period.

Many fabliaux concentrate on the *vilain* milieu exclusively. Those that do are more often than not concerned with food or such comic takes on bodily functions. One of the basest and most vulgar fabliaux at first glance, *La crote,*[28] mixes a discourse of consumption and exchange with crude scatological and sexual humor. A peasant couple's wager in a vulgar game is at stake, implying that the milieu and the humor of the tale are *vilain* indeed. *La crote* belongs to a group of fabliaux that more resemble a modern dirty joke or anecdote rather than a fable. The uncomplicated plot is that of a guessing game and Jodogne classifies it as a *devinette* (19–21). Through physical and verbal play, *La crote* redefines gender roles while remaining within a set of *vilain* expectations. The wife is clever, but in a humorous twist we see that it is impossible for her to get the upper hand, even if the husband proves himself a true *vilain* in the process. The narrative is short and though not so sweet, deemed to be entertaining in the prologue, ". . . li fablel cort et

Chapter Three

petit / Anuient mains que le trop lonc" [. . . fabliaux that are short and small are less boring than those that are too long] (vv. 4–5). A husband, to amuse himself, asks his wife to guess what he is holding in his hand. As the fabliau audience might well expect, she guesses that it is his penis. However, the unknown object turns out to be his testicle—it remains unclear whether his mistake would be received with laughter by the audience. As a retort, the clever wife bets her husband that he too would be unable to guess what is in her hand even with three guesses. He touches and smells the mystery object, baffled at first. It is only through his more refined sense of taste that he is able to name the object—excrement! The humor lies in this unexpected disgusting substance and in the fact that earlier in the text she considers her husband to be a mere foolish *sot* (v. 51), whereas after this gustatory test she vows never again to wager with him after the discovery of his masterful skill. This text lacks a precisely stated written moral, but we may deduce both humor and didacticism related to gender roles if we read between the lines.

Erotic and Verbal Culinary Comedy

The fabliau corpus relies on both linguistic play and physical surprises for its humor, its morality, and its treatment of sexuality. Norris J. Lacy makes the vital remark that "whereas . . . the fabliaux are narratives about narration, it is also correct to conclude that, even before that, they are fundamentally language about language" (*Reading* 95). Both language and physicality are employed to humorous ends in the graphic erotic culinary comedy of the fabliau genre. Gender-bending humor exploits food along with wordplay and visual slapstick. We may begin here with Gautier le Leu's *La Veuve* [The Widow] and its simple yet effective wordplay. In a series of sexual innuendos, we learn that the hungry and lonely woman hungers for a big sausage and raw meat (vv. 123–27). Her pursuit of a man is likened to the actions of a hungry bird of prey during the hunt. Substituting meat for male genitalia represents more than mere euphemism here; culinary discourse is thus transformed into obscene diction, treating the excess of two appetites together. In this verbal culinary humor, we see the same type of comedy present in fabliaux that mention hunger, cooking, and eating in relation to sexuality and gender, to those where this juxtaposition of food and sexuality is central to the action of the narrative. Simon Gaunt has found ambiguity and inconsistency of the treatment of gender throughout much of the fabliau corpus. Gaunt sees the fabliau universe as destabilized, where nothing is necessarily as it seems. In relation to gender, Gaunt also considers the fabliau as a form of subversion of canonical literary genres and of class mobility.[29] Food serves as a further subversive element in this text.

Talking about eating acts as a verbal substitute for addressing sexuality in many fabliaux in which orality is stressed. Not only are genitalia and mouths associated with or transformed into foodstuffs (and vice versa), but the analogy between eating and sexual acts appears often, as do more complicated and sometimes humorous scenarios. In the vulgar *Porcelet* [Piglet] the woman's genitalia are described as a hungry pig, and the male's semen, as wheat. All is natural until the pig also partakes of Bran. In typical fabliau degradation of woman, the narrator depicts her vagina as a debauched glutton for "grain," thus meriting the title.

Yet another apparently nymphomaniac fabliau couple uses a hungry horse metaphor to describe the female body and its desires in *La dame qui avoine demandoit pour Morel sa provende avoir*. Humorously, they even give the horse/vagina a name, Morel. Morel is constantly hungry for oats. As audience expectations are nearly always catered to in the fabliau, the husband shows that he can feed the horse with his own wild oats, carrying the extended equestrian metaphor to its fabliau-logical conclusion. Oats, grains, and certain vegetables had strong sexual and aphrodisiac associations at this time, as Bruno Roy has found in the late-eleventh-century medical treatise the *Liber de Coitu*: "Les végétaux, graines, au moins, dans le seul texte du *De coitu*—anis, ail des champs, carotte, ellébore, roquette, séséli (*Seseili tortuosum* Linné), lin, pivot, radis, trèfle, navet, chanvre, ortie, etc." (288).

Once again, food and sexuality are combined to create a transformation and provoke laughter. Orality of consumption and discourse are at stake here, involving opening one's mouth to eat, speak, or for sexual activity. Furthermore, the lust that is

Chapter Three

shown in *Morel* mocks courtly love textual traditions by beginning with a short portrait and praise of their love characteristic of romance. Verse 4 mentions *cuers et cors* together (a familiar rhyme in romance) but the rest of the tale concentrates on the urges of the body rather than the passions of the heart. Transgressions act to fill the belly or to fill the narrative. As we have seen in the fabliau examples and as Raskin's semantic theory of humor states, sexual humor scripts may be implicit or explicit and often in jokes "sexual language is substituted for sexual behavior . . ." (148). Male sexual inadequacies are mocked in the fabliaux, in particular in *Morel* and *Porcelet*, narratives that recall in a comic fashion not only the Sexual Inexperience joke script, but also a hungry version of the folkloric *vagina dentata*.

Many such fabliaux use the juxtaposition of food objects with the body to show the inadequacies of sexual activity and love in marriage, in particular as contrasted to courtly ideals of love. In *Le souhait* [The Wish], male sexual inadequacies are aggravated by dinner and drink. The consumption of food and drink prevents and replaces sexual consummation. This fabliau is set in the private space of the marital dinner table. The unfortunate husband drinks too much at his welcome home meal after returning from a long absence. Ironically, the audience, better informed than the characters, may guess what may occur in the bedroom with the lusty wife following the drunken meal. Pitiable and silly, he is rendered impotent by his inebriated state.[30] The wife, long deprived of marital relations in the absence of her husband, is disappointed with his debilitating gluttony. Her frustration appears in her dreams of a market that sells only penises rather than food or goods. There are many possible critical and humorous messages we may interpret here, addressing the excesses of both female libido and male careless gluttony or weakness.

L'Esquiriel [The Squirrel] treats human sexuality through metaphors of animals and food. Comedy derives from play on words as well as action and situation. Raskin's scripts of Sexual Ignorance or Inexperience offer apt semantic labels for this jokelike tale of sex-related culinary comedy. The irreverent story begins with a young woman forbidden by her mother to speak of male genitalia. A clever suitor takes advantage of this chaste maternal decree in order to satisfy his sexual desires by calling his penis a squirrel and claiming that his testicles are eggs that the squirrel has laid. The biological impossibility and absurdity of male squirrels laying eggs adds to the already ridiculous nature of the metaphor and plays on the woman's ignorance of human anatomy. However improbable the analogy may be, the young woman remains as gullible and naïve as any other duped fabliau character. When the woman asks if the squirrel eats nuts, she regrets that she herself has eaten many nuts the previous day and has none left to share. Here the animal desire to eat is equated with human sexual desire. The knight seizes this opportunity to further his ruse, saying that the squirrel could enter the lady's stomach through her vagina and then feast on the nuts allegedly digesting in her belly. This extended metaphor for male genitalia as rodent is continued as the lady allows the so-called squirrel to search for food everywhere on and in her body. The comical and scatological circumlocution continues as the male orgasm is described as the animal eating his fill and spitting, crying, and vomiting after eating. Another element of vulgar culinary comedy intervenes in the end when, following intercourse, the still credulous woman becomes distraught that she may have broken one of the squirrel's eggs.

In terms of comic scripts, the type of sexual joke that includes verbal *double entendres* and oppositeness (Raskin 148–52) becomes evident. In the fabliaux of *L'Esquiriel*, *Porcelet*, and *Morel* the food references provide the necessary opposition in this type of sexual joke. This fabliau sexual joke script would most likely have had a mixed audience and mixed reactions for this evocation of food related to sexuality.

In a further comic exploration of the body and its appetites, some fabliaux are notable for both verbal and physical substitutions of sexuality for eating. *La dame qui se venja du chevalier* [The Lady Who Got Revenge on the Knight] (Noomen, *NRCF* 7 : 331–50) offers a different vision of transgressive sexuality and eating. Food play, game, and joking are evoked in this tale with a comically happy conclusion. In order to satisfy her adulterous desires, one fabliau woman feigns hunger, asking her fairly well-to-do *châtelain* husband to go out and hunt to provide for her. Her food cravings are very specific. He must return with venison, which she claims is the real object of desire. The obliging and blissfully ignorant husband does her bidding without question or hesitation: "Vos en arois / Orendroit, puisque le volez" [You will have some right away since you want it] (vv. 48–49). The "some" remains ambiguous, amplifying the sexual tension. Ironically, his pledge may also be read as a *double entendre* referring to both sexual and culinary desires. When the hunter returns with his prize game to join his hungry wife in bed, she delays consummation of his lust by suggesting he remove his boots. She then sends him away for candles and wine to supplement their meal and provide a pleasant setting, "Li sires li fet aporter / Lumière tost sanz arester" [The lord had light brought to her with no delay] (vv. 136–37). After several delays to their meal, the wife challenges the husband to look under the covers for the cowering lover. The meal is an exteriorization of mental and verbal sexual play. The husband, who has blind faith in his wife's fidelity, does not draw his sword because he interprets her actions as a laughable joke: "Li sire en a ris et gabé / Puis dist: Bien me savez gaber" [The lord laughed and made jokes. Then he said: you really know how to make me laugh] (vv. 199–200). It is the incongruous addition of food here that causes the husband to laugh and believe he has been the victim of a practical joke rather than adultery. The combination of culinary comedy and the irony of the ignorant protagonist incites the audience to laugh along with him in an indication that this type of narrative, involving transgressive consumption and trickery, would have been considered comic.

As with the culinary comedy of the Perceval tradition in romance, comedy is produced when fabliau characters take language too literally. A brief example of this appears in *La vieille qui oint la paume au chevalier*, where the ignorant woman does not understand the metaphoric concept of bribing someone through "greasing their palm." This fabliau plot follows Raskin's script of Blind Obedience. It targets corruption and pokes fun at the elderly, often treated as stupid, or gullible or demented. The evil knight has wrongfully taken a woman's cows. The neighbor suggests she "grease his palm." The narrator characterizes the nameless archetypical elderly woman as naïve so it comes as no revelation that she comically rubs lard on the knight's hand rather than slipping him money to convince him. To her amazement and our own, this absurd action based on a miscommunication works. Another instance is to be found in *Les perdrix*, where the fleeing priest mistakes the husband's ambiguous talk of the stolen partridges for a threat of castration.

In *Du prestre ki abevete*, a *vilain* and his wife are enjoying their dinner when a peeping-Tom priest spies on them through a hole in the door. He then accuses the couple of fornicating. They explain that they are merely eating, so the clever priest invites the husband to get up from the table and see for himself through the hole in the door. The priest takes the husband's place at the dinner table and proceeds to engage in sexual acts with the wife. Perhaps this would not come as a surprise to an audience familiar with fabliau logic. During the act, the priest explains that he is eating. The husband is gullible, but not completely stupid, exclaiming that if the priest had not said anything, he would have thought he was making love to his wife. Comically the priest responds that he had thought the very same thing earlier. By means of the priest's discourse and transgressive voyeuristic gaze through the private door, eating and sexual activity are equated, and gastronomic appetites are combined. As is not uncommon in the fabliau genre, lechery and sexual play is associated with mealtime.

The writer plays with the literal nature of language and the power of verbal persuasion. Comic irony is present in the difference between the duped character's perception and that of the audience here, as the audience laughs or smiles at the misunderstanding that leads to the somewhat predictable cuckolding of the gullible husband.

Jean Bodel's *Du vilain de Bailleul* [The Peasant of Bailleul] (Noomen, *NRCF*, vol. 5) makes a similar move.[31] It is one of many fabliaux presenting the ruse at mealtime theme. A husband returns home for his noon meal. While waiting for his meager *bouillie* porridge, the *vilain* husband is convinced he is dying of hunger. The wife sees his moaning and his naïveté as an opportunity for adultery. To add insult to injury, she has prepared a barrel of wine, roast capon, and cake covered with a towel in preparation for her lover the priest (vv. 15–19); still the husband is persuaded he is suffering from deadly starvation. The wife exacerbates his hunger through repetition,

Chapter Three

repeating that he is pale, that his life is slipping away, that he is surely dying. Convincingly, the wife explains to her famished spouse that he has in fact died of hunger, telling him that a dead man is unable to do anything. She then engages in sexual acts with the priest in front of the gullible husband. The gullible husband remains persuaded that he is dead and unable to act. Again, the comic element here derives from his hunger and from verbal play. Both of these texts use the culinary setting and linguistic play to instigate sexual activity. Similarly, in *Du prestre ki abevete,* verbal play occurs alongside a visual description, when the cuckolded *vilain* husband watches his wife committing adultery with the priest. Beyond this verbal play is of course the social criticism that many peasants did die of hunger in this period, while members of the church often had ample provisions. The comic criticism of the fabliaux depicts real fears and obsessions surrounding subsistence, food availability, and corruption.

The linguistic play in *L'Esquiriel* is similar to the humorous verbal intercourse in *Aloul,* in which the priest refers to his penis as a food object to be consumed, suggesting that the woman have his "large, medicinal root for breakfast."[32] In *Aloul* there is also a physical comedy of errors involving cooking and genitalia. Like many other fabliaux, *Aloul,* though referred to as a *"flablel"* in the title, is a pastiche of elements from other contemporary genres. It presents the fabliau stereotypes of the lusty priest and the unfaithful wife.[33] She is the familiar *mal mariée* and as for her husband, "Ce dist l'escriture qu'Alous / Garda sa fame com jalous" [So says the written story of Aloul: / Like a jealous man he kept his wife] (v. 255). The fabliau audience, medieval or twenty-first century, would not be surprised to discover an oppressed wife who seeks vengeance on her possessive husband as well as her own sexual fulfillment. The infidelity comes as no surprise, "que il est cous" [that he is a cuckold] (v. 259). But other surprises and transgressions await the audience. The tale soon turns from sexual play to food play, with an unexpected comic twist for the priest's desiring body.

While his wife enjoys the company of a cleric, Aloul sends his hungry, stubborn cowherd to fetch bacon from the cellar while his companions make a fire. The narrator comments that in the meantime the cowherds recounted stories and soon turned to talk of eating; in a pejorative comment, he notes that cowherds are never happy until they have eaten. In a mocking wink to the audience, the *fableor* shows that these *vilain* country folk care only for food and tall tales, and associates eating with narrative.

The unsuspecting head cowherd feels around in the dark of the storeroom, mistaking a hung priest's buttocks for lumpy soft rennet and his penis for a pork sausage hanging up to dry. Sausages are inherently funny foods, and here the narrator highlights the comic association with the male body. The cowherd marvels at the wealth of drying meat; this implicitly humorous remark demonstrates the stereotype of fat gluttonous priests so prevalent in the fabliaux and mock-ecclesiastical texts of the time. As the cowherd attempts to slice off a morsel, the priest, still alive, falls on him, breaking all his bones. Unaware of any crime, the injured cowherd curses the butcher who must have hung the pig there. The others come to investigate, only to find that the meat has apparently scampered off on its own. Here the fabliau logic is rather humorous in its improbability; it is obvious that meat cannot run away, but the ignorant assumption of the cowherds provokes laughter in an audience who views both priests and *vilains* in a pejorative and often silly light. Surprisingly, ecclesiastical culinary humor thus centers on priests' bodies as items of sexual and dietary consumption. In the *Roman de Renart*, branch XVII, Renart castrates a monk whose chickens he steals; one of the miniatures illustrates the fox running off with the body parts in his mouth. Culinary comedy and misuse of priestly flesh is not limited to this episode. Mistaken identity and unexpected use of such transgressive bodies amplifies comic deception.

Of Pigs and Priests: Religious and Anticlerical Culinary Comedy

Physical comedy and mistaken identity happen repeatedly at night or in dark spaces in the fabliaux. The dark cellar of a home or the shadows of a stable provide perfectly believable settings for the intentional switch or the mistake, as in the barn in *Estula*; in other fabliaux, or indeed in romance, characters

Chapter Three

fail to recognize even the most familiar of loved ones with little justification. The sense of touch is at least as important as the senses of taste and smell in the culinary comedy of the fabliaux. When unexpected human bodies appear in the culinary context, the result is disruptive. Human bodies do not belong in the pantry or the larder. Thus touching in the dark that which should have been meat reveals a transgressive body. When the priest's body becomes transgressive in its inappropriate association with food, eating, and desire, his role is called into question.

Le Sacristain moine [The Sacristan Monk] (also *Le Moine segretain*) and *Aloul* share many similarities. They both engage the audience with the spectacle of transgressive eating and transgressive bodies. They imply an anticlerical moral.[34] *Le Sacristain moine* exists in six extant manuscripts and more than three different versions, attesting to its popularity. The story of the sacristan is perhaps more complex in its plot twists and turns than *Aloul*. *Le Sacristain moine* combines kitchen humor, religious humor, social humor, and sexual humor. In this narrative with an obvious anticlerical bias, a lecherous priest is killed by the vengeful Guillaume, husband of the lady the naughty holy man covets, as he attempts to pay her one hundred pounds stolen from the church for her favors. This anticlerical tale forces the cleric to pay dearly for his amorous relations with a *bourgeoise* (we learn her social status in verse 3). In a humorous scatological scene, the murderer comically tries to hide his victim in the monks' lavatory, slumped over a toilet, but the body reappears on his doorstep. As a solution, he attempts to bury the corpse in a nearby tenant farmer's dung heap. Coincidentally and unbeknownst to him, a thief has recently stolen a slab of bacon and hidden it in the dung heap. At first Guillaume, who is just following typical logic for a fabliau protagonist, thinks he has found another dead monk. The punch line is that in reality it is not a cadaver, but rather a pig. This is the mirror image of the *Aloul* script. Meanwhile, the thief Tibout sends someone to fetch the "bacon" from his stash to roast it for a feast with friends at the inn. It is not until they begin to carve up the cooked flesh that they notice that it is tough like a willow branch and that it wears shoes; in this comically understated scene, they seem only mildly surprised by the footwear.

In addition, verbal comedy arises when nobody present remarks that it is in fact a monk, only that it is wearing hose and shoes. In the slapstick action of the episode, the pig falls abruptly onto Tibout the thief, because of its dry smoky rope we are told, knocking him violently into an old trough. He declares comically that they have traded a monk for their pig! The animality of the clerical profession is depicted in many other fabliaux, where the holy men are driven by their lecherous and gluttonous natures.[35] Here, in a twisted fabliau exchange, the pig renders this cynical and anticlerical association between priest and animal unmistakable.

In a further affront to social constructions of identity and appearance, as a solution to the problem of hiding the body, the peasant dresses the dead monk up as a knight (with a lance) and sets him loose on a wild horse. The pair destroys everything in its path in the town and abbey, thereby concealing the identity and the crime. The majority of detail in this slapstick scene is given to the noise and destruction in the abbey kitchen, where the dead monk's mount thrashes about flinging his shield, and breaking pots, bowls, mortars, plates, dishes, and platters. No other details of damage are given, keeping this slightly morbid but humorous plot strictly in the culinary realm. The kitchen scene and the descriptive details of the utensils further amplify the silly and subversive juxtaposition of meat and corpse, priest and pork.

The sacristan is assumed by the public to be deranged, and ends up dead (again) in a ditch. The repetition of the mistaken identity and of the reappearing falling body amplifies the humorous situation. In the end, the murdering husband claims the hundred pounds and the real stolen pig, probably as some kind of fair recompense for his clever ruse in the logic of fabliau justice. The possibility of cannibalism and the morbid resemblance, corporeal and culinary, between monks and pigs provoke laughter. The male body is ridiculed and characterized as dirty, decadent, and gluttonous through the association with swine. The idea of the tricked trickster, or the one who does the duping being duped in return, is central to many fabliaux. In the *Sacristain*, the humor and indeed vengeful pleasure involved in this reversal of fortune are heightened by culinary references.

Chapter Three

The devil also figures heavily in some versions, further adding to the black humor and anticlerical tone. The likening of priests to cured bacon and lard is a common topos of the fabliau corpus, where priests are often depicted as the most *vilain*, lecherous, and dishonest of all characters. Revenge on corrupt priests, often culinary in nature, is common in the fabliaux, and often extreme. Graphic descriptions of their bodies, often tortured or misunderstood, mark the fabliau. Priests' bodies are often described as fat, hinting at gluttony, with their genitalia likened to meat. Castration is a common threat to priests' bodies in the corpus. Philippe Ménard explains expectations about this type of extreme punishment, "pour un homme du moyen âge il est normal qu'un méchant soit affreusement mis à mal" (78). This type of extreme punishment is often much more corporeal than the type of penance and punishment seen in the romance world.

Religious food humor, a common type of culinary comedy, with and without the sexual element, is seen in some fabliaux and, as described in the following chapter, in the *Roman de Renart*. These fabliaux focus on gluttonous, lecherous priests. Verbal culinary religious comedy is, for instance, a salient feature in *Le prestre qui manga des meures*. However, the *Sacristain* is as concerned with the general shortcomings of human nature as it is with the priesthood.[36]

Le prestre qui fu mis au lardier again draws the derogatory and symbolic connection between the clergy and pork when the priest's body is placed in the larder, situated thus in a space associated with animals and with food storage and consumption. This narrative sets male *vilain* artisan wits against feminine wiles and priestly sneakiness. The narrator of this anticlerical episode of culinary comedy prefaces the intrigue by warning us that it is vulgar indeed, and only to incite us to laugh at a certain Nicolas. Nicolas is a poor *savetier* whose wife has cuckolded him with the local priest. Comically, Nicolas's curious young daughter asks why it is that when her father goes to the market the priest comes over and they dine on sumptuous pies and rich pâtés made especially for him. She demands to know, in all innocence, why she is only served bread when she sups with her father. Nicolas the crafty cobbler concocts a false reason to leave, then returns early from the market to watch the adulterous lovers enjoying a bath and his food. When the shoemaker surprises them by knocking, the scheming wife hides the lecherous priest in the *lardier* [larder]. A *lardier* was a cupboard for lard, or bacon, sort of a meat safe or small pantry common in many medieval households. She announces ironically that the hot bath and dinner are ready for her husband. He announces he must leave for the market again in order to sell the old larder. He puts the old piece of furniture on his cart, and the priest's sigh of relief turns to a gasp of fear. The priest says a prayer, and Nicolas says he thinks his larder speaks Latin, so he wants to take it to the bishop. Nicolas draws a crowd to sell the talking kitchen cabinet, and vows to crush his erudite *lardier* with a mallet if it does not continue to speak Latin. The priest's brother saves him from scandal by purchasing the "talking" *lardier*. The narrator implies that Nicolas has won by earning money and taking away the priest's adulterous desire. The morals of the story, though humorous, touch on human nature and class relations. The cheeky narrator gives three lessons to conclude his tale: first, to be careful of the watchful eyes of young children, for Nicolas's honest daughter revealed the scandal; second, that the worst fate will fall on a clergyman who takes on a cobbler; third and perhaps most obviously, that one should be careful not to find oneself in a similar larder. It is no coincidence that the setting is the kitchen and in the pantry. The central element of culinary comedy, the larder, thus represents an immoral, deceitful act. As we have seen, pigs and pork-related items constitute a social critique, a class judgment on the unscrupulous clergy.[37] Moreover, in the medieval chain of being, pork was considered the lowliest meat, after mutton and veal, with chicken being considered nobler fare (because as a bird it is higher off the ground and often fire roasted, therefore closer to air and fire and God).[38] Pigs carried much religious signification in this period, because:

> Meat played a central role in mechanisms of cultural and religious differentiation during the early Middle Ages, when the subsistence-based economy was silvipastoral and forests were measured in terms of the number of pigs they contained. In this context, it is hardly surprising that pigs were regarded as both a symbol and a guarantee of otherness. The remains of St. Mark were smuggled out of Saracen territory

Chapter Three

> hidden beneath salt pork, a technique that was redolent with symbolic implications. Furthermore, in the medieval iconography of the pig's patron, St. Anthony, it was the only "real" animal (that is, without a symbolic function) to appear above the altar. (Montanari, "Food Models" 191)

Pigs have a strong connection to both the spiritual and the corporeal human. More than just a means of subsistence as an important element of Western European diet, the pig came to represent Christianity and distinguished Christians from Saracens in the minds of many.

As J. R. Simpson mentions in his investigations of animal bodies in the *Roman de Renart,* one chapter of the contemporary didactic manual *Ci nous dit exemplum* refers to pigs in a reference to Mark and Luke in its discussion of sinners.[39] This vernacular collection of *exempla* likens sinners to pigs and draws a connection with their animality. Only in the fifteenth century do we find written religious references to specific animals as emblems of the seven deadly sins with the pig representing gluttony. In the bestiaries and religious texts of the twelfth and thirteenth centuries, several different animals could represent different sins. It is clear from the above exploration of the fabliaux that the pig, or pork, represented gluttony as well as other excesses and possibly deceit. With these rich religious and secular significations, a comic connection is often made with clergy and pigs.

L'oue au chapelain is an anticlerical tale that emphasizes the ignorance of the chaplain and the craftiness of a young greedy cleric. The cleric takes advantage of his absent, gullible elder to feast on his goose. The comedy in this tale borders on the sacrilegious, as food and church are literally juxtaposed. He daubs goose fat and sauce on the church's Rood Crucifix, places a goose leg in the mouth of the carving, and convinces the chaplain that his bewitched Crucifix has in fact devoured the missing meal.[40] He blames the eaten goose on the devil or unknown enemy:

> Ne sai deable ou anemis
> S'est en vostre crucefiz mis,
> Car il a trestote mengiee
> L'oue et le gastel et l'aillee. (vv. 96–99)

> [I don't know which devil or enemy
> Got into your Crucifix,
> Because he ate the entirety
> Of the goose and cake and garlic sauce.]

This priest's only apparent fault is thus his gullibility and willingness to believe anything he hears about the cross; by extension, his faith and his ability to carry out his duties are questioned.

Nevertheless priests are not always shown to be as ignorant and unlucky as in *L'oue au chapelain,* or *Le prestre qui manga des meures*. In another goose tale, *Le prestre et la dame*, an unlucky husband bets a goose in a wager against the lecherous priest. The husband is drunk, losing both the bird and his wife to the priest. If priest's bodies are likened to bacon and pigs in the texts above, other narratives show them to warrant this derogatory animal connection. The crafty priest takes advantage of the silly husband's drunken state to sate his sexual and gastronomic appetites in the simple tale of the *Le prestre et la dame*. Similarly, the fabliau of *Le Cuvier* [The Tub]—not to be confused with the much later *Farce du Cuvier*—is a typical anticlerical tale relating the antics of a lusty wife who cheats on her husband with a clergyman. It is not necessarily completely misogynistic or feminist, but feminine wiles and improvised ruses are highlighted through the use of culinary comedy. This tale is almost theatrical in nature and involves physical comedy. The wife invites her lover to the home for a romantic tryst and for a bath in a borrowed tub. When the return of the absent husband startles them, she flips over the *cuvier* to hide her lover from him. The unsuspecting husband proceeds to lay a tablecloth and prepare to eat on top of the basin under which the guilty priest continues to cower. The humor resides in the irony of the idea that the ignorant husband is about to sup on top of his adulterous wife's lover, and in the literal juxtaposition of food consumption and sexuality.

As he prepares for his meal, the servant of the neighbor who has loaned the *cuvier* to the wife enters to retrieve it. The unsuspecting female friend quickly understands her role as accomplice and becomes the comic adjuvant. The wife tells her accomplice to give a message to her mistress that the mistress

Chapter Three

is not aware of the great need that the wife has for the tub. Here culinary comedy is combined with the humor of her veiled excuses. The perceptive servant, experienced in clandestine assignations, guesses that the wife has a cleric hidden from her husband underneath. This female complicity implies that all women are experienced in adultery and that clergymen are often their lovers. The moral emphasizes this, saying that if she had not had so much experience, the servant would never have guessed correctly. In a hasty conclusion, the wife pays a passerby to exclaim "au feu!" Thereby she provides the opportunity to free her trapped lover from underneath the husband's dinner table during the commotion. Thus in the disruption of his meal, the needs of the female body surpass the male's appetite and hunger. In a type of resolution common to several fabliaux narratives, she hides her infidelity successfully, and maintains the status quo of marriage. Order is restored and expectations are fulfilled. Her carnal appetites and cunning use of food reinforce the often misogynistic view of the wily wife in this genre.

Food and the Body

In *De Haimet et Barat*, as mentioned above, cross-dressing and references to the female body are used as part of a mistaken identity device in a ruse involving food. This represents a scene of sexual humor in a text otherwise devoid of erotic elements; in this case the element of sexuality (which could be viewed as obscenity or vulgarity) is incongruous and therefore invites laughter. Here food and superstition are combined with gender play. When the duped Travers goes to retrieve his stolen ham, he suggests to his wife—or so he believes—that she touch it three times to her genitalia for good luck against possible thievery. The *Haimet et Barat* episode offers the most blatant connection between culinary comedy and sexuality that occurs in the fabliau corpus. Here food is to be rubbed directly on female genitalia in order to preserve and protect it before cooking. At first this appears to be a reference to the power of female sexuality, a power so often the subject of the *fabliaux*. Though he believes he hears his wife's voice, Travers is in actuality speaking to one of the cross-dressing thieves who asks to complete this culinary sexual act in the privacy of the bedroom. Mistaken identity is the source of humor here, along with the notion that as a male, the thief is unable to touch the ham three times to the female genitals, referred to in typically vulgar fabliau diction as the *cul et con*. The husband obliges the desire for privacy and the thief runs off with the meat. The superstition that the meat must touch the female body in order to protect it is underlined (and echoes the wife's participation in hiding the bacon in *Haimet et Barat*). The relation of food to the human body in the fabliaux is complex. In the fabliau genre, food is not merely related to the stomach and the digestive tract, but also to female and male sex organs. Culinary comedy and the multisensual experience of eating are combined with sexual innuendos and erotic comedy in the texts investigated; other erotic elements are common throughout many fabliaux, but are beyond the scope of the present study.

Comically, in the *Jeu de Robin et Marion*, the female body is mistaken for a food object during a courtly feast. Just a few lines after the king has asked Robin "how one knows if a creature is female" and Robin responds that one must look at its *cul* (v. 520), the protagonist proves his ignorance of the female body and actually tries to consume a part of Marion's body. Marion scolds the men because she is offended by the question about the body "li demande est laide" (v. 524), then exclaims that she has been attacked. As we have noted earlier, her sexuality is tied to food from the beginning because she keeps apples, cheeses, and bread in her bodice. Her body is thus a combined locus of sexuality and of consumption and food storage. In culinary comedy, cheese substitutes for female breasts, face, or buttocks, just as the sausage or the root substitute for the penis in the fabliau *Aloul* above. In the theatrical work, it is the shape and the odor of food and body parts that the lustful, gluttonous Robin confounds. There is a fabliau-like comedy of culinary errors:

> MARIONS:
> >Encore i pert il; esgardés!
> >Je cuit que mors m'a ou visage!
> ROBINS:
> >Je cuidai tenir .i. froumage,
> >Si te senti je tenre et mole.

Chapter Three

> Vien avant, seur, et si m'acole
> Par pais faisant. (vv. 531–36)
>
> [MARION:
> The mark is still there; look!
> I think he's bitten me on the face!
> ROBIN:
> I thought I was holding a cheese,
> And I smelled you soft and ripe.
> Come, darling, and hug me
> To make up.]

In the fabliau of *Estormi*, the *fableor* places violence on the body at the center of the conflict and humor surrounding food. The botched cleanup of evidence following the murder of three lecherous priests is told in a comical manner. Culinary language adds to the comedy of the situation, through exclamations: "Ne m'i leront a nuit mengier!" [They will not let me eat tonight!] (*Estormi* v. 453) and "Ne pris .II. oes lor granz Merveilles!" [Their great miracles are not worth two eggs to me] (v. 457). One of the criminals swears, "Par foi, or ai-je mon pain cuit" [By my faith, now my bread is cooked] (v. 480) in the English idomatic sense of "my goose is cooked." Finally with his shovel, Estormi hits the priest who has apparently come back to life, "Qu'aussi la teste li esmie / com fust une pomme porrie" [Thus he squished his head like a rotten apple] (vv. 501–02). *Estormi* ends with a meal and a didactic message "not to drink out of the same cup as these men," literally or metaphorically; such an appropriate moral could be applied to most of the unfortunate fabliau victims in the episodes of culinary comedy encountered above.

Conclusions on Food in the Fabliaux

Whether in language or action, it is often the familiar human element of eating or food preparation rendered incongruous or unexpected that makes a scene humorous. The fabliau protagonists' ignorance, naïveté, and gullibility are often presented as class and gender stereotypes. Such human failings are a vehicle for ironic comic effects. Narratorial interventions often conspire with the audience, who is privy to knowledge the character does not have, to heighten the irony. Predictability—such as the common fabliau setup where a priest and bacon appear together in the beginning of a narrative foreshadowing future mistaken identity—also provides humor to the audience probably waiting for the ensuing comic confusion or case of mistaken identity.

The Superior Theory of humor sheds further light on these texts, as most fabliau culinary comedy finishes with one party reaping the rewards of the other unlucky party; in order for one to enjoy great fortune, and to sate one's appetites, both gastronomic and sexual, the other must suffer great misfortune. It is rare that everyone is happy at the end of a fabliau narrative, for cruel and humiliating humor is everywhere. Laughter is provoked by the suffering and hunger of others. Many fabliau narratives therefore encompass humorous plots and punch lines involving reversals of fortune. Food is often the catalyst for change and for crime, especially in the urban world of the fabliaux. Thieves are especially adept at saving their own bacon through their own cunning deception and the stupidity of others. Priests and women often fall victim to their appetites. Jokes mocking them follow the semantic humor scripts of Cunningness/Craftiness, Stinginess, Sexual Ignorance, Sexual Opposition, and others. These short fictional narratives create instability in existing power structures, playing on stereotypes. In the fabliaux, food humor is anticlerical, antipeasant, antibourgeois, attacking nearly every social group as well as gender roles; what is more, using consumption as a point of departure, fabliau culinary comedy is self-evaluative of the sinful side of human nature.

Chapter Four

Hungry like the Wolf, Sly as a Fox
Le Roman de Renart

> Renars qui moult sot de treslue
> Et qui avoit grant faim eüe
> Se met baaillant au frapier.
> —*Le Roman de Renart*

A cycle of beast fables, the *Roman de Renart* is about animal appetites.[1] The animals live by the code: eat or be eaten. Through the beasts' actions human class hierarchies, social institutions, and family structures are represented. As Bergson suggested as part of his definition of comedy, humor is a response to unconventional or nonhuman behavior on the part of human beings. Such is the case in the animal as human comedy of the *Renart* cycle. Renart the fox is an aristocrat and Noble the lion is the king in a world populated by chickens. The animal community is depicted in stereotypical fashion. Cats chase mice, wolves are cunning hunters, and bears climb trees for honey. They inhabit a world characterized by pretense, deceit, and ruse. Victims, adversaries, and accomplices come and go as they are tricked and defeated in turn. Looking at text and illustration, this chapter evaluates the function and effects of both physical and verbal culinary comedy in this zoomorphized representation of human nature and culture.

Philosopher Elizabeth Telfer points out that today most Westerners "... devote more time, money, and attention to food than is needed to stay alive, or even to stay healthy and active. We do this because we think that as a result our food will give us a great deal of pleasure" (24). In contrast, lower- and middle-class medieval existence could not afford such luxury of time or expensive food. Food production was a daily struggle for many people, and food choices were not broad because for many communities, food was for subsistence and not pleasure. Though the animal characters in the *Roman de Renart* are driven to act by their appetites, they demonstrate an obsession with food as a means to pleasure. Renart and other animal characters take pleasure in obtaining and preparing food even at times when they are not starving. On one level, some of the animal characters are gluttons, with food as the principal pleasure in life. On yet another level, they take pleasure in the attention needed to dupe others out of food or obtain food that is better than their daily fare of hunted small game.

The characters of the *Roman de Renart* are a reflection of contemporary iconography and zoomythology. A brief look at contemporary French *bestiaires*, compendia of animals and their signification, gives us insight into this hungry animal universe. Gabriel Bianciotto, in the preface to an anthology edition of bestiaries, reminds us that "de l'Antiquité au Moyen Age s'est donc perpétuée, presque sans changements, une vision résolument non réaliste et fantastique du monde animal" (14). In light of such an implausible vision of animals, it becomes clear that the medieval creature world is rich in meaningful signs. Michel Zink sees the medieval literary use of the animal—whether a faithful familiar of the chivalric hero, a symbol, or an anthropomorphic character—as an "instrument du sens" (48).[2] Though it is certain that most animals held allegorical functions in this period, in *renardie*[3] culinary comedy focuses more on the animals' human nature contrasted to their animal actions. The animals' actions reflect human behavior and human nature as in Aesop's *Fables*, known to this period in the form of *isopets*.[4]

The *Roman de Renart* presents a complex anthropomorphic game of changing animal-human identities.[5] Combarieu Du Grès sees this as a game of masks and roles:

> En ce qui concerne les personnages animaux, les jeux de masque qui altèrent les identités reposent sur trois procédés au demeurant bien connus dans le *Roman*: les passages constants d'une représentation de l'animal en tant que tel à une représentation humanisée et vice versa; les tours que les animaux se jouent à eux-mêmes ou jouent aux hommes et qui les amènent à ruser, c'est-à-dire souvent à se déguiser, à jouer des rôles, à endosser des personnalités autres

Chapter Four

> que la leur, au point que, précisément, on ne sait plus quelle elle est; la rencontre avec les hommes surtout lorsque celle-ci, ce qui est rare, s'effectue par le biais des dialogues, renversant les rôles traditionnels de chasseur et chassé. (361)

Thus animals take on human identities; conversely humans, like the peasant Liétard, adopt these animal roles as hungry hunters themselves.

A cursory survey of vernacular encyclopedic bestiaries, many dating from the early to mid-thirteenth century and therefore contemporary with several branches of the *Roman de Renart*, a collaborative composition that evolved over decades, reveals ideas about animals that shape the characters.[6] Conversely, certain bestiaries that postdate some branches show probable influence of the *Roman de Renart* (though this intertextuality is not the focus of the present study). Pierre de Beauvais's *Bestiaire,* an early-thirteenth-century French bestiary, gives us some insight into contemporary representations of and beliefs about animals such as the wolf, the lion, and the fox. The fox is referred to as Renart in this bestiary and shares some aspects of the fictional hero. The lion, as to be expected, is a strong and just king, with many biblical connections; his weak point is that he is afraid of the white cockerel. Man is said to be merciful to the weak, like the lion. The bestiary wolf is associated with the devil, gluttony, and violence. The wolf is mysterious and dangerous, as we would expect given the superstitions and negative perceptions surrounding the animal throughout history; it hunts at night and has devilish candle-like eyes that may attract sinful humans. The wolf, Pierre tells us literally, represents the devil and the fallen angel, and has the ability to take on the strength of others. Pierre details physiological manifestations of the wolf's evil nature. The wolf is crafty and stealthy, as in its calculated habit of staying downwind from shepherds' dogs. The equally devious fox, called *Renart* as well as *goupil* in bestiaries postdating the *Roman de Renart*, is portrayed as a wily trickster who plays dead to attract his prey.

In the bestiaries, as in the *Renart,* animal behaviors are linked to biblical and symbolic associations, some of which are associated with food or hunger. The fox's trickster nature is highlighted in contemporary bestiaries. Guillaume le Clerc de

Normandie's *Bestiaire divin* and Pierre de Beauvais's *Bestiaire* (both ed. Bianciotto) explain how the species of *goupil* is known for many ruses. The fox of the *Roman de Renart* also does engage in this playful deceit. The *bestiaires* elucidate the stealthy behavior in detail; the fox tricks its prey by rolling in red dirt to imitate blood, bloating the stomach, holding its breath, and lying still in wait for birds to arrive. The fox exhibits this behavior when motivated by hunger. It then turns on the scavengers and catches them by surprise. This ruse appears in the *Vol aux poissons* food-stealing episode.[7] Pierre associates the fox with the devil, because the devil also plays dead and entraps the vulnerable in dangerously convincing ruses. In addition, the fox is known for pillaging and for his appetite for chickens. The species' diabolical penchant for trickery targets those who live the way of the flesh. Pierre's moralizing *Bestiaire* warns that humans who partake in the devil's work, like the fox, enjoy getting fat from flesh eating. In this text foxes, like humans, also allegedly engage in the diabolical activities of fornication, homicide, stealing, and lying or false witness. The fox is also anthropomorphized in these bestiaries in a pejorative manner, characterized as deceitful, mischievous, and, above all, thief-like. The fox also becomes a symbol of the immorality of the flesh; namely, of gluttony and carnal temptations. These behavior traits are explored with humor in the *Roman de Renart.*

Throughout the *Roman de Renart,* there is little doubt that animal actions and characterization gloss both bestiary preconceptions of animals and contemporary perceptions of human social constructs. The anthropomorphic animals' cravings and antics are easily recognizable as barbed critiques of human nature, as they are centuries later, for example, in the seventeenth-century indictment of the court in La Fontaine's *Fables.* Criticism of mobility or corruption in the human world is better negotiated by analogues in the fictional animal kingdom. The juxtaposition of the two kingdoms reveals much ambiguity in the part animal, part human nature. Human analogues are transparent and may attract the sympathies, laughs, and frowns of the audience. Animals fall victim to the human flaws of greediness, laziness, hypocrisy, gullibility, and flattery. They attempt to seize power or wealth as humans do in courtly society.[8] Renart is characterized by his assiduous pursuit of food, wealth, and the upper hand, inhabiting a universe that presents a vision of hunger and violent inequality where cunning ruses are the only means of survival. As in the fabliau genre, the ignorant and the gullible seldom triumph unless luck intervenes. The heavy burden of daily survival is lightened by humor for both animals and humans. There is a considerable amount of recurrence and repetition with variation in the cycle, offering an amplified comic effect to audiences familiar with more than one branch.

The community of animals is as important as any individual character in this sociable fictional universe. Their community is brought together by the search for protein-rich food, a common goal that helps to construct their group identity. The communal ambiance of the narratives lends itself to a comedy of errors involving members of the group. Characters do not develop or grow in the same way as in courtly romance. The interest of the texts resides in characters' movements within the hierarchy of their community and the repetitively humorous situations in which the animals find themselves. It is a society of jealousy, deception, and suspicion, similar to that of the fabliaux. Disillusionment, selfishness, and distrust mark the characters' psychology. In Renart's community, might does not make right—cunning does, especially when motivated by hunger. Contrary to the Incongruity Theory of humor, rarely do the animals act outside of audience expectations, and such predictable behavior is the source of much laughter.[9] Moreover, the Superiority Theory is applicable to the beast epic, as laughter most often occurs at the expense of others.

In around 30,000 words in a composition spanning about a century (from the early 1170s to 1250), episodes concerning the search for food and eating are a common characteristic of the twenty-odd branches of the *Roman de Renart*. Not one branch neglects to mention food, and culinary comedy abounds. The *Roman de Renart* is parodic in nature, with pastiches and mockeries of romance, *exempla*, liturgy, and especially epic. Epic struggles are not between warring nations, but rival animals. The best-known and most often adapted example of hunger motivating animal action is perhaps the narrative surrounding Renart's hungry hunt for his prey, Chantecler le coq. Many tales begin with a description of Renart's or Isengrin's extreme hunger and plans to hunt or otherwise find food in the face of starvation conditions. The animals, weakened and agitated by hunger, go in quest of nourishment in a land marked by famine in over half the branches. The search for food, or the hunt, is primary animal instinct. However, intelligence, craftiness, and ruthlessness are essential for subsistence in both the animal and human domains. Hunger motivates most of the animals, which must resort to trickery to nourish themselves.[10] Many of the animals suffer from malnutrition or are motivated by gluttony, so conflict adjacent to food is thus a natural recurring topos. At the same time, the beast fables present a very realistic view of human famine and of the role that sustenance has in the political and economic relations between social classes.

Setting has an important role in the comico-realism of these narratives. Just as the fabliaux are often set in the private space of habitations, the *Roman de Renart* is usually confined to animals' hunting grounds and habitats. Occasionally animal characters transgress boundaries to seek food in human private homes or in the public milieu. The *Roman de Renart* shares some of the fabliau politics outlined above, with a particularly powerful evaluation of human foibles set in the marketplace, the farm, the court, and religious places. The farm is a logical locus of action for animal-human exchanges involving food.

Food and Hunger

Most of the branches of the *Roman de Renart* contain food episodes. I do not propose an exhaustive account of food in the *Roman de Renart*, but rather an exploration of how food functions together with comedy in the context of a cycle of texts full of challenges to the powerful expectations of social and narrative convention. Hunger invites quests for food (the object is to *querre viande,* as in branch V, *Le bacon enlevé* or *Renart et le grillon*) or provokes desperate acts of deception. Hunting—or questing, in anthropocentric terms—for food is central to the structure of many branches as well as to the overall unity of the beast fable cycle. In several branches the narrative structure follows a progression from empty stomach to full belly.[11] In this environment, farm animals and wild animals are portrayed as equally famished while a privileged few enjoy

Chapter Four

bountiful harvests and successful hunts. The folly or necessity of their hungry actions is left to audience interpretation. Many branches begin with a stable situation, and the desperate actions of a hungry animal then create disorder. The original order may be restored, but it is called into question through this hungry disruption. Unscrupulous animals and humans often do get their just desserts when irony and comedy arise with eventual deceptions, complications, and coincidences.

Gluttony is a central theme just as it is in the fabliaux. Gluttonous actions represent both sinful nature and authoritative positions in medieval European Christian culture, since eating well and overeating can be signs of spiritual weakness as well as indications of wealth and power. The one who controls the most food without losing it in the *Roman de Renart* has the upper hand. In contrast to the fabliaux, here gluttonous behavior is more of a social commentary on inequality among classes than it is a commentary on human psychology or morality. Overeating, insatiable appetites, and hording are sources of comedy in the *Roman de Renart* universe, where hunger is the norm. In one episode the wolf eats too much, letting his guard down and allowing himself to be tricked by the fox. He becomes trapped when his distended full belly will not allow him to escape. When gluttons and criminals are punished in the *Roman de Renart* (or the fabliaux) it is evident that either ingenuity, or morality, or both, intervene to reestablish order. "Cil qui tot convoite, tot pert" [The one who covets everything, loses everything] (III, v. 432) is the implicit moral throughout the *Renart*. Greed and gluttony thus lead to immorality and misfortune. Similar morals are reflected in the thirteenth-century didactic manual *Le chastoiement d'un père à son fils,* which includes the figures of Renart and Isengrin in, for instance, *exempla* 3, 4, 5, 9, 20, and 23. *Exempla* number 20 shows Renart in a typical attempt to cheat Isengrin out of cheese. We may deduce the moralizing and edifying effect Renart tales may have had on the audience or later writers from such moralizing intertextual references.

Food storage, preservation, and hording occur often in human and animal kingdoms (e.g., *Renart* branches XVII, IX, and XXIV). Liétard is the most striking figure of the human *vilain,* a wealthy peasant, who stocks his pantry and preserves his bear meat to save it from spoilage, from his hungry neighbors, and from his nosy lord. A detailed description of the conservation process amplifies the importance of the pantry as both a survival and security item. The stealthy, greedy Liétard drains the animal's blood, brings the bear carcass home on a silent cart greased with animal fat, then skins it according to the rules, with a sharp knife, washes the meat, hangs it, salts it, and hides it from others in his *saloir* (vv. 1030–60). His wife, a stereotyped image of the sneaky woman, helps him devise the plan for the stealthy safeguarding of the meat. But Liétard does not trust his own valet with the bear meat, because he is not a family member. Nor does he trust his hungry one-time accomplice, Renart, and rightly so. *Primaut et le lardier du vilain* [Primaut and the Vilain's Larder] and *Renart et le bacon du vilain* [Renart and the Vilain's Bacon] are both similar stories of animals attempting to cheat *vilain* human figures out of food. John Flinn has shown the presence of "la satire des vilains" in branches IX and XVI (102). We have seen how greedy stockpiling of meat leads to crime and comedy in the fabliau genre, where "bacon" is a tempting trophy. In the *Roman de Renart* such surreptitious and covetous actions are no different, denoting hungry, desperate, and greedy communities of humans and animals, suggesting the moral of the story. Though socioeconomic mobility is not as common or as feasible in the beast fable as in the fabliau, in *renardie,* animals and humans can, through a rapid change of circumstances, obtain riches and copious food or be reduced to rags and hunger. Typically such ironic reversals of fortune involve food.

Hunger is a crucial motivation in many of the branches (e.g., branches I, III, IV, V, XI, XII, XIV–XVIII, and XXV). Food supplies are short, illustrated by episodes such as branch II, where a farmer and his family are devastated when Tiecelin the crow steals just one round of cheese from him. In branch XI, for instance, extreme famine threatens Renart's immediate family. His children and wife cry from painful hunger. Their discomfort is emphasized in a short but poignant passage, with the triple repetition of *dolent,* "painful." In a reference to contemporary problems of malnutrition, women's health, and infant mortality rates, Renart's wife admits she is pregnant, and fears losing the baby because of malnutrition:

Chapter Four

> Devant li est venu Rovel
> Son fils qui de faim vait plorent,
> Et Hermeline meintenant,
> Et Malebrance et Percehaie
> Qui molt par font cere dolente.
> . . . .
> De lor mere sont molt dolent
> Qui ploure de fain tendrement
> Et molt par fiste dolente chere.
> Renart li diste: "Amie chere,
> Por qoi vos voi je si ateinte?"
> "Sire, fait el, ge sui enceinte,
> D'enfant ai tot le ventre plein.
> Mes certes je ai si grant fein
> Que j'en cuit perdre mon enfant." (XI, vv. 10–24)

> [Renart's son Rovel
> Came up to him crying of hunger
> And Hermeline now,
> And Malebranche and Percehaie
> Who had very sad expressions.
> They are very sorry for their mother,
> Who weeps with hunger, tenderly,
> And presents a very sad countenance.
> Renart said to her, "Dear love
> Why do I see you suffering so?"
> "Sire, said she, I am pregnant,
> I have my belly full with child.
> But certainly I am so hungry
> That I think I will lose my child."]

In an accusing tone, the desperately malnourished wife, Hermeline, suspects Renart has eaten recently and scolds her husband for being so typically selfish and dishonest while she, the children, and her unborn child go hungry:

> "Renart, trop estes a aise,"
> Dist Hermeline, "que ge cuit
> Que tu n'as pas le ventre vuit.
> Tu es plus a aise que gié
> Que tu as hui Blancart mangié
> Qui molt ert cras et rognez
> Moi et mes enfanz es les tuens
> Lez de fain morir a mesese." (IX, vv. 2147–59)

["Renart, you are too much at ease,"
Said Hermeline, "that I think
That you don't have an empty belly.
You are more comfortable than I,
Because you ate Blancart,
Who was meaty and fatty
While I, and my children (and yours)
You leave to die of hunger in misery."]

Though hunger is a grave condition and the animal community must kill, trick, or steal to eat, humor is made of their situation and is amplified through repetition.

The animals' play—and particularly food play—has a critical function that is at once satirical and parodic. In the pseudo-reality of the *Renart,* satire of human institutions and literary conventions involves make-believe or deceptive pretense as well as games with food as an object to be won, lost, or toyed with. Harsh yet comic social criticism of the aristocracy, of unjust laws and unfair hierarchies, of corrupt merchants, and of the nature of the *vilain* flavors the *Renart*. There is perhaps more obvious literary parody in the *Roman de Renart* than in the fabliaux, directly mocking conventions of epic, lyric poetry, or courtly romance.[12] For example, in branch XI, we hear echoes of the lyric or romance conventional topos of the *reverdie* of springtime. As in these other genres, the animals are awakened by birds singing, the verdure of fresh leaves on the trees, flowers in bloom, and balmy weather. Also similar to topoi in other twelfth- and thirteenth-century lyric and narrative genres, the change in seasons brings on a desire to enjoy the bounty and beauty of nature. The contrast of winter and spring represents scarcity and abundance for the animal world. Springtime heralds happiness and abundance for the beasts, but in a way that is different from that for the lovers of troubadour poetry or chivalric romance. The parodic *Renart* twist on this common device is that this springtime rejoicing is accompanied by the animals' hunger after a long winter's starvation or hibernation. Instead of enticing them to think of acts of love or to satisfy lust as in lyric or romance, they feel the seasonal urge to seek their prey and fill their aching bellies. In the springtime,

Chapter Four

> Ce fu en la douce saison
> Que cler chantent li osellon
> Por le tans qui ert nes et purs,
> Que Renars ert dedens les murs
> De Malpertuis son for manoir.
> Mai molt ot son cuer triste et noir
> Pour sa viande qui li lasche. (XI, vv. 169–75).[13]
>
> [It was in that season
> When the birds sang loudly because the weather is clean and pure
> That Renart heard it within the walls of his castle, Malpertuis,
> But he had a very sad and black heart
> For he was missing meat.]

In this humorous parodic passage, Renart's mood is thus gloomy, not amorous, as he pines for his meat, not his beloved.

Comic Realism

Along with descriptive passages of nature, there is a strong element of realism in several branches. Many realistic descriptions are connected to food or to Renart's *vilain* or noble victims. Mouth-watering descriptions of expensive food items abound for: fish, eels, anchovies, meat, sausages, salt pork, ham, cheese, and poultry. Renart, Isengrin, and Tibert are carnivores (in many branches, such as the story of Renart, Isengrin, and the *jambon* in branch V).

The animal heroes prefer cooked and prepared meat products, those suitable for human consumption, such as andouilles and charcuterie. Isengrin, when in his anthropomorphic guise, prefers to stock hams at his home rather than limiting his diet to the cliché of sheep hunting. The three predators shy away from cabbage and other available vegetables in favor of flesh and seafood, mimicking the diet of the rich and noble. But they are also occasionally too lazy or too small for game hunting. They prefer to rob the wealthy *vilain*, their perpetual nemesis and easy target. The higher-ranking members of the human social strata, as well as rich peasants such as Liétard, have copious food stores; he explains how he built wealth and reserves through hard work:

> Venu en auques en dis ans
> Que deners avoie gisans
> Bien entor cent livres ou plus
> Sans autre chose le sorplus.
> Terres et vignes, bues et vaches,
> Forment et vin, lait et formaches
> Avoie plus, la Deu merci,
> Que vilein qui fust pre de ci. (vv. 413–20)

> [Coming from nothing, in ten years
> I had earned well over a hundred pounds or more
> Without counting the rest.
> Land and vineyards, oxen and cows,
> Wheat and wine, milk and cheeses,
> I had, thank God,
> More than any other peasant around here.]

Liétard also makes a pleasantly rich blackberry liqueur, the fruit of his abundant private garden.[14] Food and wine continue to be indicators of mobility within human societal class structure, particularly among the growing merchant class and upwardly mobile peasant class as depicted in the *Roman de Renart*. As this *vilain* declares with pride, he is indeed one of the best-provisioned peasants in the *Roman de Renart* and in much of Old French literature (due to hard work, ambition, and his highborn wife).

Risibly, the animals are shown searching habitually for an easy meal while many humans hoard foodstuffs. Sometimes these predators target dim-witted and inattentive human characters rather than hunting for themselves. These ruses criticize human failings. For instance, in branch III, Renart comes upon a group of gullible traveling fishmongers who are transporting ocean fish, herring, lampreys, and eels. There are many realistic details of their cargo and their trade. Notably, there is a precise list of fish, and the narrator remarks that they had plenty of fresh herring because they had a good sailing wind from the north all last week.[15] The same fishmongers are also concerned with the quality and possible market price of Renart's hide, in a discussion of the realistic value of fur pelts. When Renart steals some of their catch, the narrator includes a realistic description of how his hungry family prepares their stolen meal. They wash Renart's legs, perhaps in observance of courtly

Chapter Four

human hand washing rituals, and take the eels from around his neck. They skin the eels, cut them in slices and resourcefully slide them onto knitting needles. The hungry family finally prepares hot coals from their reserve of wood to grill them (vv. 168–76). Based on what we know from medieval culinary treatises, the technique of grilling rather than boiling shows that the Renart family still has aristocratic tastes even though they are suffering from starvation, as boiling was often a more economical approach common among cooks of lower socioeconomic status.

The animals' lives are marked by periods of extreme famine, as mentioned above, alternating with opulent humanlike feasts with their families and peers. As in Arthurian romance and several fabliaux, mealtime is structurally important as the setting for action, conflict, and humorous situations. Wedding feasts are as elaborate as in the romance world, as, for example, in Poincet's wedding celebrations, where the focal point of the festivities is a plentiful meal. Renart *jongleur* sings while Tibert and Brun serve the copious dishes:

> Totes sont pleines les cuisines
> Et de capons et de jelines;
> D'autres vitailles i avoit
> Selonc ce que chascun voloit.
> Et li jugleres lor chantoit.
> ....
> Aprés mangier savez que firent?
> Hastivement se departirent. (Ib vv. 2891–95, 2899–2900)

> [All of the kitchens are full
> With capons and chickens;
> There were other dishes
> According to what each person wanted.
> And the minstrel sang to them.
> Do you know what they did after eating?
> Hastily they all left.]

Eating is all that matters at this greedy feast found in the tale of *Renart Teinturier* and *Renart Jongleur*, with no time for additional talk or celebration; this both implies the careless gluttony of the animals and criticizes the emptiness of the trappings and customs of courtly feasts.

Sly as a Fox: Food and the Character of Renart

Cunning ruses are Renart's forte, particularly in the case of food.[16] The propensity for trickery and ruses throughout the branches of the *Renart* is another common point with the fabliau genre. If "trickery ... is what the fabliau is all about in the broadest sense" (Schenk, *The Fabliaux* 55), this is equally true of the *Roman de Renart* in nearly every sense. Renart goes from outlaw to emperor to clergyman to doctor, occupying several positions in between, relying on wits and verbal skill to give him his advantage. Deception involving food, whether verbal or visual, is at the center of many branch structures. Whether the fox uses his handsome coat or his eloquent words to attract his victims and steal their food, Renart's charisma and irresistible powers of persuasion always aliment his appetite. Dominique Boutet sees a positive image of Renart in the oldest branches:

> ... Renart est un être astucieux, dénué de scrupules mais plaisant, dans ses échecs comme dans ses succès: symbole d'intelligence confrontée à d'autres intelligences, ou victorieuses de la force bête que représente un Isengrin, il est un héros sympathique. (257)

In later branches Renart becomes more vicious, violent, and underhanded and perhaps less inviting of audience sympathies. Renart can play dead, as does the fox in the bestiaries, to fool the simplest bourgeois or play complex verbal word games to persuade the king. He expresses disdain for animals of varying social positions and *vilain* humans. No one who has food in his or her possession is safe from his subterfuge. Unlike fabliau protagonists, Renart has multiple targets for his dupery; Chantecler le coq and Isengrin are far from being his only competitors. Renart does not often have to expend effort to seek his prey, for a parade of victims from the animal world passes by for his amusement and profit.

In the *Enfances Renart,* branch XXIV, supposedly the fox's origins are taken from a mysterious book entitled *Aucupre*. This section recalls the *Enfances* of the heroes of the chansons de geste. The quasi-biblical genesis of the crafty fox explains many of his actions. Renart the fox is an animal created by Eve,

Chapter Four

and thus doomed to sin and sneaky behavior as part of the group of wild animals who went into the forest and were not tamed like those issuing from Adam. The implication is that he benefits from feminine wiles, intuition, and intelligence. Conversely, through this connection with Eve, Renart also receives the misogynistic feminine characteristics as seen in the fabliau, among others: devious, tricky, mischievous, greedy, and underhanded. We also learn that his mother was a glutton, explaining his constant famished state and the hunger that motivates many an adventure. His Aunt Hersent has an insatiable appetite, while his Uncle Isengrin is a gullible glutton. Renart's vision of heaven is of a gourmet paradise; the gluttonous fox envisages a glorious safari of edible game, including goats, hares, cows, and sheep (also XVII, vv. 902–07):

> Je sui en paradis celestre
> Ceens a riche pecunaille
> Ceens puez veoir mainte aumaille
> Et mainte oreille et mainte chievre,
> Ceenz puez tu veoir maint lievre,
> Et bues et vaches et moutons. (IV, vv. 268–75)

> [I am in celestial paradise
> Here it is rich in cattle
> Here you can see many livestock
> And many goats
> Here you can see many hares
> And oxen and cows and sheep.]

The narrators create a sly, driven, and persistent image of the character of Renart. The ruse becomes even more central to the narrative—structure and humor—than in the fabliau. The strategies utilized by the scheming Renart to find nourishment are at the base of the comic action of many branches. But there is more to the cunning Renart than just gastronomic dreams and pleasures. Renart does not merely show his teeth or use his powers of persuasion to obtain food, he also does it for the pure pleasure of winning, taking revenge, or tricking others. It is comedy through humiliation; feelings of superiority bring laughter. Culinary pleasures are also constituted as physical, animal pleasures and may therefore be viewed as sinful and gluttonous.

In part because of his relentless, cunning nature and in part because of his feminine biblical origins, in the mid-thirteenth century Renart becomes a symbol for the triumph of Evil in the world. By extension, he is an effective analogue of human evil. Simpson has shown that with an animal figure, the beast fable is better able to represent human sins than other contemporary didactic genres:

> What makes the *Renart's* version of the topos of the sinful human as animal all the more unique is that it is able to extend the tale and to produce a body of material that can explore the ramifications of animality in narrative on a scale beyond the comparatively much shorter and much more closed *exempla* and discussions that deal with animality found in theological works. (20)

Renart and the other animals are already fallen sinners, and we may understand more about human sin through an extended, complex narrative of their analogous actions that reflects humanity's shortcomings. It is for the reason of pre-existing animal sin that Simpson suggests, ". . . the animal body offers poor odds in any metaphysical wager" (22).

We recall that Renart is no ordinary fox, nor is he a *vilain paysan*. Renart is an aristocrat in a zoomorphic kingdom. He is a noble, a baron, and never forgets his place. He has a castle, Maupertuis, and rides a proud *destrier* when he sets out for adventure. Renart's enemies and victims are often *vilains*; he steals their goods, robs them of fish or pork, and even drowns them. Still, when the tantalizing odor of freshly roasted meat overtakes him, he is not above stealing partridges and food from underneath the copious table of the king (recounted in the *Chasse au Renart* branch).

Culinary Comedy and Mock-Religious Discourse

Culinary comedy is not limited to the class struggles of the secular sphere in the *Renart*. Renart is God-fearing and often prays for victory in his exploits, as do the other animals and members of his family. The mock-epic *Moniage Renart* depicts Renart in a pietistic light. Moreover, the confused Bernart the Ass calls Renart a saint in his sermon. Though a believer in

Chapter Four

God his protector, Renart is staunchly anticlerical and often turns up his nose at Christian dogma and the institutions of the Church, of which he is skeptical. Like many fabliau characters, Renart is not above double-crossing a member of the clergy. For instance, in one anticlerical episode he tricks a priest, who has just kindly blessed him, into a grossly unfair trade; along with his occasional partner in crime, Isengrin, he takes the priest's fattened gosling in exchange for his own stolen priestly garb. Through his mock-religious discourse and irreverent anticlerical antics, he mocks the church, but his faith remains strong.[17]

The juxtaposition of culinary comedy and the religious characterizes the *Andouille* episode (branches IV/XVa). The vocabulary is mock religious and gastronomic as Renart and the other animals engage in wordplay about food. They speak of sermons, penitence, heretics, the Last Judgment, damnation, the congregation. The tone is liturgical and at times didactic. Sausages and andouilles were the butt of many a joke in medieval and early modern times, and perhaps because of their shape, ingredients made of intestines, and availability, such meat products were inherently funny. Later, the *Sermon joyeux de Saint Jambon et de Sainte Andouille* uses similar alimentary imagery with a mock-religious tone (text in Koopmans 47–56) while Bowen notes that "Saint Boudin and Saint Andouille were already old jokes in Rabelais' time . . . " (19). In the *Andouille* episode, food serves as a means to comment on, debase, and mock the church and spirituality. The hero's travels are plagued by hunger as usual. To set the stage for this mock-religious drama, the narrator says Renart's stomach growls for Tibert the cat, to gobble him up in a bout of revenge. Food soon becomes the object of their conflict. Then Renart and Tibert the cat happen upon an andouille sausage. They discuss who should have it and the possibility of sharing. Tibert announces he will carry it to the nearby cross for them to eat, but Renart scolds him for dragging the andouille in the dirt. The fox makes a comical, cunning attempt to take the sausage from Tibert, saying that it will be cleaner and safer in his mouth. Sharing seems the obvious option, since the two have made amends, but Renart artfully turns his discourse toward religious topics, in a tone not unlike contemporary mock sermons. In so doing, an andouille becomes The Andouille with a capital "A," comically transformed into a religious object. The blessed Andouille, or Andouillette in the diminutive, is *saintifiée*, "sanctified" (vv. 204–05). It becomes *sacrée* when it is attached literally to the cross. The comical mock-religious dialogue centers on eating the sausage at the nearby Crucifix, as the animals become fervent believers in the spiritual and gastronomic properties of the Andouille. Their reverence for the sausage is linked to other (nonhumorous) spiritual food as in the Eucharist.[18] But food is more important to this community than is spirituality or liturgical discourse. Food humor thereby debunks religious discourse, poking fun at clerics, the liturgy, relics, and human institutions.

In another adventure, *Renart, Tibert et l'andouille joué aux marelles* [Renart, Tibert, and the Andouille Game], branch XXVI,[19] Renart seems to have forgotten sermonizing about the sausage. Mock-spiritual verbal silliness turns to an active game. The andouille shape invites laughter, as do connotations associated with the andouille such as the insult "une triple andouille," meaning a complete imbecile, or the phrasal verb "faire l'andouille," meaning to act or play the fool. These idioms and the *Renart* episodes including the andouille are humorous in part because of its phallic associations, in part because of its odorous pork chitterling filling. He comes upon Tibert the wild cat along with Fremont, Blanche the ermine, and Roussel the squirrel. This episode centers on food games. The group of animals is engaged in a game that involves an absurd, wasteful usage of the now apparently mundane andouille; they attempt to ridicule Renart, who is known to "faire l'andouille" on occasion. This game provides the setting for trickery involving food. The playful transformation and unexpected usage of food has the resulting effect of culinary comedy. The group has found a nicely trussed andouille that Renart covets. They had been planning to share the fortuitous sausage among the four of them; Renart is an unwelcome fifth mouth. He is often an unwelcome diner in someone else's feast, as we see again with the King's game in the *Partage* episode. In a simple ruse that toys with the cat's appetite, Renart distracts Tibert with a mouse and claims the andouille for his own dining pleasure. When Tibert begs him to share, he responds with an

Chapter Four

offer similar to the offensive offer of the harness Isengrin proposes elsewhere; he offers undesirable leftovers from the andouille.

In the beginning of the *Andouille* incident, Tibert the cat launches into a diatribe against human nature and sin (vv. 39–58). He laments in his century the number of evil people in the world, how people are reluctant to help one another, how one attempts to trick one's neighbor, how there is a general lack of sincerity and loyalty. He concludes that crime and trickery do not pay, and that one always receives the punishment one merits, warning Renart that betrayal and wrongdoing never come to any good. In a sense, he gives both the state of affairs and a didactic code of conduct for the animals in the *Roman de Renart* universe as well as for humans outside the text. This episode harkens back to the epic parody that is the *Enfances Renart* with the treatment of the relation of animals to Original Sin. In a prolonged discussion of the sin of the Andouille, gluttony and improper eating are both alluded to. The sermon speaks of martyrdom, penitence, damnation, and *l'Assemblée* to warn that lying leads to damnation. Renart uses the consumption of food—an oral act—along with lying—a verbal act—in his oratorical ridiculing of spiritual discourse. Many such instances of this nonsensical alimentary orality exist, as the *Renart* continues to play with meaning.

The *Moniage Isengrin,* also a parody of a chanson de geste subgenre as in the *Moniage Guillaume,* provides yet other opportunities for religious wordplay. Once again, food is used to make a mockery of even the most basic of religious discourse.[20] Renart induces Isengrin to undertake a false monastic life, which proves to be a great burden to the wolf. This derisory ruse ridicules both Renart's rival and the tenets of monasticism. Moreover, the wolf is gullible when he falls victim to Renart's twofold strategy to obtain food and to call into question Christian doctrine. The hungry Renart covets Isengrin's fish, so he uses a verbal attack to obtain the object of his desire. Renart tries to persuade Isengrin through his word game that the word *fish* to which he refers is in reality the "fisherman" or "fisher(s) of men." This twist, like that of the Andouille/andouille, mocks liturgical discourse through the unexpected and inappropriate juxtaposition of food and religious allegory. Similarly, in *Le duel* Renart becomes a "fisher of men" not for expected spiritual reasons, but literally to fill his belly with fish. Culinary signs are superimposed on and confused with religious signs, and this mixture thereby begins to question meaning in narrative.

Social Satire

On another level, turning from religious culinary parody to food-based social comedy, we recall that several episodes include urban interaction in *Renardie*. Urban life, with its mercantile negotiations and its trickery, is represented in a cynical fashion. Merchants and bourgeois humans and animals become Renart's victims and the butt of many a joke. In one episode, Renart simultaneously obtains a seafood feast and achieves a sharp social criticism of traveling merchants.

In the episode of Renart and the eels in branch III, desperation and necessity call for ingenuity and provide much comic action. The narrator amplifies the description of his famished state through repetition. Renart has used up his reserves (vv. 6, 17); famine is threatening and distressing the dismayed animal. It is winter and Renart's family is starving as we see Renart in a less aristocratic light. He has nothing, nor is there anything for him (in the human persona) to buy with which to comfort them, in a critique of the monetary marketplace economy (vv. 7–8). Once again, his errant travels are motivated by hunger as necessity demands he leave his abode in search of food. Rather than having his noble family suffer, he decides to profit from the foolhardiness of *vilain* merchants. The comic narrative illustrates a growing aristocratic bias against the merchant class. Following the expected comic formula, he does not have to reflect long on his situation before a vulnerable *vilain* arrives on whom he may prey. In this case, some unsuspecting fishmongers become his quarry. Renart's skill and superiority over the ignorant below-average merchants invite our laughter.

As usual in the fabliaux and the *Roman de Renart*, it is not a question of what will happen or who will triumph, but rather what sort of ruse will be devised and how the narrative will be resolved, in *Le vol aux poissons*. In his ever-admiring tone, the sympathetic narrator reminds the audience that Renart has no

Chapter Four

equal when it comes to tricking people (vv. 34, 45). Renart's most simple ruse to steal food is based on animal instinct. With a few moments of foresight, he plays dead in the middle of the road and lies in wait as the fishmongers arrive. To further add to the suspense as Renart plays dead in the road, the narrator asks the rhetorical question, "Oïstes mais tel traïson?" [Has anyone ever seen such betrayal?] (v. 48). Apparently unaware of animal behaviors in contemporary bestiaries, in their greediness and desire to get something for nothing, the fishmongers appraise the carcass and decide his clean coat will earn a healthy sum. They ignorantly place him on the top of their cart with the fish, as the miniature illustrates. Renart lies in wait, then helps himself to a pile of herring and makes off with a load of eels slung around his neck. Renart's reaction is indicative of the theme of the text and perhaps of the audience's own reaction: "Mes Renart n'en fet que sourire, / Que mout a entre fere et dire" [But Renart could only smile / Because there is a big difference between what one says and what one does] (vv. 793–94). He has the audacity to pause to thank the fishmongers, gloating as he makes his escape. His successful getaway is comic.

Renart is never completely at ease even in his own home with fish on the fire for his next meal. In a humorous episode that follows, *La pêche à la queue*, Isengrin sees the smoke rising from the kitchen and recognizes the odor. Adhering somewhat to convention, Isengrin asks for hospitality in exchange for news. Renart simply laughs in his face and interrogates him. The refusal of hospitality is yet another comic criticism of convention and society, particularly that found in romance.

In a clear adaptation of Aesop's fable of *The Fox and the Crow*, Tiecelin the crow also becomes the victim of Renart's culinary ruses and thievery.[21] In this adventure, Renart's hunger is once again the motivation from the outset, and cheese is the object of desire. As he is admiring the charm of nature around him, he feels the first needling of hunger. The narrator exaggerates the hunger comically; Renart cannot think of how to appease it and he hesitates to ponder his situation for a while. Meanwhile, Tiecelin the crow swoops down on a nearby stock of cheese that has been put out to dry. In an inattentive moment, the female guardian leaves the cheeses, and Tiecelin is able to steal one just as she returns to catch him. She throws rocks and pebbles and scolds the bird, but to no avail. Tiecelin just responds with proverbial language, yelling back that when someone asks who stole the cheese, she will have to say it was her because, as the proverb goes, "the incompetent guard feeds the wolf." Coincidentally, he retreats to the tree under which Renart is resting to enjoy this booty; he pecks at and savors the yellow cheese then the rind as the envious Renart looks on. To further underline Renart's hungry jealousy, the narrator mentions that the dry cheese went down with ease through Tiecelin's beak. Foreshadowing the punch line of the Cunningness script and characterizing Renart with humor, the narrator reminds us that he is fond of cheese as well as of the one who is its master. Though the *Roman de Renart* is less overtly moralizing than the fabliaux, if we regard parts of the *Roman de Renart* as *exempla* then it becomes evident that the animals' food provides signs for the edification and entertainment of the audience, and if we consider such episodes as entertaining, jokelike narratives, their meaning is better recovered.

Renart uses flattery (of the type that reappears centuries later in La Fontaine's use of a crow and cheese episode) in praising the reputation for singing held by Tiecelin's father, and Tiecelin's passion for organ playing, to get the bird to sing and drop the cheese. Renart thus indulges Tiecelin's belief that he is the greatest musician in the world. But the ruse is not so simple. Renart continues his flattery, adding that he has leg pain, and that the unsavory odor of the cheese is harmful to him, doctor's orders. The gullible and vain Tiecelin obliges, falling victim to flattery, as will analogous characters in La Fontaine. Ever the voice of reason and humor, the narrator asks how one could resist believing such woeful words accompanied by painful gestures. As Tiecelin descends from the tree to move the fallen cheese, Renart repeats, asking the bird how he could possibly be afraid of him in his impotent state. When Tiecelin descends, the impatient Renart attacks, getting nothing more than a mouth full of feathers. Renart tries to explain that it was a painful bout of gout that forced him to attack in spite of himself. His persuasiveness is betrayed by his overzealous appetite. Tiecelin agrees to leave him the cheese in order to save his own feathers. Ironically, the satisfied Renart

Chapter Four

exclaims that it is the best meal of cheese he has ever eaten, and that it is just the thing to cure his aching leg.

In *Renart Médecin* [Renart the Physician], branch X, the cunning fox makes amends with the estranged Lion king through his newfound medical talents. The king believes himself to be deathly ill, and no doctor has been able to cure his ailments. First, Renart uses the skins of his enemies such as Isengrin the wolf and Tibert the cat for a strong psychosomatic effect on his patient. Then he turns to herbs and potions he has obtained from a pilgrim. During this period such herbal remedies and dietary regimens were thought to have medicinal qualities, though some of them had a placebo effect or were actually harmful. At the heart of this episode is a comic portrayal of the king and his gullible nature and comic commentary on the "quack" medicine of the day. Renart rubs the king's nose in his herbs, provoking a barrage of flatulence and sneezing. Though the expelling of "bad air" was seen as beneficial to some patients, the excessive, unexpected, and non-royal actions are humorous. Several lines are devoted to this digestive cure; undoubtedly this kind of culinary toilet humor would have alimented audience laughter or smiles as we may suppose was the case with fabliaux such as *Jouglet* and *Le pet du vilain* [The Peasant's Fart]. Miraculously, Renart actually helps the king, who is relieved by the induced flatulence and the strength of the herbs he sniffs and the supposedly medicinal food he ingests.

The cunning persuasion of those who are ignorant and the gullible is Renart's forte, to much humorous effect, as in one example that reveals Renart's verbal play when one morning, Renart goes hungry to his uncle Isengrin the wolf's house. When his feigned illness proves an insufficient ruse to obtain the prized pork, Renart declares woefully that he has not eaten recently, that he does not feel well, and that he has even lost his appetite. His aunt Hersent, concerned for his health, feeds him a hearty meal of kidneys. The sly Renart only has eyes for his uncle's three handsome hanging salt porks. Stealing bacon is a common goal for the animal vilains of the *Renart* cycle just as it is for desperate fabliau characters, with similar links to connotations of sexuality, Christianity, and social climbing. Renart hints with subtlety that the bacon is not secure; thieves will surely come and steal it, he warns. He comically hints that all of Isengrin's neighbors are capable of this criminal act. This witty quip addresses human nature and relations between *vilains*. With this idea firmly implanted in his rival's head, Renart is able to steal the bacon, having already persuaded him that someone else was at fault (a ruse similar to that in the fabliau *Boivin*). Two days later, he returns in the night to steal the meat, eating his fill and hiding the rest under the straw of his bed. Isengrin is truly duped, and the narrator predicts other similar furtive actions and verbal trickery, saying that Renart will do even better later, taking advantage of everyone, especially his uncle. The comic mode of the *Enfances Renart* is inaugurated with Renart's own laughter as he scurries off with a victorious flourish of his cape.

Interaction between Renart and the miserly *vilain* Liétard is a portrayal of animal-human relations.[22] The human and animal communities become integrated in the lengthy narrative of branch IX, *Liétard, Renart, et la mort de Brun* [Liétard, Renart, and the Death of Brun] in which animals now speak with humans, rather than just silently stealing food as in other episodes, where before ". . . face aux hommes ils redeviennent '*bestes mues*,' fuyant devant les meutes, tentant d'échapper aux coups de bâtons" (Combarieu, "Des Animaux" 36). In later branches such as IX and X, the animals become adjuvants in human schemes. They also betray their new human accomplices in order to pull the wool over their gullible human eyes. In relating the interplay between Liétard and Brun and Renart and Liétard, human characters become more than just rustic farmers or greedy merchants from whom the animals procure easy feed while fearing the consequences of their angry weapons. Nor do humans remain the dangerous trapper or hunter throughout the cycle. In branches IX–X the human is rather a fool to be taken advantage of or to prey upon in more complex ways. This branch presents a parody par excellence of the *vilain*. The self-serving *vilain* Liétard conspires with Renart against Brun, then turning on his collaborator to join forces with Timer the mule against his former ally in a satire of human hypocrisy and instability in socio-political relations. The human Liétard and the animal hero Renart are brought together through hunger and gastronomic desires. Brun's carcass is kept in Liétard's *saloir* for preservation.

Chapter Four

Liétard and his wife are stereotypical representations of the *vilain*: hypocritical, greedy, tricky, underhanded, but also—fortunately for Renart—as credulous and gullible as the *vilains* of the fabliaux. He remains uncourtly despite his wealth. In the opening lines of the episode, Liétard is described as one of the most affluent peasants of the time, prosperous with substantial savings and eight of the best cattle in the region. A model citizen, this *paysan* is an early riser and a hard worker. But, like most literary representations of *vilains*, he is naive, falling victim to Brun and Renart. Liétard is perhaps deserving of his fate, in the animal-centered logic of the *Roman de Renart*. As will be further demonstrated below, this is just one example of the comical manner in which animal order substitutes for human order and finally subverts it in the latter branches.

The evil peasant farmer treats his livestock poorly, overworking and abusing Rogel (also Rougeaud), his best ox. Rougeaud, burdened by fatigue and heavy loads, irritates his master with his slow plodding pace. Though this is natural for a beast of burden to some extent, Liétard has upwardly mobile intentions and is proud that he toils to become more productive than the average *paysan*. Liétard exclaims that he wishes bears and wolves would devour this ox. Ironically, who should appear but the stealthy and hungry Brun the bear?[23] Brun is motivated by revenge on the farmer's pesky dogs. Adding to the comedy of the situation is Brun's culinary reverie. His desire for beef overcomes him, as he says his whiskers quiver in anticipation "de la char Rogel crasse et tendre" [of Rogel's fatty and tender flesh] (IX, v. 106). Brun then turns to lengthy discourse on how he will fight Liétard for his prey; suddenly—and humorously—he realizes that there should be no struggle, since the peasant has promised him this carnivorous feast. Brun is sure Liétard will be grateful to him for answering his exasperated pleas. Satisfied with his situation, he leaps forth from the underbrush in anticipation. Brun then begins to reason with Liétard, reminding him that he promised the ox with the farmer's own self-fulfilling vow, "Que max ors poüst manger" [that a bad bear could eat it] (v. 171). Liétard replies with a tacit confused gaze, not amused, though the audience certainly would be entertained by the irony, the same form of ironic culinary comedy present in the fabliau of the *Prestre que menga les meures*. There is comedy in the repetition of Brun's persuasive discourse (vv. 163–207), telling him to oblige without smirk or grimace, and to get back to work where a good peasant belongs.[24] Intimidated and befuddled, Liétard sweats and worries about an attack on his entire herd of oxen that he no longer takes for granted under the threat of a more powerful figure. He also fears for his own life. He reasons that it is better to lose one cow than eight. Then he turns to prayer, believing it to be a more powerful solution than violence. In tears, Liétard tries to negotiate, promising to turn over the ox to Brun the following day in the tone of accepting dismay of one who has fallen victim to the bullying, corruption, and unfairness so rampant in thirteenth-century society. But Brun knows, like any fabliau or *Renart* audience, that such future promises are not often respected. Brun refuses to delay his dinner. He does not wish to be taken for a fool (v. 257), and explains that he lives by the cunning Renart's motto: "Tien ge cest sen, molt vaut saisine" [I hold to this motto, a bird in the hand is worth two in the bush] (v. 254).[25] His language becomes increasingly proverbial, as Brun uses adages to convince Liétard to renounce the promised beef. Brun's verbal trickery is perhaps not as adept as Renart's, but his verbal promises are meant to dupe the peasant, in a Renardian ruse indeed. Liétard convinces him to wait, promising to feed the cow hay and oats to fatten him up. Wordplay is central to the humor of this scene. In addition, the *vilain* himself turns to proverbs to comfort himself about his impending loss. "You reap what you sow" and "Once the wine is poured you must drink it" are his appropriately culinary proverbial utterances that are amplified by the culinary comedy of the tale.

Like Renart, Brun expresses strong antipeasant sentiments, calling them liars (IX, vv. 277–84).[26] Brun suggests that the *paysan* class always acts in bad faith. Showing his profound distrust, he then suggests that no lord set a tax-evading peasant free on his word. The human peasants and *vilain* are shown to be worse than any animal counterparts. Brun's actions convince the wealthy *vilain* to give up on commerce altogether. When Renart arrives he insults the *vilain*, or *paysan*, calling him an idiot and contrasting his stupidity with his own ingeniousness while recapitulating his culinary adventures and victories over

165

Chapter Four

the inferior Isengrin. The fox then repeats the bear's (and perhaps the narrator's) mistrust of *vilains*:

> Mes j'auroie povres merites
> De toi si con je croi et pens.
> Vilein ment volonters tot tens. (IX, vv. 624–26)
>
> [But I would get a meager pay
> From you, that's what I think of you
> Peasants lie deliberately all the time.]

Thus Renart devises a plan to obtain Brun the bear on behalf of the peasant, but fears Liétard will swindle him out of his fair recompense because of the inherent deceitful nature of his lower social ranking. Renart in turn wants to claim the bovine prize for himself. The peasant obliges and is so thankful for his help that he offers chickens and capons to further demonstrate his gratitude. Renart concocts a scheme to deceive Brun and kill him by distracting him by imitating the clamor of a hunting party in the woods. Being the carnivorous connoisseur that he is, Renart instructs Liétard to drain his blood, perhaps knowing that this lengthy culinary preparation could possibly provide an opportunity for him to steal the meat for himself, so "meus vaudra la char a manger" [the flesh will be better to eat] (v. 702). For the peasant, Brun the bear is transformed, losing all anthropomorphic qualities as the hunt begins. The bear meat becomes the object of his desire. He dreams of skinning the beast with his sharpened knife. He does not wish for a settling of scores, but "Avoir char d'ors en son larder" [to have the bear flesh in his larder] (v. 740). After having butchered the deceived bear savagely, Liétard becomes greedy. He mistrusts his less wealthy *vilain* neighbors. He vows to hide the carcass, lest dishonest and greedy peasants discover the bounty of meat in his larder. The peasant fears equally his feudal lord, saying that no amount of money could save him if the count or his entourage discovered his unauthorized meat (vv. 977–79). This would have been considered an infraction of game hunting laws, in which game was increasingly reserved for nobles. Thus the nature of both classes is called into question by his secretive and comically paranoid actions.

The juxtaposition of human and animal spheres in branch IX has long been problematic to critics, posing questions on interpretation and dates of composition, as noted by Batany in his review of editions and manuscript variants (125–26). The narrator tells us repeatedly in branch IX that Renart is motivated by hunger. He does not believe the peasant wife's attempt to convince him to wait for fatter poultry as recompense, in an illustration of stereotypes of greedy, *vilain* desire for instant gratification and rapid wealth. Renart eventually gets the upper hand and enjoys Liétard's birds. The victory of animal over man in this episode (as elsewhere, e.g., the trial of the fur trader in branch XVII) overthrows the expected order of life, questioning justice in an unexpected satirical fashion. Liétard is wary of both his poor peasant neighbors and his unforgiving feudal lord. But the narrative does not side with Liétard or these two real extremes of medieval society. Instead it is Renart the animal, the other, who truly disrupts the human order of things. Renart's actions and his words serve to question the human communities and institutions. The fox's attack on the peasant and other more high-ranking humans is a comic reversal of role that attacks both class structures and linguistic structures. This representation of the *monde à l'envers*, where animals win food and power, represents a scathing criticism of human social institutions, and even calls into question audience expectations of verbal conventions in narrative. *Vilains* and aristocrats are shown to be deficient, whether animal or human.[27]

In a fabliau view of human failings in private life, culinary comedy in the *Renart* often occurs in private homes. The ironic culinary comedy here stems from the formula of the duper who is duped, often in his or her own home. Renart often takes advantage of his uncle Isengrin when it comes to food. In another episode, the two come upon a *vilain* merchant carrying a load of salt pork. In a rapid reflection on this sudden opportunity to eat, Renart is persuasive, saying that he will procure the meat and then give it to Isengrin to eat his fill, selling the rest. Renart reminds his uncle that he is the best salesman around, and that he will only take one third of the profits. Because he does not have the same sense of superiority over humans or upwardly mobile drive as Renart, Isengrin is scared of *vilains*, who often

Chapter Four

beat him, and so lets himself be convinced by the proud and confident ruses of Renart. Renart's tactic is to appear feeble and battered so that when he appears in front of the *vilain*, the man will give chase, thinking him easy prey, as suggested in the *Bestiaires* of the time. The plan works because of the *vilain's* greedy nature. He wants Renart's hide, which he knows is worth more than the price of his bacon. Happily he declares that he wants to sew some of the hide on his coat as a trophy and sell the rest. Isengrin takes advantage of the hunt, running out to take the pork when the *vilain* drops it to run after Renart. Later the outlaw animals return to the woods, the proper hideout for such marginal characters, where Isengrin has carefully wrapped the pork in leaves to keep it fresh. He refuses to give Renart his fair share, in revenge for other actions. Instead he offers Renart the *hart*, far less desirable than the juicy morsel of pork that he takes for himself. The proud fox refuses, as he knows he will get his revenge another time.

The borders between the world of nature and the world of human society are blurred when it comes to food preparation and culinary comedy. The divisions between animal and human behavior become ambiguous in the scenes we have explored above, and food habits represent one of the most essential distinctions. Jacques le Goff has applied Lévi-Strauss's dichotomy of *le cru et le cuit* to Chrétien's *Yvain* and courtly romance. Roger Bellon has suggested a similar application to the *Roman de Renart*. The starved Renart eats raw chickens, crows, and other birds. Renart eats the birds raw, and only on occasion does he prepare them; in branch IV, Renart kills three hens, eats two raw on the spot, and runs off with the third to cook at home (he becomes distracted by his thirst and a nearby well). Eggs are also prized, especially Dame Coppée the hen's large eggs. Many manuscript miniatures show Renart with a bird in his mouth or devouring the uncooked freshly caught birds, feathers and all, as discussed further below. He is proud of this and recounts his meals more than once. However, Renart does enjoy well-prepared cuisine; in branch VII, the narrator comments on his uncivilized meal, represented by the uncouth (and humorous) lack of a tablecloth as he gobbles his prey without cooking it. Revealing realistic cooking details, the noble Renart shows his awareness of differences with human food preparation when he must go without. Contrary to his gourmet tastes,

> Onc n'i oi savor de cuisine,
> Ne vert sauce ne ail ne poivre
> Ne cervoise ne vin por boivre. (VIII, vv. 30–32)[28]

> [So I did not have flavor in the cooking,
> Neither green sauce nor garlic nor pepper
> Neither beer nor wine to drink.]

He laments not cooking his meat, and having a meal without sauces, seasonings, trimmings, or beverages. Renart shows the gastronomic expectations of an aristocrat who is accustomed to the flavors and seasonings of a well-cooked human meal, and however absurd it would be for an animal to be such a *gastronome,* we accept anthropomorphized qualities for the most part and expect the animals to behave as humans.

Most of the animals consume their food raw at some point, but Renart and his wife and children engage in realistic food preparation. They prefer cooked food, and their favorite dishes would not be distasteful to their human counterparts. There are many indications that the beasts prefer cooked, humanized food. Isengrin is attracted by the smell of broiled eels at Renart's house, being prepared by his sons as any noble family would roast them. Renart's hungry fox family

> Ont les anguilles escorchees.
> Puis les couperent par troncons
> Et les espois font de plancons
> De codre et ens les ont boutez.
> Et li feus fu tost alumez
> Que buche i ot a grant plenté.
> Lors ont de toutes pars venté.
> Si les ont mises sus la brese
> Qui des tisons i fu remeze. (III, vv. 169–76)

> [Skinned the eels.
> Then they cut them into slices
> And speared them with skewers made of hazel tree wood.
> And the fire was soon completely lit,
> Because there was a good supply of logs

Chapter Four

> They blew on it from all directions
> They put them on the hot embers
> That the logs had been reduced to.]

When he is not running around the forest, Renart enjoys his gracious and noble household in which he grills meat or fish and also eats at properly set tables, with linens, water service, and several courses, as Bellon also notes (5–6). The culinary detail of the cooking scene amplifies Isengrin's frustration at Renart's characteristic good fortune and adept deception.

Culinary Comedy in Text and Image: The Renart Miniatures

Now that we have considered the textual manifestations of culinary comedy in the *Renart,* we turn to a succinct look at the phenomenon in image. The images selected for illustration in the *Roman de Renart* cycle can tell us much about audience perceptions of the work in the decades following composition and copying, and also shed further light on the importance and functions of culinary comedy. The most common scenes in the *Renart* manuscript tradition illustrate the animals at Noble the lion's court, or Renart chasing birds or engaged in ruses. These illustrations represent a contemporary response to culinary comedy and other forms of play in the *Renart.* Play in manuscript miniatures reflects the nature of play in the texts, amplifying meaning and providing unambiguous images of a satirical nature. Rubricators and artists interpreted texts, whether working with short titles or the entire narrative, thus giving us a tangible, visual look at what readers may have thought was significant, funny, poignant, or entertaining.[29] Such interpretative images would have enriched reading, understanding, or performance of the beast epic for decades, sometimes centuries, following composition.

Not all manuscripts containing *Roman de Renart* branches are illustrated. Those that are filled with miniatures constitute a unique reading experience shared perhaps by a limited audience; nevertheless, we may gain insight into how the romances may have been interpreted by illustrators, rubricators, and audiences. MS BN f.fr. 12584 is a fourteenth-century copy of

Hungry like the Wolf, Sly as a Fox

the *Roman de Renart* with rich illuminations and numerous elaborate color miniatures. It is notable that the illustrations were done around the time of famine in the thirteenth-century and early-fourteenth-century (with a so-called little ice age beginning around 1300), lending further satirical significance to images of food. With illustrators' conceptions adhering more to contemporary iconography and *Bestiaire* portrayals of animals, the animals are not very anthropomorphized in their general appearance, but activities such as sleeping in a bed with covers, eating at table, or riding horses suggest the dual aspect of their existence. In considering a number of the representative miniatures portraying food, tables, cooking, fishing, or hunting for prey, we discover that a significant percentage of the total miniatures illustrate food and culinary ruses. Here the corresponding function of culinary comedy in both text and image becomes evident, as illustrated by the miniatures in MS BN f.fr. 12584, for example the image on folio 66 entitled "Renart et les anguilles." Other *Renart* manuscripts include longer titles and rubrics describing this episode. As this comic illustration shows, we recall that in this adventure Renart, through his pervasive cunning, procures eels, or herring fish, from a traveling merchant. It is significant that the comic episodes of trickery involving fish throughout the *Renart* are amplified by miniatures on the following folios: f. 66 shows the detail of the cart with the eels that Renart steals from the merchants by playing dead; f. 68 illustrates the "Pêche aux anguilles." Folio 77v. shows two miniatures including fish with Renart, Isengrin, and Tiecelin, with the *titulus* "Renars menga molt volontiers." At least three manuscripts depict this episode in a miniature, showing Renart, the eels, and his *vilain* victims. The fish cart adds another realistic detail. A few images show the animals after the ruses have been successful. They illustrate the joy and bounty of the kitchen and the table, glossing the text in an amplification of the importance of consumption in the text. Folio 67 shows the cooking of the stolen eels on spits over an open fire at Renart's home, and folio 103v. shows Renart, Isengrin, and their pilfered fish and a table. These images, often adhering to elements of the Cunningness script, depict comic happy conclusions where hunger and the injustice of society may be overcome through cunning ruse and/or crime.

Chapter Four

In his bestiary animal mode, Renart feeds off birds and their young. Domestic chickens and more exotic breeds alike tempt his palate. His attacks on birds serve two purposes: survival and spectacle. While Renart's appetite is satisfied, the audience's own visual pleasure is heightened by the resulting spectacle. The sheer number of images depicting Renart with birds or poultry compared to other scenes is evidence of their powerful visual effect. Several miniatures show Renart's penchant for poultry, in a series of miniatures repeated with variation, for example: folio 4 shows appetizing chickens in a cage; f.39 Renart is shown taking and eating white birds; f.60 shows Renart eating a white chicken again; f. 91 shows Renart and others eating birds; f. 94 shows him eating birds in front of the cat. Still others portray plump appetizing birds, before they fall into the fox's clutches. Probably the best known of all the Renart fables is that of Renart and Chantecler le Coq, inspiring countless adaptations across linguistic borders for centuries (branch IIb, *Renart et Chantecler le coq*). In this tale, Renart catches and prepares to eat the bird, which is appetizingly "bon et cras et grant" [good and fat and big] (XIV, vv. 153–54). Renart derives pleasure from his playful interaction with Chantecler, but finally does not eat him in this branch. Since food production is as important as consumption, the hen that lays big eggs is another important character. Renart is punished for his sin in an appropriate, food-related manner. Ironically in the text of *La mort de Renart* [The Death of Renart], we are told that he will be prevented from eating chickens in heaven! (vv. 1008–16). Daydreams of his favorite pastime, as well as his dreams of a poultry paradise, are dashed down by the ironic poetic justice so common in *Renardie*.

Food is a major preoccupation of the animal characters as it was for humans over the period of the *Renart's* composition. This preoccupation is revealed in both text and image. Other visual representations of culinary comedy and food ruses in this manuscript exist in the following images: f. 22, with the *titulus* "Renart veut manger son confesseur" [Renart wants to eat his confessor], showing violent animal instinct with humor; f.16 shows the ill king in the episode of *Renart médecin* and his edible remedy; f. 67 shows Isengrin, stuck in a wall with a food dish. Folio 65 is a nearly blasphemous representation of the comic antireligious humor in the episode of the Andouille, the cat, and the cross. Other images do not feature food ruses, but show the significance of the functions of food throughout the branches: f. 14v. shows Renart at table with text describing his meal; ff. 25–26 show a full-page feast; f. 59 has Renart cooking; ff. 94–95 show table objects; f. 96r. shows bread.

The illustration of Renart's chicken stealing and castration of a monk where Renart is shown with human genitalia in his mouth is reminiscent of fabliaux narratives in which human body parts are mistaken for food objects. MS Oxford, Douce 360 f. 21, shows Renart stealing chickens in the Chantecler episode, making a crafty escape with one slung over his back while angry *vilains* come at him. The rubric for this illustration indicates familiarity with the story and emphasizes the elements of ruse and play in this familiar scene of Renardian culinary comedy: "Si comme Renart emporte .i. coc que il a pris en .i. par centre pluseurs gelines. Et une fame et vilains le chaçoient a chiens et a bastons et le coc s'en eschapa par barat" [How Renart took one rooster that he took from the midst of several hens. And a woman and peasants chased him with dogs and sticks; and the cock escaped by a ruse]. The image does not, however, show Chantecler's subsequent cunning escape from the jaws of the fox. With the sly fox at it again, folio 29 of MS Douce 360 displays the Aesopian tale of Renart, the crow, and the cheese; the miniature shows the cheese about to fall into his clutches as a result of another successful culinary ruse. As with the other miniatures, this image serves two functions; it structures the narrative and enriches the meaning and implied or stated morals. Moreover, in MS BN f.fr. 12583, f. 1, the first miniature, though it is found at the beginning of branch one, shows an episode from the end of the cycle, with Renart rising from his own (sham) funeral while grabbing a chicken for his next meal, indicating the importance of culinary comedy from the beginning through the very end of this social satire; this manuscript does not contain *La mort de Renart*, but makes reference to it visually while at the same time underlining Renart's roles as hunter, eater, and trickster par excellence.

Chapter Four

Conclusions: Food Play and Beast Epic

The device of culinary comedy in the *Roman de Renart* engages the animals and the audience in complex play, both visually and verbally.[30] In the *Jugement de Renart* recapitulation and evaluation of Renart's life, the element of *barat/baraz*, meaning play or trickery, is highlighted: "Renart qui sait trop de barat" [Renart who knows too many tricks] (I, vv. 805–06), and is the focus of the entire cycle of beast epic. Ruses and counter-ruses are among the few constant and plentiful elements in the animals' otherwise desolate realm. In a cyclical narrative structured by games, characters themselves are aware of the omnipresent trickery and deception in their universe. Craftiness is valued over might, with cunning subterfuge as the beastly modus operandi. As in the fabliaux, the outcome of gamelike alimentary ruses is largely predictable in beast epic, as the characters play with their food to much comic effect. Sometimes there is no clear winner in the endless contests of wit, which implies play for play's sake. Verbal play and physical play may be comic and subversive as demonstrated in the preceding analysis.

In his conventional trickster role, Renart's ruses are acted out in the spirit of play. He enjoys deceiving, putting on airs, creating false pretenses, and pretending. His ruses are often associated with a game, in which the object is food. But the fox gains more than just his prized food at the end; he derives pleasure from tricking others and being deceitful or playing make-believe. Renart's reaction to the plight of others, as a consequence of his ruses, is often laughter, as when Isengrin becomes trapped while fishing, ". . . Renart commenca a rire" [. . . Renart started to laugh] (III, v. 430). The suffering of those he has duped brings pleasure to the sly fox. The eternally hungry Renart is at his most devious when the prize is edible and his adversary may be humiliated by the loss of a food object. Hunger aside, Renart is motivated by vengeance, pride, and the spirit of competition. Renart is a trickster, unscrupulous but amusing. However, Renart is held accountable for some of his food play. In a sense, since he pretends to be human, foxy games lead to human consequences. A royal death warrant in addition to trials about chickens and dead mice are the results, with hanging as the punishment for the gluttonous animal hero.

Just as Renart himself enjoys laughing at the misfortunes of others he has tricked, the self-proclaimed goal of one of the first *Renart* narrators is to incite audience laughter:

> Pierres qui de Saint Clost fu nez,
> S'est tant traveilliez et penez
> Par priere de ses amis
> Que il nous a en rime mis
> Une risee et un gabet
> De Renart, qui tant set d'abet. (I, vv. 1–6)[31]

> [Pierre who was born in St. Cloud
> Worked so hard and toiled,
> By request of his friends,
> To put into rhyme for us the
> Laughter and trickery
> Of Renart, who has so many ruses.]

Ostensibly catering to his audience's taste for amusement, the supposed narrator Pierre de St. Cloud concentrates his effort on comedy. Thus the humorous food tales analyzed above and many others constitute joking satire, a parody of human flaws, directed at audience reception.

The game, in both senses of the word, hunted prey or amusement, with food as the object, serves to criticize inequality in the animal domain, and by extension in human society. Renart, along with his predatorily savvy accomplices and perceptive adversaries, penetrates the human world in its farmyards, marketplaces, and pantries. The value of food as sustenance or nourishment is given primacy in the *Roman de Renart* whereas excess, gastronomic pleasure, and gluttony are secondary. The representation of the animal community's rapport with food reconstructs and reinforces human paradigms. Comic animal actions involving food demonstrate the underhanded corruption of an unscrupulous society. In a cynical view of human nature, we see that humans and animals are willing to go to any ends to satisfy their desires. Culinary comedy thus underlines the cunning of the animal community while demonstrating the animality of human nature.

All of the branches feature hunger or the depiction of food sources in the growing tradition of thirteenth-century French comico-realism. Many branches portray animal

Chapter Four

tactics, strategies, failures, and triumphs in ongoing competitions over food. Food humor is amplified through repetition with variation in text and image, notably visually in the *Roman de Renart* miniatures showing the animals' interaction with each other, with humans, and with food. Hierarchical relations are called into question when food and play are combined in a disruptive manner. No social class is spared from scathing portrayals of greed, gluttony, hypocrisy, and deception—from the lowly peasant to the barons of Noble the lion's court. The physically strongest or most politically powerful does not always win in this telling social satire. The alimentary ruse is a powerful weapon, but cannot ensure survival. Trick and ridicule show the possibilities for upward mobility and differences in societal institutions that may result from contesting the status quo. The guiding rule of food play in *renardie*, eat or be eaten, echoes the constructions of human political, mercantile, and social rapports. Food humor—in the form of ruses and games—questions the status quo and subverts order. The search for food and eating constitute a comic reshuffling of hierarchies. Common points among the diverse elements of the beast fables, hunger and the search for food are representative of animal communities' fight for survival in an unfair world, and if most actions are motivated by food and hunger in the *Renart*, then the use of culinary comedy is more significant than it seems at first glance. A poignant depiction and bitter satire of human hardships that bedeviled both audiences of romance and less privileged members of the public are revealed through the animals' hungry antics.

Renardian culinary comedy, through transgressive consumption and playful orality, disturbs both linguistic and social order, ridiculing real life and earlier fictional representations of it.[32] The fox's desires for food and food play are never satisfied. Renart's verbal culinary comedy questions conventional roles and destabilizes meaning. The physical food play is not only satirical of human social institutions, but also calls into question audience expectations of literary conventions as well. The cycle presents multifaceted generic characteristics, from mock epic to chivalric romance, from vulgar fabliau to moral *exempla*. Through parody and pastiche, these genres are not taken seriously. There are comic and critical echoes of romance quests and epic battles. Characters range from the starving peasant to the flattered king. Some tales have implicit morals or proverbs while others mock religious sermons and didactic discourse, as in the wordplay surrounding the Andouille.[33] A common point that ties together the diverse structure, tone, and content of different branches, composed over decades, is the powerful concurrence of food and humor.

Conclusion

Food, whether it serves as nourishment or as the object of a quest or ruse, becomes a powerful comic mechanism across the genres explored. Comic culinary discourse has been the focus in this illumination of the function of humor in fictional vernacular narratives. Food consumption is as essential to culture and narrative as clothing, gestures, ceremonies, even language, and as rich in signification. Furthermore, eating is as saturated with convention, symbol, and commonplace as the conventionalized literary genres themselves. Food is used as a tool to reveal criticisms of social constructs and literary conventions. The preceding chapters have demonstrated how foodstuffs may become funny objects when connected with incongruous, inappropriate, or humiliating actions. Food also amplifies sexual or social humor when it is a familiar object used in an unfamiliar, inappropriate, or unexpected situation. Generating humor of incongruity and superiority are two primary aspects of culinary comedy. From socially inept epic heroes to hungry knights-errant and mischievous fabliau housewives, out of the ordinary food usage invites laughter at the failings of one's own social strata or at other groups.

In romance, those characters that begin their knightly careers as young unknown heroes, such as Perceval, Fergus, and Hunbaut, along with respected and more permanent members of the Arthurian court, such as Gauvain and Lancelot, can let their hunger get the best of them and act outside of the behavior that the audience anticipates, undermining courtly ideals and creating comic distance. Culinary comedy is a comedy of action, of words, and of manners. In these courtly texts the dynamics of appetite and table manners, or indeed the lack of them, are exploited for comedy and irony, flavoring narratives with humor, exaggeration, and biting criticism of generic conventions.

Chrétien de Troyes's romances and many that take inspiration from them include a series of significant encounters with food. In romance, food humor is situational and physical in general, with verbal wit, as with Gauvain's comical pleas to finish his meal in *La Vengeance Raguidel*. Improper table manners make a mockery of the Arthurian court and conventions of courtly genres. Considering the demographics of the time, it becomes apparent that daily struggles for nourishment proved a catalyst for the satirical treatment of everyday woes in an otherwise courtly genre. Parodic criticism of an overly idealized vision of courtly life and literary formulae is also present. Decades later, romancers appear to be showing that French courtly conventions have become dry by the thirteenth century, losing meaning for audiences and *remanieurs*, commonness and strictness inviting a different twist on familiar motifs. There is a notable evolution in the use of culinary comedy from Chrétien to his followers. Essentially, indications of crisis in twelfth-century romance brought about nostalgia and humorous criticism in thirteenth-century narrative. The satire of courtly feasts calls into question the moral values of social convention and the aesthetic and implied moral values of literary convention as well. Through the innovative forms of humor, irony, and criticism created by culinary comedy, everything old becomes new again in the romance genre.

By contrast, in the other genres examined here, culinary comedy does not target convention in the same manner as in romance. In the fabliaux and throughout the *Roman de Renart*, episodes concentrate on social satire of several target groups in addition to generic transgression. These narratives may be characterized by their cynic tone and mischievous mood. In the fabliaux and beast fables, many a trickster's ruse entails food. Both genres employ food humor based on caricature and stereotypes of certain groups, poking fun particularly at the below average, the ugly, the ridiculous, in line with the Aristotelian conception of comedy. Verbal comedy and physical comedy alike are common forms of food humor in these short fictional pieces. Verbal *engin*, ruses, and playfulness mark the narratives

Conclusion

of the fabliaux and the *matière de Renart*. Repeated patterns, or scripts, occur with variation in the food ruses so common in these two genres. Class-based culinary comedy is essential to the *Renart*, whereas sexual culinary comedy is at the center of many ribald fabliaux, in which love is far from being courtly or spiritual.

The *Roman de Renart* and fabliau characters use food to subversive ends, to carve or reshape their niche in social or household hierarchy. Representations of food and the device of culinary comedy are essential because these narratives address issues of everyday life, human nature, and human needs. Several similarities in the use of culinary comedy in these two genres become apparent. Both genres show and mock different incompatible models of society. Trickery involving food transgresses class boundaries. Peasants, priests, knights, women, and merchants may achieve victory or be dashed down by Fortune's wheel depending on the situation. Both genres evaluate and redefine roles. Fabliau narratives are sharply satirical, criticizing human nature and societal institutions through scatological, erotic, social, or ridiculous anecdotal humor. The culinary comedy of the fabliaux reflects the reality of life for *vilains*, bourgeois, merchants, and others. In some fabliaux, culinary comedy deconstructs categories of society and gender roles through subtle irony and ambiguity. Often read in modern times as crude and vulgar, the fabliaux include culinary humor based on realistic details about bodily functions or dysfunctions, needs, and desires. The inappropriateness of food games and gluttony can represent excess and comic spectacle rather than subsistence in the fabliaux.

Though it serves especially significant functions in twelfth- and thirteenth-century French literature, we find that culinary comedy is not limited to the texts studied.[1] We may cast a momentary glance beyond these contemporary genres to other implications and possibilities for the approach of culinary comedy, inviting further application of this approach to later periods. Later, François Villon laments poverty and hunger, sometimes with irony and humor that grow out of this tradition. Villon is very concerned with the injustice of *la faim* in his urban environment, using their discussions of hunger to criticize society. Villon (like Rutebeuf) treats hunger as a symbol for all poverty and injustice, and he treats it with humor, sarcasm, and irony. Conversely, Villon portrays excessive consumption of food and wine in conjunction with sexual excesses. The combinations of culinary comedy with scatological, erotic, social, and religious humor witnessed in medieval French texts may be found in different forms centuries later throughout Western Europe, as throughout the late medieval French farces (notably *La Farce du pâté et de la tarte*) and the familiar examples in Rabelais and Cervantes.

Turning toward possibilities for the application of the approach of culinary comedy to early modern literature and Rabelais, we are struck instantly by the portrayals of food and excessive consumption; the mounds of tripes, thousands of milk cows, giant mouthfuls of *langue de bœuf,* and the salad with pilgrims in it that are an extension of medieval culinary comedy.[2] Indeed, hardly a page of Rabelais's *œuvre* may be turned without revealing a feast or drinking. Culinary comedy in Rabelais tends toward the absurd and incongruous. Gargantua and Pantagruel are both characterized by excessive and transgressive eating in their childhood, recalling the Old French epic *enfances*. Audiences of Rabelais cannot fail to be struck by a landscape littered with sausages, andouilles, smoked beef tongue, fish, eels, bread, butter, flour, fruit, wine, and plentiful spoonfuls of mustard. These food items serve to mark excess, violence, and absurdity; they may also act as sexual symbols, weapons, and political metaphors. In the *Quart Livre,* Pantagruel and his entourage experience a sort of food fight. Rabelais's transgressive use of the image of the andouille is reminiscent of the *Roman de Renart*. Well-known monstrous names such as Gaster, Engastrimythes, and Gastrolâtres make reference to the body and consumption in a work that engages us in culinary comedy through descriptions of bodily functions and excessive eating. Looking forward in time, with such humorous, exaggerated, and often scatological treatments of the human or monstrous stomach, it is probable that Rabelais was familiar with a number of medieval French food fights and medieval motifs involving food humor.

In twelfth- and thirteenth-century France, some knights in epic or in verse romances prefer fighting with roast chicken or bread loaves rather than their swords. Robin finds that the way

Conclusion

to Marion's heart is through her stomach. Some immoral fabliau priests would fancy wine over holy water. Renart, the noble fox, chooses well-prepared human feasts over raw animal prey. Young epic heroes attack the kitchen cupboards as they would attack the enemy. Culinary comedy serves as both social satire and literary parody, playing with institutional social conduct and alimentary codes. Finally, culinary comedy surrounds questions of subsistence in society as well as the complex pleasures of eating and of play. On a textual level, tired conventions of twelfth-century genres degenerate into a knockdown-drag-out food fight in later narratives. *Rire, barat,* and *gaber* become the central focus of many narratives structured by food. Like Aucassin, who reacts with laughter to a gender-bending, status quo–testing food fight—"Les coumence a regarder / S'en prist a rire" [He started to look at them and he began to laugh] (*Aucassin* XXI, vv. 12–14), audiences of any century cannot help but smile at the different types of battles being fought and won through medieval culinary comedy.

Notes

Chapter One
Food Fight: Medieval Gastronomy and Literary Convention

1. Lévi-Strauss's concept of *le cru et le cuit* in *Les manières de table* addresses the cultural anthropology of food, positing a connection between cooking or culinary sophistication and the evolution of culture.

2. The role of human values that are static or evolving is treated in the landmark study by Milton Rokeach, *The Nature of Human Values*.

3. See Burrow on gestures and Burns, *Courtly Love Undressed*, on clothing conventions.

4. In *Holy Fast and Holy Feast* Carolyn Walker Bynum shows food as an empowering force for women in spiritual discourse.

5. Anne Cobby gives a close reading of the text and explores its parodic treatment of courtly formulae, especially in portraits of the hero and heroine (*Ambient Conventions* 55–81). She makes the astute remark with which my analysis is in agreement, that in *Aucassin et Nicolette*, "... humour is not only an aim but also an aid to the direction of our judgment" (57). See also Szabics on conventions of courtly love and the idea of *prouesse* in *Aucassin*.

6. All translations from the Old French are my own except where otherwise noted.

7. The *estrange* other—that is, the unknown, the unexpected, the different, the *merveilleux*—was on occasion a source of humor for medieval poets. Philippe Ménard considers laughter surrounding the *merveilleux* (376–416).

8. When I use the term *transgression*, as applied to bodies, to language, to literary and social conventions, to texts, and to spaces, I align myself with Stallybrass's use of the term as in his application of the notions of transgression and boundary in medieval literature, Peter Stallybrass, "Boundary and Transgression: Body, Text, Language."

9. Another realm with unusual food habits is found in the romance of *Claris et Laris*, in which the inhabitants confine their food production and consumption to fruit (vv. 25421–622). Bountiful, perpetual feasting is shown as other and otherworldly in *Guingamor* (vv. 422–532).

10. This rich narrative poem has intertextual links to *La Chanson de Roland, Erec et Enide, Tristan, La Folie Tristan, Pyramus et Tisbé, Floire et Blanchefleur,* and *Clarisse et Florent,* for example.

11. See Herman Pleij on the idealized alimentary world of Cockaigne covering several periods. For a discussion on Bakhtinian theory applied to varied aspects of medieval literature, see the volume edited by Thomas J. Farrell.

12. This custom is a familiar commonplace throughout medieval literature, especially in Chaucer.

13. For more on representations of courtly space, see especially *Espaces romanesques*, edited by Michael Crouzet.

14. The meal and consumption also take center stage in Chrétien's *Cligés*, in which the court enjoys more than six prepared dishes while the servant Thessala serves the enchanting *breuvage* (reminiscent of the love potion in the Tristan tradition) to the unsuspecting emperor.

15. Colors of foods and sauces were also highly symbolic and golden sauces sought after: " . . . above all the great feast was a pageant of colour and brightness—the brilliance of the hangings and covering cloths, the glow of gold and silver vessels, the varied hues of the clothes of the principal diners and the heraldic colours of the livery of the many servers who carried their food and drink through the Hall to the dais" (Wilson, "From Medieval Great Hall" 32).

16. Norris J. Lacy addresses the importance and function of custom in narrative in his "Coutumes, merveilles, et aventures."

17. Unexpected rude behavior when combined with inappropriate excess is humorous. Moreover, it is comical when a character is portrayed principally in light of these bodily needs.

In parts of Chapters 1 and 2, I have drawn on material in my "Kitchen Knights in Medieval Literature: Rainouart, Lancelot, Gareth"; copyright 2005 from *LIT: Literature, Interpretation and Theory,* 2005, 16 (2): 189–212. Reproduced by permission of Taylor & Francis Group, LLC, http://wwwtaylorandfrancis.com.

18. A fabliau title that has also been translated in English as *The Abundance.*

19. Many decades later, Villon makes light of the poverty, hunger, and the plight of urban student life.

20. On this aspect of Keu's personality as well as other jokes, see John L. Grigsby's study of *gabs* in Old French literature.

21. In contrast, see also Chrétien's *Yvain,* verses 2839 ff. for a portrayal of a hermit's daily meal.

22. *Blandin de Cornouaille,* a fourteenth-century text, is the only other possible known Occitan Arthurian romance, and many scholars debate this label. See also De Caluwé, "*Le Roman de Blandin de Cornouaille et de Guillot Ardit de Miramar:* Une parodie de roman arthurien?" The romance of *Jaufré* is one of longer Arthurian verse romances, spanning around 11,000 lines of octosyllabic rhyming couplets. The romance can be found in manuscript BNF 216422, which has been dated c. 1200–28 (Bibliothèque Nationale de France, Paris).

23. For a general study of this vice, the reader is referred to the recent cultural history of gluttony in Francine Prose, *Gluttony.*

24. See Adrian Tudor's discussion of negative portrayals of drinking in his "Hangovers from Hell" study of the *Vie des Pères.*

25. *Felon* has many meanings, such as "evildoer" or "criminal." *Culvert* is basically a synonym for *vilain,* both words meaning "scoundrel," "lowlife," "serf," "peasant," etc.

26. Drunken knights appear in romance too, though they are rare. For example, Lancelot encounters a group of drunks in the thirteenth-century romance of the *Merveilles de Rigomer.*

27. Overdrinking is a common form of transgression or *démesure* in many genres. In Marie de France's twelfth-century lai of *Guigemar*, the hero drinks of a potion and falls so drunk from the beverage and from love that he does not ever think he will become sober.

28. For example, *Aliscans* vv. 3837–40, 4455–85, and 4841–43 and *Chanson de Guillaume* laisses III–VIII, CLIX–X, and CLXV.

29. A useful general study on the *enfances* making reference to such texts is provided by Jeanne Lods.

30. See Theodor and Ménard on categories and examples of humor in the chanson de geste.

31. Saly studies birds in the late-medieval bourgeois and aristocratic diet.

32. In another *monde à l'envers* reversal involving food, in the *Folies Tristan* the hungry hero goes against convention in appropriating food. Tristan comically states the reverse of normal hunting practices, saying that he intends to hunt small birds with his hounds and the larger game with his falcons (vv. 505–14). In contrast, see Danielle Buschinger for a comparison of realistic and fictional portrayals of food and eating in the German and French Tristan tradition.

33. Culinary comedy also exists in the English and Italian romance and fabliau traditions, Chaucer, Malory, Boccacio, and several French-English romance adaptations. Malory's kitchen-boy-come-knight Gareth is mocked by Kay and is the source of much humor. The late-medieval Italian tradition also includes culinary humor, with exaggerated images such as a mountain of parmesan and sausage drapings in an idyllic land with unlimited portions of ravioli.

34. For further theoretical explanation on the importance of such texts in cultural history, see Horandner, "The Recipe Book as a Cultural and Socio-historical Document."

35. The thirteenth-century Occitan moralizing *ensenhaments* teach courtly household etiquette and mention cooking and serving practices as well as some table manners.

36. Nicole Crossley-Holland, in *Living and Dining in Medieval Paris*, makes the case for the authorship of this text as Guy de Montigny, a knight serving the Duc de Berri and residing in Paris and Champagne.

37. The early-fourteenth-century didactic manual *Enseignements* also includes instruction on food. Antiquity produced Apicius's *De Re Coquinaria*, but it was not known in the twelfth and thirteenth centuries. It was later printed in Italian and German in the fifteenth century.

38. An edition of approximately contemporary prominent Anglo-Norman culinary documents is provided by Constance B. Hieatt and Robin F. Jones. In Italy, the verse *De Quinquaginia Curialitatibus ad Mensam* by Bonvesin de la Riva is a contemporary Latin text that delineates table manners, from how to share bread politely to how not to lick one's fingers, from hand washing and cleanliness to not petting the dogs under the table, from not resting one's elbows on the table to how best to use one's spoon. It stresses temperance, here meaning not eating too much, nor too little.

39. This later romance has been studied recently in terms of biography by Michelle Szkilnik.

40. Jean's origins are similar to Gareth's in Malory, as a cook and knight known as "Kay's Kitchen Boy," who is responsible for much kitchen humor, as I have shown in "Kitchen Knights in Medieval Literature."

41. Glixelli's edition of this text includes a detailed evaluation of extant manuscripts.

42. For socio-historical perspectives on the significance of hunting, see Cartmill.

43. An example of this occurs in the *Roman d'Alexandre* in text and image, as discussed below.

44. *Pois au lard* is a recipe served by peasants and aristocrats alike that occurs throughout the Middle Ages, as well as in Rabelais, as for example in the cookbook found in the library in *Pantagruel*.

45. Translations from Adam de la Halle's play *Le jeu de Robin et Marion* are cited from Schwam-Baird's edition and translation.

46. Also may refer to the herb wild thyme.

47. In the fabliau of *Frère Denis* the narrator delineates the tripartite hierarchy of medieval society: nobles, clergy, and peasants (vv. 1–25). The problematic interaction of the three provides the intrigue of this complex genre. Conflict among the three is often played out over food.

48. Christopher Dyer has noted that English chronicles mention famine in the eleventh and twelfth centuries and that there were bad harvests at the end of the twelfth century and beginning of the thirteenth century (54–55).

49. Indeed, reflections of such hardships occur throughout medieval European literature, as for example in the *Décameron* and Chaucer. Lynette R. Muir's *Literature and Society in Medieval France* treats general military, religious, and social concerns of the time in relation to their literary representations.

50. See the volume *French Humour* edited by John Parkin for general theoretical views on the evolution of French humor over the centuries.

Chapter Two
Uncourtly Table Manners in Arthurian Romance

1. Preliminary sections of this chapter appeared in my "Culinary Comedy in French Arthurian Romance," *Medievalia et Humanistica* 30 (2004): 15–31, a journal edited by Paul Clogan. Excerpts have been used with permission of Rowman & Littlefield, Lanham, MD

2. The narrator of *Hunbaut* shows us he is aware of his relation to Chrétien's romances: "Ne dira neu nonque je robe / Les bons dis Crestïen de Troies" [No one will say that I rob the good stories of Chrétien de Troyes] (186–87). Though the later poet does not rob Chrétien per se, there is certainly both imitation and response in his work.

3. Anne Cobby (*Ambivalent Conventions*) looks at how romance and epic convention and formula are parodied in *Aucassin et Nicolette*, the fabliaux, and the *Pèlerinage de Charlemagne*.

4. Norris J. Lacy treats Gauvain's trivialization in his "Gauvain and the Crisis of Chivalry in the *Conte du Graal*." He explores humor and romance convention in his recent "Convention, Comedy, and the Form of *La Vengeance Raguidel*" in *Arthurian Literature XIX*. The thirteenth-century romances of the *Mule Sans Frein, Le Chevalier à l'Épée*, and *Giglois* all criticize or mock the once impeccable Gauvain. Keith Busby's volume *Gauvain in Old French Literature* is the reference on the evolving character of Gauvain in Medieval French literature. For a discussion of Gawain in the English romance tradition, see the introduction to Hahn's *Sir Gawain: Eleven Romances and Tales* (1–8).

5. Food has increased religious significance in the prose romances, as discussed by William L. Boletta. See also Andrea Williams for a comprehensive recent study of the Grail romance tradition, especially her illuminating discussions of structure and metaphoric structure.

6. For more thoughts on convention and status, consult Le Goff's "Vestimentary and Alimentary Codes in *Eric et Enide*."

7. Also critical of the state of the Arthurian court and its values, a lament of the loss of the golden days, where real love thrived and real adventure was a plentiful opportunity for glory, appears in the opening of Chrétien's *Yvain*.

8. In the English tradition, *Sir Gawain and the Green Knight* exemplifies the importance of all of these conventions. Manuscript illustrations and miniatures too evince a greater interest in the preparation and consumption of even simple meals, as for example the manuscripts of the *Roman d'Alexandre*, which show food merchants and techniques of cooking poultry, alongside images depicting essential plot elements. In extant manuscripts of Chrétien's *Perceval*, important events such as the young hero's arrival at Arthur's court and the Fisher King's castle feature food and miniature feast scenes with full table settings. Perceval's entry into Arthur's court during a feast where guests are already seated for dinner is illustrated in Paris, Bibliothèque Nationale, f. fr. 12576. His arrival at the Fisher King's table is illustrated in Paris, Bibliothèque Nationale, f. fr. 12577, where the table is set with a table cloth, a knife, a pitcher, and serving dishes.

9. Other scenes of cooking, serving, and carving occur in *Erec et Enide* verses 4256–64, 2007–11, 6395, 3162–72, and 6872–74, including the wedding feast.

10. Along with culinary comedy, other devices may disrupt the conventions of the feast. In the contemporary Occitan verse romance *Jaufré*, for instance, the merveilleux becomes a transgressive element into the Arthurian feast. A monster appears to test and attack King Arthur and his knights, verbally and physically questioning their status and power.

11. *Durmart le Gallois* is found in a unique copy, MS Berne 113 (Bibliothèque nationale suisse, Berne, Switzerland). Other epic and mock-epic feast scenes make equal use of convention; for instance in the epic banquets of the *Pèlerinage de Charlemagne,* the Franks enjoy a well-set table and superb spread of venison, wild boar, a selection of poultry, and plenty of wine and claret, served in a jocular atmosphere.

12. Similarly, the romance of *Giglois* reinforces aristocratic and bourgeois values with culinary and other conventions.

13. "Food habits" is the term applied to ". . . the ways in which humans use food" (Kittler and Sucher 2).

14. Sara Sturm-Maddox touches on Perceval and some of these episodes in a discussion of their intertextual, or transtextual, relationship to the *Continuations* and the prose romances, in particular the *Queste del Saint Graal.*

15. Following instructions literally also results in culinary comedy in the fabliaux, as with the narrative in which a woman literally greases a knight's palm, as discussed in the following chapter.

16. In the chanson de geste *Raoul de Cambrai,* the hero also tells his mother not to worry about anything but staying home, eating, and drinking liquor (vv. 1103–06).

17. Perceval, at least, has some gastronomic background. The rustic and naïve epic hero Doon de Mayence leaves his home lacking knowledge of wine, money, and many other elements of society.

18. Charles Foulon looks at realism and narrative ambiguity in Perceval's four meals. He sees the meals at the Château du Grail and at la Tente as excess and the meals with the Hermit and at Beaurepaire as lacking. See also Vincensini for a related discussion of meals in the Perceval tradition from the point of view of myth analysis.

19. This is vol. 4 of the William Roach et al. edition of the *Continuations* (126, 198).

20. See Norris J. Lacy's overview of the role of the king, the court, and Arthurian chivalry in romance ("Typology" 40–42).

21. For a multifaceted discussion of contemporary audience expectations, see the articles by Lacy, Busby, and Blumenfeld-Kosinski in *The Legacy of Chrétien de Troyes*, vol. 1 (ed. Lacy, Kelly, and Busby). For a useful index of texts influenced by Chrétien, see Mölk or Schmolke-Hasselmann.

22. Blake Spahr has investigated analogues of Chrétien in the Dutch and French versions of *Fergus*. D. D. R. Owen has also considered political and literary connections, including many "comic reversals."

23. Sleep is another comic bodily need. In the thirteenth-century Manessier *Continuation*, Gauvain too falls asleep during a religious lesson (v. 17798).

24. E. Jane Burns, in *Bodytalk,* and Simon Gaunt in *Gender and Genre,* have explored gendered bodies. Burns looks in particular at female orality, utterances, and transgression.

25. In the Gerbert *Continuation,* Perceval quests after his stolen shield. Multiple-quest structures are not limited to the prose romances. Douglas Kelly has studied multiple quests and double quests with two knights ("Multiple Quests" 260).

26. See North's study on the qualities of the ideal knight in different Old French genre (c.1090–1240) including strength, physical bravery, moral courage, endurance, good looks, and good birth.

27. It is comical and unexpected that Fergus's mount is a hearty workhorse, rather than a knight's noble *destrier.*

28. Linda Gowans has provided a landmark study on the evolution of the figure of Keu, or Kay, in literature and legend.

29. A similar incident occurs in the *Livre d'Artus* when Arthur partakes of the robber knights' wine and invites himself and his maiden to a feast.

30. Other thirteenth-century texts depict such hardships, for example Ramon Llull's *Libre del Ordre de Cavayleria*, a Catalan text with French, Scottish, and English adaptations.

31. MS Paris, Bibliothèque Nationale f. fr. 1553 of the *Fergus* embellishes here, with a comical and graphic variant where he tries to get rid of the robbers' bodies and their putrid odor.

32. This is a realistic portrayal of the scarcity and popularity of bread. Several contemporary texts emphasize the rarity of finely milled, quality all-wheat bread, for instance the *Jeu de Robin et Marion* in which clean water and wheat bread entice attendance at a picnic.

33. See Scully on the complex semantic field of *temperare* and its cognates in medieval cuisine, a term related to consistency such as mixing, moistening, thickening, and more ("Tempering" 3–13). I would add that this cooking term could be viewed as similar in some ways to the medieval literary term describing the combining and unifying phenomenon of narrative *conjointure* so valorized by Chrétien de Troyes.

34. Echoing both this interest and the romance heroes' desperate search for a hearty meal on the road, the mid-thirteenth-century *trouvère* and *bon vivant* Colin Muset is known for having expressed a universal human feeling about the necessity and the pleasures of even a simple meal. In one *chanson*, he writes that he has little desire to do battle or lay siege when he has roast fowl to enjoy, implying that gastronomic needs and gustatory pleasures supercede war or duty.

35. In her critical edition of *The Romance of Hunbaut*, Margaret Winters provides evidence for the date of the poem's composition on the early end of this range.

36. In Chrétien's *Perceval*, vv. 327 and 457–58, the hero is familiar with this reputation. Perceval criticizes Arthur, asking how the king can possibly be the maker of knights if one cannot get him to utter a word (vv. 882–89).

37. Norris J. Lacy's perceptive analysis of the evolution of the figure of Gauvain in *Hunbaut* shows character evolution; ". . . he does something that for him is rare: he changes" ("The Character" 305). The Aristotelian sense of the comic would require a similar character transformation. See also Keith Busby's comprehensive work on the figure of Gauvain in Arthurian romance.

38. Spit roasting of poultry and game was a common practice in this period, appearing in many romance and Psalter manuscript illustrations, such as the miniatures accompanying one manuscript of the *Roman d'Alexandre*.

39. The manuscript of *Hunbaut* breaks off soon after this passage.

40. Many monstrous figures appear in the romance, such as the panther that swallows knights and horses whole.

Chapter Three
Much Ado about Bacon: The Old French Fabliaux

1. Parts of this chapter on the fabliaux were presented at the 38th International Congress on Medieval Studies in Kalamazoo, Michigan, in May 2003.

2. The contemporary thirteenth-century Occitan Arthurian verse romance of *Flamenca* describes the pleasant Christmastime odors of the spices in this same fragrant Montpellier marketplace.

3. Cobby points out intergeneric and intertextual relationships in this period where ". . . the parodic fabliaux, broadly speaking, use the language of courtly literature to establish their literary background . . ." (*Ambivalent Conventions* 56).

4. See also Jodogne.

5. See Brusegan for an analysis of different ruses in the fabliau corpus. She sees the couple's financial state as playing an important part in ruses.

6. The larder is a type of pantry.

7. Lorcin offers a useful survey and typology of cuckolds in the fabliaux. She indicates that although no fabliau includes *cocu*, "cuckold," in the title, there are at least thirty-seven that treat female marital infidelity in various ways. She investigates the phenomenon that in the majority of cases (twenty-five) the husband is cuckolded but happy, usually through his ignorance of the situation orchestrated by the mischievous wife. Lorcin concludes that we cannot find fault with most cuckolded fabliaux husband, but rather with their wives: "Mais dans la majorité des contes, le mari n'a commis aucune faute. Son seul tort est sans doute d'être souvent absent. C'est la femme qui est coupable, à cause de sa sensualité excessive, à cause du besoin irrésistible de ruser, de mentir, de comploter . . . Cocu ou pas, le mari est content si sa femme est de bonne humeur" (Lorcin, "Le feu" 185).

8. Kathryn Gravdal explores this period in terms of the social and literary opposites of *vilain et courtois*. Gravdal also divides stylistics as *mediocris stylus* and *gravis stylis*, thus making a distinction between highbrow and lowbrow humor. Through comedy, and especially culinary comedy, the fabliaux combine humorous criticism of both *vilain* and *courtois*.

9. This ironic scene of transgressive eating has a less comic analogue in Thomas's *Tristan*, where the adulterous woman has to eat her lover's heart. It is also reflected in the Philomena tradition.

10. Realistic descriptions of hunger, food preparation, and eating occur in the fabliaux. Perhaps this realistic yet comic portrayal allows audiences to recognize situations, or even to laugh at themselves as suggested in Bakhtin's notion of the socially sanctioned carnival. The elements of material culture highlighted in the fabliau food episodes are often culinary objects, such as tables, wine barrels, pieces of meat, and objects of food preservation such as pantries and meat hooks.

11. This text has classical analogues; see the article by Roy J. Pearcy.

12. Lisa M. Heldke's "Foodmaking as a Thoughtful Practice" sees growing and preparing food as requiring and generating emotional and erotic energy (222–23). It also discusses communities and relations between foodmaker and food, among foodmakers, foodmakers and eaters, etc.

13. Brusegan refers to Boccacio's *salvamento* motif, in which a woman resorts to ruses to save herself from punishment (152); she also finds the ruse to be a mode of protection (154).

14. Brent A. Pitts discusses truth and lies in his article on the fabliaux and "Truth-seeking Discourse."

15. This text was edited and translated into modern French by Gabriel Bianciotto (49–50).

16. This is the English title given by most translated editions.

17. At the end of one manuscript, we see that the tale was recorded by the Prevost de Provins, who allegedly paid Boivin for his narrative.

18. See Bennett for a discussion of Bakhtinian carnival in Boivin de Provins.

19. Barat is a proper name that would have had the connotation of *barat/baraz*, "trickery."

20. Two mentions of how one has had his culotte underclothes stolen by the others lend just a hint of sexual humor.

21. Cabbage is an element of realistic detail in this story of peasant plight. In contemporary texts, Rutebeuf (also a fabliau poet) laments his own poverty and poverty in certain ranks of society. Themes of poverty and hunger are thus developed further, along with the use of humor and irony, by François Villon.

22. This translation is from Shira I. Schwam-Baird's edition of Adam de la Halle's *Le jeu de Robin et Marion*.

23. Henri Rey-Flaud investigates this narrative in his "Le vilain ânier."

24. In branch IX/X of the *Roman de Renart, Les Vêpres de Tibert le Chat*, we find the same type of culinary scatological humor, when Tibert's wordplay and riddle makes allusion to food and painful flatulence. This is mixed with anticlerical humor, as Tibert pokes fun at a priest by subjecting him to his toilet humor and riddles.

25. Levy considers the many manifestations of the devil and language related to the devil.

26. Flatulence is the subject of comico-realism throughout this period, in Chaucer, and elsewhere.

27. This translation is from Shira I. Schwam-Baird's edition of *Le jeu de Robin et Marion*, by Adam de la Halle.

28. More explicitly identified as *Le dist de la merde* in another manuscript.

29. In *Reason and Society in Medieval France*, Murray explores both upward and downward mobility, showing movement and friction between the feudal aristocracy and the wealthy bourgeois of this period.

30. Adrian P. Tudor's "Hangovers from Hell" addresses diabolical drinking in a different context.

31. This narrative is one of many that announces its truth and *auctorité*: "Se fabliaus puet veritz estre, / Dont avint il, ce dist mon mestre" [If a fabliau can be true, so it happened, as my master says] (*Du vilain de Bailleul* vv. 1–2 [Noomen, *NRCF* vol. 5]). The comic and didactic *Baillet le Savetier, ou Le pretre au lardier* also shares some common points. Both are parodies of urban working classes and priests. Jeanette Beer provides an in-depth study of narratorial claims to truth.

32. Mandrake root was associated with fertility and the creation of humanity in the Garden of Eden.

33. Perhaps no coincidence, she is named Hersent, like Isengrin's feisty wife in the *Roman de Renart*.

34. Cobby (*Anticlericalisme*) provides a study of anticlerical themes and images throughout the fabliaux corpus. Walpole mentions antireligious humor, character humor, and low-style humor in relation to the chanson de geste.

35. See Brian J. Levy's chapter on "Comic Inversion: A Fabliau Bestiary" for an analysis of the use of different animals in the Old French fabliaux.

36. Roy J. Pearcy has presented convincing evidence for sources in Ovid.

37. In addition to the pejorative association between pigs and members of Christian religious institutions in this period found in the fabliaux and elsewhere, Muslim characters (who are not pork eaters) use "pig" as an insult to the Christians in the *Conquête d'Orange* (XLI).

38. Drinkers' masses also made fun of priests in this period. For more on the chain of being, humors, and the relation of food to God, the ele-

ments, and social strata, see: Greico 309–11 and Civitello 55–57. See also Mark Burde's dissertation on parodic and anticlerical mock sermons, many of which involve food and drink.

39. A critical edition is to be found in: *Ci nous dit: Recueil d'exemples moraux*, edited by Gérard Blangez.

40. The idiom "Faire mangier de l'oue" [To force someone to eat goose] is an Old French saying, meaning to deceive someone (Levy 47). Another goose fabliau, similar to a beast fable, is Jean Bodel's *Dou lou et de l'oue* [The Wolf and the Goose].

Chapter Four
Hungry like the Wolf, Sly as a Fox: *Le Roman de Renart*

1. References to *Roman de Renart* titles follow J. R. Simpson's revision of Kenneth Varty's standards, as all manuscripts and scribes do not divide up the branches in the same manner. I also include branch numbers where necessary for clarity. For a chronological schema of the branches, the reader is referred to Scheidegger 33 ff., and for a concordance of branches as treated by different critical editions (Martin; Fukumoto, Harano, Suzuki; Roques), see Scheidegger 11–14.

2. Michel Zink's "Le monde animal et ses représentations dans la littérature française du Moyen Age" and Marcel Durliat's "Le monde animal et ses représentations iconographiques" provide a broad examination of animal roles in medieval French literary and artistic production.

3. I use the term *Renardie* to mean the fictional animal universe within the narrative; however, it may also be used to refer to Renart's brand of deception, as in Reichler's *La diabolie: La séduction, la Renardie, L'écriture*.

4. Brucker provides a useful thematic exploration of morals in adaptations of Aesop's fables from the twelfth through fourteenth centuries.

5. A distinction between naïve anthropomorphism and conventional anthropomorphism is drawn by Marie-Louise Tenèze (2).

6. Beyond the focus of this study, the *Roman de Renart* inspired many lengthy later adaptations and continuations that also include much food humor.

7. Eels were a staple in the medieval and early modern diet, and the source of some comedy later in Rabelais.

8. William Kibler has studied political satire in branch XVI.

9. See Bordo on the ideology of hunger.

10. In a contribution on eating and drinking in the Middle Ages, Combarieu investigates the theme of hunger, also seeing hunger as the primary occupation of all the animals, for "la faim apparaît d'abord comme un motif d'inspiration réaliste si on considère Renart, Isengrin et les autres en animaux" ("Manger" 415).

11. Jacques Le Goff describes the *Roman de Renart* in terms of food as an "*épopée de la faim*" (*Civilisation* 206).

12. Kathryn Gravdal classes the *Renart* as a literary parody, showing imitation of epic in her *Vilain et Courtois* (82–112).

13. In Old French, *la viande* may refer to meat, or to food in more general terms, though Renart undoubtedly seeks animal flesh here.

14. See the volume of essays on this peasant vs. animal branch, edited by Dufournet, *Le goupil et le paysan: Roman de Renart, branche X*.

15. Robert Delort's study provides some useful preliminary details and desiderata on fish (herring, eels) and fishing in this period, "Les animaux en Occident du Xe au XVIe siècle."

16. For a careful consideration of the moral significance of Renart's actions, see Subrenat's article which asks "Renart est-il bon, est-il méchant?" Vessela Guenova has provided a comparative study of the function of the ruse in general in the *Roman de Renart* and Rabelais.

17. *Le puits* is an anticlerical, antimonastic tale that also includes transgression of religious doctrine, as Renart's thirst motivates him more than does his spiritual devotion to holy images. Renart is merely attracted to the water in the well, and Isengrin is only interested in it because he thinks it may contain sheep.

18. The spiritual importance of the Eucharist needs no explanation here. Carolyn Walker Bynum draws a link between eating and female ecstasy (126–27).

19. This branch dates from c.1205–50 and is thus contemporary with the peak period of fabliaux production. Perhaps the later date explains the emphasis on play as part of the vogue of parodic literature at this time.

20. Just exactly who is being mocked here has been the subject of much scholarly discussion; for example, Simpson has seen it as the Cistercians making fun of themselves or as a Bernadine attack (120–21).

21. Branch II, c. 1174–77. The scribe notes that this tale is by Pierre de Saint Cloud, who was a contemporary of Chrétien de Troyes, composing the first branch c.1170–79.

22. See Boutet for another perspective on this branch, focusing on appearance and reality, masks, and the carnivalesque.

23. Bears appear elsewhere in the Old French tradition; for instance in the romance of *Yder* Guenièvre is rescued from one.

24. Brun also relies on physical strength rather than clever ruses, as one of the characters more closely resembling an animal at times. Roger Bellon confers: "Seul Brun ne fera jamais appel au moindre bon tour, car il est conscient de la supériorité de sa force physique, qui lui permet d'étrangler un bœuf et donc de s'imposer face au vilain sans armes, et en même temps confiant en la parole donnée . . ." ("*Fole*" 22).

25. Oxen and cows are an important commodity in the literature of this period and the object of many *exempla*-like and joke-ike narratives. In the fabliau of *Brunain, la vache au prestre*, a devout *paysan* couple follows the opposite logic of this proverb when they give their only milk cow to the local priest because they think that God will reward them "twofold" for any charity they give. Though the corrupt priest had the intention of taking the cow to keep for himself, the peasants believe that God has rewarded them according to the adage when their cow returns home with another (the priest's) cow attached in an apparently miraculous proof of their prayers.

26. Elsewhere, the *vilain* peasant Bertaut is treated with similar disdain.

27. *La Chasse au Renart* episode is especially rich in gastronomic detail. It hints at an attack against the dominant aristocratic class and ideology as well.

28. From cookbooks and descriptions of meals in romance, we know that garlic and pepper were primary seasonings for poultry in this period. *Le verjus* is a common condiment in this period, made from green grapes and/or herbs. Wine and beer accompanied meals in many settings.

29. Keith Busby interprets the relation between text and image in different miniatures and rubrics, focusing on the *Roman de Renart* in pages 226–53 of his *Codex and Context*. He includes several miniature reproductions.

30. For the seminal debate on play in medieval culture, see Huizinga's *Homo Ludens* and Jacques Ehrmann's "*Homo Ludens* Revisited."

31. This is branch XVIII in the Roques edition.

32. Note in particular Scheidegger's *Roman de Renart, ou le texte de la dérision*, which addresses jokes and critical humor in the *Renart*.

33. Bowen suggests that Rabelais associates *anguilles* and *andouilles*, eels and sausages, in part because of their homophony in the *Quart Livre*.

Conclusion

1. For instance, the humor from Boileau's satirical *Repas Ridicule* to such culturally diverse comic food films as *La Grande Bouffe, Delicatessen, Tampopo, Like Water for Chocolate, Chocolat, Big Night, Last Orders, Tortilla Soup, Monsoon Wedding*, and *My Big Fat Greek Wedding*.

2. The role of food in Rabelais has been treated by other scholars and is beyond the scope of this study; for instance, it is explored by Michel Jeanneret, highlighting the relation between spectacle, hyperbole, and nourishment. On early modern cooking manuals and different types of consumption in Rabelais, see also McMahon.

Bibliography

Adam de la Halle. *Le jeu de Robin et Marion*. Ed. and trans. Shira I. Schwam-Baird. New York and London: Garland, 1994.

Adams, Alison. "The Shape of Arthurian Verse Romance (to 1300)." Lacy, Kelly, and Busby 1: 141–56.

Adamson, Melitta Weiss, ed. *Food in the Middle Ages: A Book of Essays*. New York: Garland, 1995.

Aliscans. Ed. Claude Régnier. 2 vols. Rpt. Paris: Champion, 1990.

Apicius. *De Re Coquinaria / L'Art de la cuisine*. Ed. and trans. Jacques André. Paris: Belles Lettres, 1965.

Aristotle. *Aristotle on Poetics*. Trans. Seth Bernadete and Michael Davis. London: St. Augustine's Press, 2002.

Attardo, Salvatore. "The Analysis of Humorous Narratives." *Humor: International Journal of Humor Research* 11 (1998): 231–60.

———. *Linguistic Theories of Humor / Humor Research I*. New York and Berlin: Mouton de Gruyter, 1994.

Aubailly, Jean-Claude, ed. *Et c'est la fin pour quoy sommes ensemble: Hommage à Jean Dufournet, littérature, histoire, et langue du moyen âge*. 3 vols. Paris: Champion, 1993.

Aucassin et Nicolette. Paris: Flammarion, 1993.

Bakhtin, Mikhaïl. *L'Œuvre de François Rabelais et la culture populaire au moyen âge et sous la renaissance*. Trad. Andrée Robel. Paris: Gallimard, 1970.

Batany, Jean. "Renart et le vilain Liétart: Brindilles le long d'une 'branche.'" Aubailly 1: 125–37.

Bédier, Joseph. *Les fabliaux: Etudes de la littérature populaire et d'histoire littéraire du Moyen Age*. 6th ed. Paris: Champion, 1964.

Beer, Jeanette. *Narrative Conventions of Truth in the Middle Ages*. Geneva: Droz, 1981.

Bellon, Roger. "*Fole parole* et *bon barat:* La ruse dans la branche X du *Roman de Renart*." Dufournet 9–34.

———. "Lévi-Strauss en Renardie: Manières de table, cru et cuit dans le *Roman de Renart*." Vincensini 393–407.

Bennett, Philip E. "Carnaval et engendrement du texte dans les fabliaux." *Florilegium* 12 (1993): 63–77.

Bergson, Henri. *Le rire*. Paris: Presses Universitaires de France, 1947.

Bianciotto, Gabriel, ed. *Bestiaires du moyen âge*. Paris: Stock, 1980.

Bibliography

Bloch, R. Howard. *The Scandal of the Fabliaux*. Chicago: U of Chicago P, 1986.

Bober, Phyllis Pray. *Art, Culture, and Cuisine: Ancient and Medieval Gastronomy*. London and Chicago: U of Chicago P, 1999.

Boletta, William L. "Earthly and Spiritual Sustenance in *La Queste del Saint Graal*." *Romance Notes* 10 (1968–69): 384–88.

Bordo, Susan. "Hunger as Ideology." *Eating Culture*. Ed. Ron Scapp. Albany: State U of New York P, 1998. 11–35.

Boutet, Dominique. "Renart, le plaisir, le rire, et le mal: Réflexions autour de deux branches du *Roman de Renart*." Aubailly 1: 257–68.

Bowen, Barbara C. "Lenten Eels and Carnival Sausages." *L'Esprit Créateur* 21.1 (1981): 12–25.

Brillat-Savarin, Jean-Anthelme. *La physiologie du goût*. Ed. Jean-François Revel. Paris: Flammarion, 1988.

Brucker, Charles. "Société et morale dans la fable ésopique du XIIe et du XIVe siècles." Aubailly 1: 281–92.

Bruckner, Matilda Tomaryn. *Narrative Invention in Twelfth-Century French Romance: The Convention of Hospitality (1160–1200)*. French Forum Monographs 17. Lexington, KY: French Forum, 1980.

Brusegan, Rosanna. "La fonction de la ruse dans les fabliaux." *Strumenti Critici* 47–48 (1982): 148–61.

Burde, Mark R. "Cannibals at Communion: The Poetics of Alimentary Desire in Four Medieval French Ecclesiastical Parodies, circa 1200." Diss. Washington U in St. Louis, 1997.

Burns, E. Jane. *Bodytalk: When Women Speak in Old French Literature*. Philadelphia: U of Pennsylvania P, 1993.

———. *Courtly Love Undressed: Reading through Clothes in Medieval French Culture*. Philadelphia: U of Pennsylvania P, 2002.

Burrow, J. A. *Gestures and Looks in Medieval Narrative*. Cambridge: Cambridge UP, 2002.

Busby, Keith. *Codex and Context: Reading Old French Verse Narrative in Manuscript*. 2 vols. Amsterdam: Rodopi, 2002.

———. *Gauvain in Old French Literature*. Amsterdam: Rodopi, 1980.

Buschinger, Danielle, and André Crépin. *Comique, satire et parodie dans la tradition renardienne et les fabliaux: Actes du colloque des 15 et 16 janvier 1983*. Göppingen: Kümmerle, 1983.

Bynum, Caroline Walker. *Fragmentation and Redemption: Essays on Gender and the Human Body in Medieval Religion.* New York: Zone Books, 1991.

———. *Holy Feast and Holy Fast: The Religious Significance of Food to Medieval Women.* Berkeley: U of California P, 1987.

De Caluwé, Jean-Michel. "*Le roman de Blandin de Cornouaille et de Guillot Ardit de Miramar:* Une parodie de roman arthurien?" *Actes du VIIe Congrès International de Langue et Littérature d'Oc et d'Etudes Franco-Provençales.* Modena: Cultura Neolatina, 1978. 55–66.

Camporesi, Piero. *Bread of Dreams: Food and Fantasy in Early Modern Europe.* Trans. David Gentilcore. Chicago: U of Chicago P, 1989.

Cartmill, Matt. "Hunting and Humanity in Western Thought." *Social Research* 62.3 (1995): 7.

La chanson de Guillaume. Ed. François Suard. Paris: Garnier, 1999.

Le chastoiement d'un père à son fils. Ed. Edward Montgomery, Jr. Chapel Hill: U North Carolina P, 1971.

Chrétien de Troyes. *Romans.* Ed. Michel Zink. Paris: Librairie Générale Française, 1994.

Ci nous dit: Recueil d'exemples moraux. Ed. Gérard Blangez. 2 vols. Vol. 1. Paris: Société des Anciens Textes Français, 1979.

Civitello, Linda. *Cuisine and Culture: A History of Food and People.* Hoboken: Wiley, 2003.

Clark, Michael. "Humor and Incongruity." *The Philosophy of Laughter and Humor.* Ed. John Morreall. Albany: State U of New York P, 1987. 139–55.

Cobby, Anne Elizabeth. *Ambivalent Conventions: Formula and Parody in Old French.* Amsterdam: Rodopi, 1995.

———. "L'Anticléricalisme des Fabliaux." *Reinardus: Yearbook of the International Reynard Society* 7 (1994): 17–29.

De Combarieu Du Grès, Micheline. "Des Animaux et des Hommes: Se Parler / Se Battre (Etude sur la Branche X du *Roman de Renart.*" Dufournet 35–56.

———. "Manger (et Boire) dans le *Roman de Renart.*" *Manger et boire au moyen âge: Actes du Colloque de Nice.* 2 vols. Vol. 2. Nice: Les Belles Lettres, 1984. 415–28.

———. "Le même e(s)t l'autre: Etude sur les *Vêpres de Tibert le Chat.*" Aubailly 1: 361–73.

———. "Bonnes et mauvaises manières de table dans la *Chanson de Guillaume* et *Aliscans.*" *Banquets et manières de table au moyen âge.* Aix: CUERMA, 1996. 281–302.

Bibliography

The Continuations of the Old French Perceval of Chrétien de Troyes. Ed. William Roach et al. 3 vols. Philadelphia: 1949–84.

Cooke, Thomas D. *The Old French and Chaucerian Fabliaux.* Columbia, MO and London: U of Missouri P, 1978.

———. "Pornography, the Comic Spirit, and the Fabliaux." Cooke and Honeycutt 137–62.

Cooke, Thomas D., and Benjamin L. Honeycutt, eds. *The Humor of the Fabliaux: A Collection of Critical Essays.* Columbia, MO and London: U of Missouri P, 1978.

Cosman, Madeleine Pelner. *Fabulous Feasts: Medieval Cookery and Ceremony.* New York: George Braziller, 1976.

Crossley-Holland, Nicole. *Living and Dining in Medieval Paris: The Household of a Fourteenth-Century Knight.* Cardiff: U of Wales P, 1996.

Curtin, Deane W., and Lisa M. Heldke. *Cooking, Eating, Thinking: Transformative Philosophies of Food.* Bloomington and Indianapolis: Indiana UP, 1992.

Delort, Robert. "Les animaux en occident du Xe au XVIe siècle." *Le monde animal* 29–31.

Dufournet, Jean, ed. *Le goupil et le paysan: Roman de Renart, branche X.* Paris and Geneva: Champion-Slatkine, 1990.

Duggan, Joseph. *The Romances of Chrétien de Troyes.* New Haven: Yale UP, 2001.

Durliat, Marcel. "Le monde animal et ses représentations iconographiques." *Le monde animal* 72–94.

Durmart le Gallois. Ed. Joseph Gildea. 2 vols. Villanova, PA: Villanova Press, 1965–66.

Dyer, Christopher. "Did the Peasants Really Starve in Medieval England?" *Food and Eating in Medieval Europe.* Ed. Martha Carlin and Joel T. Rosenthal. London and Rio Grande, OH: Hambledon, 1998. 53–72.

Ehrmann, Jacques. "*Homo Ludens* Revisited." *Yale French Studies* 41 (1968): 31–57.

Farrell, Thomas J., ed. *Bakhtin and Medieval Voices.* Gainesville: UP of Florida, 1995.

Farrier, Susan E. "Hungry Heroes in Medieval Literature." Adamson 145–59.

Fink, Béatrice. "Du savoureux au sublime: Vers une poétique de la nourriture." *Recherches sémiotiques / Semiotic Inquiry* 14 (1994): 207–20.

Flandrin, Jean-Louis, and Massimo Montanari, eds. *Food: A Culinary History from Antiquity to the Present*. Engl. ed. Albert Sonnenfeld. Trans. Clarissa Botsford et al. New York: Columbia UP, 1999.

Flinn, John. *Le Roman de Renart dans la littérature française et dans les littératures étrangères au moyen âge*. Toronto: U of Toronto P, 1963.

Foulon, Charles. "Les quatre repas de Perceval." *Mélanges de philologie et de littératures offerts à Jeanne Wathelet-Willem*. Liège: Cahiers de l'ARUL, 1978. 165–74.

Gaunt, Simon. *Gender and Genre in Medieval French Literature*. Cambridge: Cambridge UP, 1995.

Geach, P. T. *The Virtues*. Cambridge: Cambridge UP, 1977.

Genette, Gérard. *Palimpsestes*. Paris: Seuil, 1992.

Gerbert de Montreuil. *La continuation de Perceval*. Ed. Mary Williams and Marguerite Oswald. 3 vols. Paris: CFMA, 1922, 1925, 1975.

Glixelli, Stefan. "*Les contenances de table*." *Romania* 47 (1921): 1–40.

Gordon, Sarah. "Kitchen Knights in Medieval Literature: Rainouart, Lancelot, Gareth." *LIT: Literature, Interpretation and Theory* 16.2 (2005): 189–212.

Gowans, Linda. *Cei and the Arthurian Legend*. Arthurian Studies 18. Woodbridge, Engl.: Boydell & Brewer, 1988.

Gravdal, Kathryn. "Counterfeiting Orality: Parody in the French Middle Ages." Aubailly 2: 661–84.

———. *Vilain and Courtois: Transgressive Parody in French Literature of the Twelfth and Thirteenth Centuries*. Lincoln: U of Nebraska P, 1989.

Greico, Allan J. "Food and Social Classes in Late Medieval and Renaissance Italy." Flandrin and Montanari 302–12.

Grigsby, John L. "Le *gab* dans le roman arthurien français." *Actes du 14e Congrès International Arthurien*. Rennes: Rennes UP, 1985. 260–63.

———. "Heroes and Their Destinies in the Continuations of Chrétien's *Perceval*." Lacy, Kelly, and Busby 1: 41–54.

Guenova, Vessela. *La ruse dans le Roman de Renart et dans les œuvres de François Rabelais*. Orléans: Paradigme, 2003.

Guillaume le Clerc. *The Romance of Fergus*. Ed. Wilson Frescoln. Philadelphia: William H. Allen, 1983.

Gutwirth, Marcel. *Laughing Matter: An Essay on the Comic*. Ithaca and London: Cornell UP, 1993.

Hahn, T. *Sir Gawain: Eleven Romances and Tales*. Kalamazoo, MI: Medieval Academy, 1995.

Heldke, Lisa M. "Foodmaking as a Thoughtful Practice." *Cooking, Eating, Thinking: Transformative Philosophies of Food*. Ed. Deane W. Curtin and Lisa M. Heldke. Bloomington: Indiana UP, 1992. 202–29.

Hellman, Robert, and Richard O'Gorman, eds. and trans. *Fabliaux*. New York: Crowell, 1965.

Henisch, Bridget Ann. *Fast and Feast: Food in Medieval Society*. University Park, PA: Pennsylvania State UP, 1976.

Hieatt, Constance B., and Robin F. Jones. "Two Anglo-Norman Culinary Collections Edited from British Library Manuscripts Additional 32085 and Royal 12.C.xii." *Speculum* 61 (1961): 859–82.

Honeycutt, Benjamin L. "The Knight and His World as Instruments of Humor in the Fabliaux." Cooke and Honeycutt 75–92.

Horandner, Edith. "The Recipe Book as a Cultural and Socio-historical Document." *Food in Perspective: Proceedings of the Third International Congress on Ethnological Food Research*. Ed. Alexander Fenton. Edinburgh: Donald, 1981. 119–44.

Huizinga, Johan. *Homo Ludens*. New York: Beacon, 1971

Hunt, Tony. "La parodie médiévale: Le cas d'*Aucassin et Nicolette*." *Romania* 100 (1979): 341–81.

Jaufré: An Occitan Arthurian Romance. Ed. Ross Gilbert Arthur. New York: Garland, 1992.

Jeanneret, Michel. *Des mets et des mots: Banquets et propos de table à la renaissance*. Paris: Corti, 1987.

Jean Renart. *Le roman de la rose, ou Guillaume de Dole*. Ed. Félix Lecoy. Paris: CFMA, 1979.

Jeay, Madeleine. "Consuming Passions: Variations on the Eaten Heart Theme." *Violence against Women in Medieval Texts*. Ed. Anna Roberts. Gainesville: UP of Florida, 1998. 75–96.

Jehan. *The Marvels of Rigomer / Les merveilles de Rigomer*. Trans. Thomas Vesce. Garland Library of Medieval Literature 60. New York and London: Garland, 1988.

———. *Les merveilles de Rigomer: Der altfranzoïsischer Artusroman des 13. Jahrhunderts*. Ed. William Foerster. 2 vols. Dresden: Gedruckt für die Gesellschaft für romanische Literatur, 1908.

Jodogne, Omer. *Le fabliau*. Turnhout: Brepols, 1975.

Johnston, Ronald, and D. D. R. Owen, eds. *Fabliaux*. Blackwell's French Texts. Oxford: Blackwell, 1957.

Kawa-Topor, Xavier. "L'image du roi dans le *Roman du Renart.*" *Cahiers de Civilization Médiévale* 36.3 (1993): 263–80.

Kelly, Douglas. "Multiple Quests in French Verse Romances: *Merveilles de Rigomer* and *Claris et Laris.*" *L'Esprit Créateur* 9.4 (1969): 260.

Kibler, William W. "Politique et satire dans la branche XVI du *Roman de Renart.*" Aubailly 2: 801–11.

Kinser, Samuel. "Why Is Carnival So Wild?" *Carnival and the Carnivalesque: The Fool, the Reformer, the Wildman, and Others in Early Modern Theatre.* Ed. Konrad Eisenbichler and Wim Hüsken. Amsterdam: Rodopi, 1999. 43–87.

Kittler, Pamela Goyan, and Kathryn P. Sucher. *Food and Culture.* 3rd ed. Belmont, CA: Wadsworth, 2001.

Koopmans, Jelle, ed. *Quatre sermons joyeux: Édition critique avec introduction, notes et glossaire.* Geneva: Droz, 1984.

Korsmeyer, Carolyn. *Making Sense of Taste: Food and Philosophy.* Ithaca, NY: Cornell UP, 1999.

Lacy, Gregg F. "Fabliau Stylistic Humor." *Kentucky Romance Quarterly* 26 (1979): 349–57.

Lacy, Norris J. "The Character of Gauvain in *Hunbaut.*" *Bibliographical Bulletin of the International Arthurian Society* 38 (1986): 298–305.

———. "Convention, Comedy, and the Form of *La vengeance Raguidel.*" *Arthurian Literature XIX.* Ed. Keith Busby and Roger Dalrymple. Woodbridge, Engl.: Boydell & Brewer, 2003. 65–76.

———. "Coutumes, merveilles, et aventures." *Chant et enchantement au moyen âge / travaux du groupe de recherches "Lectures Médiévales." Université de Toulouse II.* Toulouse: Editions Universitaires du Sud, 1997.

———. *The Craft of Chrétien de Troyes: An Essay on Narrative Art.* Leiden: Brill, 1980.

———. "Fabliau Women." *Romance Notes* 25 (1985): 318–27.

———. "The Fabliaux and Comic Logic." *L'Esprit Créateur* 16 (1976): 39–45.

———. "Gauvain and the Crisis of Chivalry in the *Conte du Graal.*" *The Sower and His Seed: Essays on Chrétien de Troyes.* Ed. Rupert T. Pickens. Lexington, KY: French Forum, 1983. 155–64.

———. *Reading Fabliaux.* 2nd ed. Birmingham, AL: Summa, 1998.

Bibliography

Lacy, Norris J. "The Typology of Arthurian Romance." Lacy, Kelly, and Busby 1: 32–57.

Lacy, Norris J., and Gloria Torrini-Roblin, eds. *Continuations: Essays on Medieval French Literature and Language in Honor of John L. Grigsby*. Birmingham, AL: Summa, 1989.

Lacy, Norris J., Douglas Kelly, and Keith Busby, eds. *The Legacy of Chrétien de Troyes*. 2 vols. Amsterdam: Rodopi, 1987.

Le Goff, Jacques. *La civilisation de l'Occident médiéval*. Rpt. Paris: Flammarion, 1982.

———. "Lévi-Strauss in Brocéliande: A Brief Analysis of a Courtly Romance." *The Medieval Imagination*. 2nd ed. Chicago: U of Chicago P, 1988. 107–31.

———. *Pour un autre moyen âge: Temps, travail, et culture en Occident*. 1977. 2nd ed. Rpt. Paris: Gallimard, 1997.

———. "Vestimentary and Alimentary Codes in *Erec et Enide*." *The Medieval Imagination*. 2nd ed. Chicago: U of Chicago P, 1988. 132–50.

Lévi-Strauss, Claude. *Le cru et le cuit*. Mythologiques I. Paris: Plon, 1964.

———. *Du miel aux cendres*. Paris: Plon, 1966.

Levy, Brian J. *The Comic Text: Patterns and Images in the Old French Fabliaux*. Amsterdam: Rodopi, 2000.

Lods, Jeanne, "Le thème de l'enfance dans l'épopée française." *Cahiers de Civilisation Médiévale, X^e–XIIe Siècles* 3 (1960): 58.

Lorcin, Marie-Thérèse. "Le feu apprivoisé: L'homme, la femme et le feu dans les fabliaux." *Les quatre éléments dans la culture médiévale: Actes du colloque des 25–27 mars 1982*. Université de Picardie, Centre d'Etudes 386. Ed. Danielle Buschinger and André Crépin. Göppinger Arbeiten zur Germanistik 386. Göppingen: Kümmerle, 1983. 185–97.

———. "Jeu de mains, jeu de vilains: Le geste et la parole dans les fabliaux." *Le geste et gestes au moyen âge*. Aix-en-Provence: CUER-MA / U de Provence P, 1998. 369–83.

———. "Le mariage dans les fabliaux français." *Cahiers d'Études Médiévales* 2.3 (1984): 333–43.

Lucien, Christopher. "Aus grans pescheurs eschapent les anguilles." *Littérature* 74 (1989): 76–89.

Marin, Louis. *Food for Thought*. Trans. Mette Hjort. Baltimore: Johns Hopkins UP, 1989.

Mars, Gerald, and Valerie Mars, eds. *The London Food Seminar*. London: London Food Seminar, 1993.

Bibliography

McMahon, Elise-Noël. "Gargantua, Pantagruel and Renaissance Cooking Tracts: Texts for Consumption." *Neophilologus* 76 (1992): 186–97.

Ménard, Philippe. *Le rire et le sourire dans le roman courtois en France au moyen âge 1150–1250.* Geneva: Droz, 1969.

Le mesnagier de Paris. Ed. Georgine Bereton and Janet Ferrier. 1981. Paris: Lettres Gothiques Françaises, 1994.

Mohaldo White, Sarah. "Sexual Language and Human Conflict in Old French Fabliaux." *Comparative Studies in Society and History* 24.2 (1982): 185–210.

Mölk, U. *Französische Literarästhetik des 12. und 13. Jahrhunderts.* Tübingen: Niemeyer, 1969.

Le monde animal et ses représentations au moyen âge (XIe–XVe siècle): Actes du XVème Congrès de la Société des Historiens Médiévistes de L'Enseignement Supérieur Public, Toulouse 25–26 mai 1984. Toulouse: U of Toulouse P, 1985.

Le moniage Guillaume: Chanson de geste du XIIe siècle. Ed. Nelly Andrieux-Reix. Rpt. Paris: Champion, 2003.

Montanari, Massimo. "Food Models and Cultural Identity." Flandrin and Montanari 189–93.

———. Introduction to Part 5, "Toward a New Dietary Balance." Flandrin and Montanari 247–50.

———. "Peasants, Warriors, and Priests: Images of Society and Styles of Diet." Flandrin and Montanari 178–85.

Morreall, John, ed. *The Philosophy of Laughter and Humor.* Albany: State U of New York P, 1987.

Muir, Lynette R. *Literature and Society in Medieval France: The Mirror and the Image, 1100–1500.* New York: St. Martin's, 1995.

Müller, Beate, ed. *Parody: Dimensions and Perspectives.* Amsterdam: Rodopi, 1997.

Murray, Alexander. *Reason and Society in Medieval France.* Oxford: Oxford UP, 1978.

Muscatine, Charles. *The Old French Fabliaux.* New Haven: Yale UP, 1986.

Noomen. See *Nouveau recueil complet des fablbiaux (NRCF).*

North, Sally. "The Ideal Knight as Presented in Some French Narrative Poems, c.1090– c.1240: An Outline Sketch." *The Ideals and Practice of Medieval Knighthood: Papers from the First and Second Strawberry Hill Conferences.* Ed. Christopher Harper–Bill and Ruth Harvey. Woodbridge, Engl.: Boydell and Brewer, 1986. 111–32.

Bibliography

Nouveau recueil complet des fabliaux (NRCF). Ed. Willem Noomen and Nico van den Boogaard. 10 vols. Assen, Neth.: Van Gorcum, 1983–86.

Owen, D. D. R. "Chrétien, Fergus, Aucassin et Nicolette and the Comedy of Reversal." *Chrétien de Troyes and the Troubadours: Essays in Memory of the Late Leslie Topsfield*. Ed. Peter S. Noble and Linda M. Paterson. Cambridge: Cambridge UP, 1984. 186–94.

Parkin, John, ed. *French Humour: Papers Based on a Colloquium Held in the French Department of the University of Bristol, November 30th, 1996*. Amsterdam: Rodopi, 1999.

Pearcy, Roy J. "*Le prestre qui menga les meures* and Ovid's *Fasti III*." *Romance Notes* 15 (1973): 159–63.

Pitts, Brent A. "*Merveilleux*, Mirage, and Comic Ambiguity in the Old French Fabliaux." *Assays* 4 (1987): 39–50.

———. "Truth-seeking Discourse in the Old French Fabliaux." *Medievalia et Humanistica* 15 (1987): 95–117.

Pleij, Herman. *Dreaming of Cockaigne*. Trans. Diane Webb. New York: Columbia UP, 1997.

Poirion, Daniel. "Aliments symboliques et symbolique de la table dans les romans arthuriens (XIIe–XIIIe siècles)." *Annales ESC* 3 (1992): 561–94.

Prose, Francine. *Gluttony*. The Seven Deadly Sins. New York Public Library Lectures in the Humanities. New York and Oxford: Oxford UP, 2003.

Rabelais: Œuvres complètes. Ed. Guy Demerson. Paris: Seuil, 1973.

Raoul de Houdenc. *Mesire Gauvain ou La Vengeance de Raguidel: Poème de la Table Ronde*. Ed. C. Hippeau. Rpt. Geneva: Slatkine, 1969.

Raskin, Victor. *Semantic Mechanisms of Humor*. Synthese Language Library: Texts and Studies in Linguistics and Philosophy 24. Dordrecht, Boston, and Lancaster: D. Reidel, 1984.

Le recueil de Riom et la maniere de henter soutillement: Un livre de cuisine et un récepteur sur les greffes du XVe siècle. Ed. Carol Lambert. Le Moyen Français 20. Montréal: CERES, 1987.

Redon, Odile, Françoise Sabban, and Silvano Serventi, eds. *The Medieval Kitchen: Recipes from France and Italy*. Trans. Edward Schneider. London and Chicago: U of Chicago P, 1998.

Reichler, C. *La diabolie: La séduction, la Renardie, l'écriture*. Paris: Minuit, 1979.

Bibliography

Reid, T. B. W., ed. *Twelve Fabliaux from MS F. fr. 19152 of the Bibliothèque Nationale*. Manchester: Manchester UP, 1958.

Rey-Flaud, Henri. "Le vilain ânier." *Littérature* 59 (1985): 85–91.

Ribard, Jacques. "Espace romanesque et symbolisme dans la littérature arthurienne du XIIe siècle." *Espaces romanesques*. Ed. Michael Crouzet. Paris: Presses Universitaires de France, 1982. 73–82.

Roguet, Yves. "Gloutonnerie, gourmandise et banquets." *Manger et boire au moyen âge: Actes du Colloque de Nice*. 2 vols. Vol. 2. Nice: Les Belles Lettres, 1984. 255–78.

Rokeach, Milton. *The Nature of Human Values*. New York: Free Press, 1973.

The Romance of Hunbaut: An Arthurian Poem of the Thirteenth Century. Ed. Margaret Winters. Davis Medieval Texts and Studies 4. Leiden: Brill, 1984.

Roy, Bruno. "Trois regards sur les aphrodisiaques." *Du manuscrit à la table: Essais sur la cuisine au moyen âge et répertoire des manuscrits médiévaux contenant des recettes culinaires*. Ed. Carole Lambert. Paris and Montréal: Champion-Slatkine, 1992. 285–92.

Rychner, Jean. *Contribution à l'étude des fabliaux: Variantes, remaniements, dégradations*. 2 vols. Rpt. Geneva: Droz, 1960.

Saly, Antoinette. "Les oiseaux dans l'alimentation médiévale d'après le *Viandier de Taillevent* et le *Ménagier de Paris*." Vincensini 2: 173–79.

Scheidegger, Jean R. *Le Roman de Renart, ou le texte de la dérision*. Geneva: Droz, 1989.

Schenck, Mary Jane Stearns. *The Fabliaux: Tales of Wit and Deception*. Purdue University Monographs in Romance Languages 24. Amsterdam: Benjamins, 1987.

———. "Functions and Roles in the Fabliau." *Comparative Literature* 30 (1978): 21–34.

Schmolke-Hasselmann, Beate. *The Evolution of Arthurian Romance: The Verse Tradition from Chrétien to Froissart*. Trans. Margaret Middleton and Roger Middleton. Cambridge: Cambridge UP, 1998.

Scully, D. Eleanor, and Terence Scully. *Early French Cookery: Sources, Original Recipes and Modern Adaptations*. Ann Arbor, MI: U of Michigan P, 1995.

Scully, Terence. *The Art of Cookery in the Middle Ages*. New York: Garland, 1995

Bibliography

Scully, Terence. "Tempering Medieval Food." Adamson 3–23.

Simpson, J. R. *Animal Body, Literary Corpus: The Old French Roman de Renart.* Etudes de Langue et Littérature Françaises 110. Amsterdam and Atlanta: Rodopi, 1996.

Spahr, Blake. "*Ferguut, Fergus,* and Chrétien de Troyes." *Traditions and Transitions: Studies in Honor of Harold Jantz.* Ed. Lieselotte Kurth, William McCain, Holger Homann, and Morgan Pritchett. Munich: Delp, 1972. 29–36.

Stallybrass, Peter. "Boundary and Transgression: Body, Text, Language." *Body and Transgression in Medieval Culture.* Spec. issue of *Stanford French Review* 14.1–2 (1990): 9–23.

Sturm-Maddox, Sara. "Food for Heroes: The Intertextual Legacy of the *Conte del Graal.*" *Text and Intertext in Medieval Arthurian Literature.* Ed. Norris J. Lacy. New York and London: Garland, 1996. 117–31.

Subrenat, Jean. "'[. . .] La dent Seint Roënau le Rechingnié': Sur les reliques dans le *Roman de Renart.*" Aubailly 3: 1307–18.

———. "Renart est-il bon, est-il méchant? (Au sujet de la branche X du *Roman de Renart*)." Dufournet 127–44.

Susskind, Norman. "Humor in the Chansons de Geste." *Symposium* (1961): 185–97.

Szabics, Imre. "Amour et prouesse dans *Aucassin et Nicolette.*" Aubailly 3: 1341–49.

Szkilnik, Michelle. *Jean de Saintré: Une carrière chevaleresque au XVe siècle.* Geneva: Droz, 2003.

Taillevent, Guillaume Tirel. *The Viandier of Taillevent: Text in Old French of Le Viandier de Guillaume Tirel dit Taillevent.* Ed. Terence Scully. Ottawa: U of Ottawa P, 1988.

Taylor, Steven M. "Comic Incongruity in Medieval French Enfances." *Romance Quarterly* 35 (1988): 3–10.

Telfer, Elizabeth. *Food for Thought: Philosophy and Food.* London and New York: Routledge, 1996.

Tenèze, Marie-Louise. *Le conte populaire français: Contes d'animaux.* Vol. 3. Paris: Maisonneuve et Larose, 1976.

Theodor, Hugo. *Die komischen Elemente der altfranzösichen Chansons de Geste.* Halle: Max Niemeyer, 1913.

Tudor, Adrian P. "Hangovers from Hell: The Demon Drink in the First *Vie des Pères.*" *Romance Studies* 29 (1997): 47–63.

Varty, Kenneth. "Sur le comique du *Roman de Renart:* Des premières branches à *Renart et le Vilain Liétard.*" Dufournet 167–200.

Bibliography

Villon, François. *Poésies de François Villon.* Ed. Emmanuelle Baumgartner. Paris: Gallimard, 1998.

Vincensini, Jean-Jacques, ed. *Banquets et manières de table au moyen âge.* Aix-en-Provence: U de Provence P, 1996.

Visser, Margaret. *The Rituals of Dinner.* London: Penguin, 1992.

Vitz, Evelyn Birge. "Desire and Causality in Medieval Literature." *Romanic Review* 71 (1980): 213–43.

Walpole, Ronald N. "Humor and People in Twelfth-Century France." *Romance Philology* 11 (1957–58): 210–25.

Williams, Andrea. *The Adventures of the Holy Grail: A Study of La Queste del Saint Graal.* Oxford and New York: Peter Lang, 2001.

Wilson, C. Anne, ed. *Appetite and the Eye: Visual Aspects of Food and Its Presentation.* Edinburgh: Edinburgh UP, 1991.

———. "From Medieval Great Hall to Country-House Dining." Wilson, *Appetite* 28–55.

———. "Ritual, Form and Colour in the Medieval Food Tradition." Wilson, *Appetite* 5–27.

Zink, Michel. "Le monde animal et ses représentations dans la littérature française du Moyen Âge." *Le monde animal* 47–71.

Index

Adam de la Halle, 31
Aesop, 141, 160, 173, 193n4
affective shift, 6–7
Aliscans, 14–15, 35–37, 185n28
andouille, 20, 150, 156–58, 195n33. *See also* food: sausages
animals
    bears, 166, 194n23
    cows, 153, 194n25
    foxes, 129, 140–77
    horses, 17, 76, 88, 189n27
    lions, 87, 140, 142, 162, 170, 176
    pigs, 20, 123, 124–25, 133–34, 192n37. *See also* food: bacon; food: pork and ham
    squirrels, 124–25
    vegetables, 3, 16–17, 29, 44, 46, 110, 123, 150
    wolves, 142, 145, 158, 161–63. *See also* Isengrin
animals, humans compared to, 78, 82, 86–88, 107, 109, 124, 131, 132, 135
animals, nature and representation of, 35, 107, 117, 134, 140–45, 155, 192n35, 193n3
anthropomorphism, 12–13, 140–41, 151–52, 170
anticlerical discourse, 33, 37, 101, 127, 128, 129–36, 139, 156, 192n24, 194n17, 194–95n25
aphrodisiac, 4, 105, 106, 119, 123
Apicius, 185n37
appetite, 14, 38, 75–76, 55, 94, 75, 76, 78, 79, 82, 97, 104, 108, 112, 122, 125, 128, 135, 136, 139, 143, 146, 153, 154, 157, 161, 162, 172, 178. *See also* hunger
appetite, female, 11, 107–09
Aristotle, 5, 33, 179
Arthur, King, 22, 23–24, 30–31, 52–54, 81, 187n10
Arthurian court, 10–11, 22, 23, 27, 30, 31, 40, 41, 50–96, 105, 187n7
Atre Perilleux, L', 59, 90
Attardo, Salvatore, 100
Aucassin et Nicolette, 9, 16–20, 22, 40, 183n5, 187n3
auctoritas, 100, 106
audience, reception and expectations, 10, 13, 17, 19, 22, 23, 25, 35, 40, 41, 43, 49, 51, 54, 55, 59, 60, 68, 71–72, 76, 81, 82, 84, 86, 87, 88, 91, 95, 107, 108, 110, 111, 113, 117, 120–21, 122, 123, 124, 125, 126, 128, 130, 138–39, 143, 146, 153, 159, 160–61, 162, 164, 165, 167, 170, 172, 174–76

Bakhtin, Mikhail, 8, 20, 37, 100, 183n11, 191n10
Balzac, Honoré de, 2
banquet. *See* feast
beast epic, 4, 40, 49
beast fables, 12, 33, 140, 179
Bel Inconnu, Le, 24, 28
Bergson, Henri, 6
Béroul, 24
Bestiaire divin, 143
bestiaries, 109, 141–43, 153, 160, 168, 171–72, 172
Blandin de Cornouaille, 184n22
Blind Obedience script, 126
Boccacio, Giovanni, 185n33, 186n49

211

Index

Bonvesin de la Riva, 185n38
bourgeoisie, 15, 21, 30, 31, 32, 41–42, 47, 56, 98, 99, 101–02, 104, 105, 112, 113, 116–17, 120, 130, 139, 153, 159
brevitas, 26, 81
Brillat-Savarin, Anthelme, 1, 2, 14

cannibalism, 21, 103, 131
Carnival, and carnivalesque, 8, 100, 191n10, 194n22
castration, 21, 108, 127, 129, 132, 173
Caxton, William, 33
Cervantes, Miguel de, 181
chanson de geste, 4, 18, 32, 33, 35–40, 39, 47, 48, 153, 158, 185n30. See also epic
Chanson de Guillaume, 15, 37–39, 185n28
Chanson de Roland, 33, 40, 183n10
Chantecler, 40, 144, 153, 172–73
chantefable, 4, 9, 15. See also *Aucassin et Nicolette*
chastoiement d'un père à son fils, Le, 106
Chaucer, Geoffrey, 183n12, 185n33, 186n49
Chevalier à l'Épée, Le, 187n4
Chiquart, 42
Chrétien de Troyes, 10, 22, 24–31, 33, 40, 45–46, 50, 51–76, 78, 79, 81, 83, 85, 86, 87, 94, 97, 179, 184n14, 186n2, 189n33
Cligés, 40, 184n14
Erec et Enide, 25, 28, 51, 52, 183n10, 187n9
Lancelot, le chevalier de la Charrette, 25, 27–28, 51, 52
Perceval, ou le Conte du Graal, 10, 28, 45–46, 50, 51, 52–72, 73–74, 94, 189n36. See also Perceval
Yvain, le chevalier au Lion, 21–22, 28, 32, 40, 45, 50, 52, 63, 80, 85, 87, 89, 184n21, 187n7
Christine de Pizan, 43
chronicle, Latin, 52
Ci nous dit, 134
Claris et Laris, 183n9
Clarisse et Florent, 183n10
clergy and priests, depictions of, 4, 11, 20, 29, 32, 33, 117, 127–28, 129–36, 138–39, 153, 156–57
clothing, 14, 26, 28, 29, 39, 115, 183n3, 191n20
Cocagne, Cockaigne, 20, 183n11
comic, types of defined, 5, 9
Contenances de table, Les, 43
conventions, courtly, 43, 51–52, 118
cook, figure of, 14, 24, 29, 37, 40, 42, 46, 89, 109
cookbooks, 40–44, 46, 48, 110, 195n28
cooking, 12, 14–16, 21, 24, 26, 29, 36, 38, 39–43, 51, 68, 69, 76, 83, 88, 98, 99, 109, 115, 117, 119, 123, 128, 136, 152, 168–70, 171, 173, 187n9, 189n33, 191n12
courtoisie, 23, 26, 43, 83
cross-dressing, 115, 136
cuckold, figures of, 101, 127–28, 132, 190–91n7
Cunningness script, 7, 111, 139
cupbearer. See seneschal
custom, 22, 26–31, 106, 184n16

De Caresme et de Charnage, 20
démesure, 33, 39–40
diet, 1, 3, 14–15, 42, 44, 45–48, 49, 120–21, 134, 150, 162

212

disgust, 14, 77, 99, 118, 122
drink and drinking, 1, 15, 26, 28, 29, 32, 33, 34, 36, 39, 42, 46, 112, 113, 124, 138, 165, 169, 184n14, 184n24. *See also* drunkenness; water; wine; thirst, epic
drunkenness, 31, 32–33, 36–37, 113, 124, 135, 184n36, 185n27, 192–93n38. *See also* drink and drinking
Du fait de cuisine, 42
Durmart le Gallois, 10, 188n11

Enfances Guillaume, 38
envy, 31, 104
epic, 4, 15, 74, 103, 194n12
etiquette, 14, 30, 33, 106, 119. *See also* table: table manners
Eucharist, 3, 194n18
Eve, 31, 153–54
excrement, 32, 119, 120, 122
exempla, 12, 32, 100, 106–07, 110, 112, 119, 121, 134

fabliaux, 4, 11, 19–22, 25, 29, 30, 32, 33, 40, 44, 45, 47, 48, 49, 97–139
  Aloul, 104, 128–29, 130, 137
  Boivin de Provins, 112–13, 114, 163, 191n17
  Bouchier d'Abeville, Le, 20, 110–11, 112, 114
  Bourgeoise d'Orléans, La, 113
  Brunain, la vache au prestre, 194–95n25
  crote, La, 20, 121
  dame qui avoine demandoit pour Morel, La, 123
  dame qui se venja du chevalier, La, 125–26
  De Haimet et Barat, 97, 116, 136–37, 191n19
  Du prestre ki abevete, 127–28
  Du vilain de Bailleul, 127–28

  Esquiriel, L', 124–25
  Estormi, 138
  fabliaux, genre defined, 97–104
  Frère Denis, 186n47
  Guillaume au Faucon, 80
  Jouglet, 104–07, 119, 121
  Lai d'Ignaure, Le, 20–22, 103
  Lai du Lecheor, Le, 103
  oue au chapelain, L', 20
  pauvre clerc, Le, 29
  perdrix, Les, 20, 104, 108–09, 117, 127
  pescheor du pont sur seine, Le, 99
  pet du vilain, Le, 119–20
  Plantez, 29
  Porcelet, 20, 124–25
  prestre et la dame, Le, 40, 135
  prestre qui fu mis au lardier, Le, 20, 100, 132
  prestre qui manga des meures, Le, 20, 107, 132, 135
  quatre larrons, Les, 113
  Sacristain moine, Le, 130–32
  souhait, Le, 124
  trois dames de Paris, Les, 32
  Veuve, La, 122,
  Vieille qui oint la paume au chevalier, La, 126
  vilain ânier, Le, 99, 107, 119–20
  vilain au buffet, Le, 22
famine, 15–16, 19, 40, 47, 48, 117. *See also* hunger
farce du cuvier, La, 135
Farce du Meunier, 121
fasting, 3, 15, 16, 39, 40, 41, 46, 61, 75
feast, 2, 10, 14–16, 19, 21–26, 27, 30–32, 35, 41, 43, 44–46, 47, 48, 65, 75, 80–81, 82, 96, 97, 102–03, 106, 112, 117–18, 125, 130, 134, 137, 152, 159, 164, 173, 187n10

Index

Fisher King, 23, 27, 65, 71–72, 187n8
fishing, 99, 171, 174, 194n15
Flamenca, 190n2
flatulence, 5, 119, 120–21, 192n24, 192n26
Floire et Blanchefleur, 28, 183n10
Florimont, 28
Folie Tristan, La, 183n10
food
  apples, 18, 31, 48, 136, 138
  bacon, 4, 44–45, 48, 114, 115, 128, 130, 132, 135, 137, 139, 145–47, 162, 163, 168. *See also* animals: pigs; food: pork and ham
  bread, 4, 15, 16, 29, 31, 37, 39, 40, 43, 44, 45–46, 48, 80, 82, 89, 112, 137, 138, 173, 189n32, 191n10
    Bread of Life 71
  cabbage, 4, 116–17, 150, 191n21
  capon, 4, 31, 44, 48, 127, 152, 166. *See also* food: poultry
  cheese, 16, 17, 18, 31, 44–45, 48, 112, 137–38
  eels, 20, 159–60, 169–71, 193n7, 195n33
  eggs, 5, 16, 17, 35, 42, 44, 109, 125, 138, 162, 178
  fish, 20, 23, 35, 37, 39, 46, 61, 90, 93, 110, 155, 158, 159–60, 170–71, 194n15
  fruit, 5, 16, 102, 151
  garlic, 37, 67, 118, 135, 169, 195n28
  goose, 4, 20, 37, 134–35, 138, 193n30
  meat, 15, 20, 23, 26, 35, 37, 42, 44, 45, 46, 60, 62–65, 70, 80, 90–91, 106–07, 112, 116–17, 122, 130, 133, 147, 149–50, 155, 163, 166, 167, 169–70, 191n10, 194n13. *See also specific meats under* food
  mutton and sheep, 4, 133, 150, 154
  nuts, 5, 118, 125
  oats, 4, 46, 123–24
  partridges, 20, 40, 107–09
  pears, 104–06, 119
  pepper, 20, 35, 65, 66, 119, 169, 195n28
  pie, 1, 2, 7, 31, 46, 48, 70, 71, 82, 132
  pork and ham, 4, 29, 44, 45, 94, 115, 118, 119, 131–32, 134, 150, 155, 157, 162, 167–68. *See also* food: bacon
  porridge, 4, 44, 127
  poultry, 4, 23, 35, 37, 40, 46, 62, 83, 90, 107–09, 133, 140, 143, 150, 152, 166–67, 168, 172–73, 174, 188n11, 190n38, 195n28
  sausages, 2, 5, 20, 122, 128, 137, 149, 156, 157, 195n3. *See also* andouille
food fight, 4, 17–20, 27, 29, 31–39, 40, 47, 81, 109
Freud, Sigmund, 8

games, 19, 101, 114–15, 121, 125, 126, 141, 149, 153, 157–58, 174–75. *See also* andouille
Gargantua, 1
Garin et Loherain, 39
Gauvain, 10, 22, 30–31, 51, 78, 81–85, 90–94, 99, 178, 179, 187n4, 188n23, 190n37

gender, 11–12, 16–17, 19, 25, 35, 109, 113, 115, 121, 122, 136, 138, 139, 189n24
General Theory of Verbal Humor, 7, 20, 26, 27, 100, 179
genitalia, 5, 21, 107–08, 122–24, 128–29, 137, 173
Gerbert de Metz, 39
gestures, 14, 161, 183n3
Giglois, 187n4, 188n12
gluttony, 2, 4, 31–39, 42–43, 46, 48, 98, 104, 106, 107–09, 112, 124, 129, 131–32, 134, 137, 141, 145–46, 152, 154, 158, 174, 175, 184n23
Graal. See Grail
Grail, 23–24, 46, 74
    Grail castle, 10, 71, 188n18
    Grail procession, 24, 91
greed, 29, 33, 143, 146–47, 152, 154, 160, 163–64, 166–68, 176
Guenièvre, 51, 194n23
Guiborc, 15, 38
Guigemar, 185n27
Guillaume, epic figure of, 9, 15, 36–39, 47
Guillaume le Clerc de Normandie, *Bestiaire divin,* 143
Guillaume le Clerc, 74–82. *See also Roman de Fergus*
Guingamor, 183n9

hand washing ritual, 25, 30, 44, 151–52
hermits, 45–46, 80, 184n21, 188n18
Hobbes, Thomas, 7
hospitality, 10–11, 22, 26–31, 43, 79–80, 83, 84, 104, 110–11, 160
hosts. *See* hospitality
humor, black, 99, 132

humors, bodily, 29, 105
hunger, 13, 15, 29, 33, 36, 37, 38, 39, 40, 46, 47, 71, 74, 76, 79, 80, 102, 112, 114, 116, 117, 122, 128, 139, 142–59, 145–49, 163, 167, 171, 174–76, 184n19, 191n10, 193nn9–11
hunting and hunters, 26, 27, 39, 40, 44, 108, 122, 125, 126, 140, 141, 142, 144–45, 150–51, 163, 166, 168, 171, 173, 175, 185n32
Huon de Bordeaux, 39
hygiene, 42

identity, 2, 14, 22, 26, 29, 36, 46, 109, 114–15, 117, 120, 129, 131, 136, 137, 139, 144
Ile et Galeron, 28
incongruity, 6, 17–18, 19, 48, 115, 117, 126, 136, 138, 144
indigestion, 5, 45, 106, 118–19, 121, 125
inns and innkeepers, 11, 29, 32, 56, 104, 111–12
Ipomedon, 28
irony, 10, 19, 21, 51, 52, 71, 72, 76, 81, 83, 111, 126–27, 135, 139, 145, 147, 161, 164, 167, 172, 191n21
Isengrin, 40, 76, 144, 146, 150, 153–54, 156, 158, 160, 162–63, 166–67, 169–70, 172, 192n33, 194n17

Jaufré, 30–31, 44–45, 47, 91, 184n22, 187n10
Jean de Saintré, 43
Jehan, 50. *See also Merveilles de Rigomer*

215

Index

Jeu de Robin et Marion, 11, 31, 44–45, 118, 121, 137–38, 189n32
Jewish diet, 3
jokes. *See* scripts, joke
jongleur, 22, 104–07, 119, 121

Kant, Immanuel, 6
Keu, 30–31, 54, 66, 76, 85, 184n20, 189n28. *See also* seneschal
Kierkegaard, Søren, 6
kitchen, 18, 22, 25, 32, 34–37, 39–40, 43, 46, 56, 62, 63, 76, 81, 85–90, 99, 98, 103, 130, 133, 152, 160, 171
knights and knighthood, 11, 15, 18, 19, 22–23, 27, 28, 30, 31, 32, 43, 47, 52, 65–67, 68, 69, 70, 72, 74, 80, 81, 83, 85, 86–90, 94–95, 99, 103, 104, 113, 125, 126, 131, 178, 189n26

La Fontaine, Jean de, *Fables,* 143
Lancelot, 25, 27–28, 51, 56, 66, 67, 77, 85–90, 95, 178
larder, 4, 20, 25, 37, 46, 100, 130, 132–34, 147, 166, 190n6
largesse, 10, 47, 57, 61, 111
laughter, 1, 16, 18–19, 21, 29, 30, 32, 36, 39, 48, 54–55, 64, 76, 87, 96, 100, 107, 138, 144, 154, 157, 159, 162, 163, 174–55. *See also risus monasticus*
lean days, 15, 61. *See also* fasting
lechery, 4, 11, 33, 101, 105, 111, 127, 130, 131, 132–33, 135, 138
Lent, 41
Lévi-Strauss, Claude, 183n1
Liber de Coitu, 123

Llull, Ramon, 33
love and lovers, 16, 19, 21, 23, 31, 51, 56, 64, 68, 73, 75, 79–80, 85, 86, 90, 91, 99, 124, 126–27, 133, 135, 136, 148–50
lust, 21, 31, 123–24, 126, 128, 135, 137, 149
lyric, 16, 22

madness, 80, 87
Malory, Thomas, 185n33
Manière de se Contenir à Table, 43
Mannessier, 23, 71–72, 188n23
manuals, didactic and household, 16, 26, 33, 40–44, 48, 119
manuscript images and miniatures, 23, 63, 82, 170–74, 187n8
marketplace, 15, 39, 41, 48, 97, 98, 107, 120, 124, 132, 133, 190n2
marriage, 11, 23, 51, 56, 105, 109, 124, 136
medicinal properties of food, 5, 15, 128, 162, 149, 151, 159–60, 163, 167, 171
merchants, 11, 47, 82, 98, 111–12, 119–20
Merlin, 101–02
Merveilles de Rigomer, 10, 21, 50, 55–57, 58, 63, 66, 74, 77, 85–90, 94, 95, 184n26
Mesnagier de Paris, 42, 46
misogyny, 11, 32, 101, 110, 154
mock epic, 9, 155, 176
monde à l'envers (world upside down), 16–20, 22, 73, 87, 90, 167
Moniage Guillaume, 37–38
Montpellier, 99, 190n2
morality, in relation to food, 31–34, 56, 65, 87, 91, 104–

216

Index

22, 143, 146, 147, 161, 173, 176–77
Morel, 124–25
Morreall, John, 6–7
mule sans frein, La, 24, 187n4
Muset, Colin, 189n34
Muslim diet, 3, 192n37

nutrition and malnutrition, 15, 26, 41, 42, 43, 47, 48, 95, 120–21, 145, 147–48

orality, 33, 123–24, 189n24

Pantagruel, 181, 186n44
pantry, 12, 20, 25, 29, 44, 99, 103. *See also* larder
Paris, 29, 32
parody, 9, 51, 55, 73, 81, 85, 111–12, 149, 158, 159, 163, 175–76, 179, 194n12
Partonepeu de Blois, 28
Pèlerinage de Charlemagne, 187n3, 188n11
Perceval, 10, 23–24, 27, 30, 33, 34, 35, 38, 43, 45, 47, 51, 52–72, 74, 78–79, 82, 91, 94, 126, 187n8
Perceval Continuations, 10, 23, 46, 71–74, 75–76, 188n14, 189n25
Perlesvaus, 74
picnic, 20, 118, 189n32
Pierre de Beauvais, 109, 142–43
pilgrimage and pilgrims, 15, 162
plague, 48
Plato, 5
Poetics, Aristotle, 5
Ponge, Francis, 2
poverty, 4, 19, 29, 47, 48, 56–57, 60–62, 64, 66, 67, 69, 98, 104, 112–13, 116–17, 167, 184n19, 191n21. *See also* famine; hunger

priests. *See* clergy and priests, depictions of
prisoners, 23, 57, 85, 87
prostitution and prostitutes, 11, 112
Proust, Marcel, 2
proverbs, 80, 84, 85, 89, 100–01, 110, 112
Pyramus et Tisbé, 183n10

quest, 15, 23, 25, 29, 74, 178
Queste del Saint Graal, La, 71, 188n14
Quintilian, 5

Rabelais, François, 1, 20, 156, 181, 186n44, 193n7, 195n2
Rainouart, 9, 28, 33, 35–38, 47, 85
Raoul de Cambrai, 188n16
Raoul de Houdenc, 50
Raskin, Victor, 7, 100, 124
realism, comic, 15–16, 51, 47–48, 51, 56, 74, 75, 77, 79, 81–82, 83, 95, 99, 103, 141, 145, 149, 150–59, 164, 168, 169, 171, 175
Recueil de Riom, 42
Régime pour tous serviteurs, 43
Release Theory, 8, 47
Relief Theory, 8, 47, 97
Renart, 3, 33, 40, 44, 47, 74, 140–77, 193n3
Renaut de Beaujeu, 20–21, 103
Restraint Theory, 8
Ridiculous, the, 5, 18, 33–34, 38, 56, 83, 179
risus monasticus, 32. *See also* laughter
romance genre, 4, 15, 19, 21–31, 39, 43–44, 45–47, 50–96, 94–95, 97, 104, 105, 152. *See also under romance titles and authors*

217

Index

Roman d'Alexandre, 82, 186n43, 187n8, 190n38
Roman de Fergus, 10, 28, 33, 38, 40, 47, 50, 72–81, 188n22
Roman de Renart, 4, 7, 8, 12–13, 25, 30, 44, 47, 48, 74, 76, 95, 98, 116, 129, 132, 134, 140–77, 181, 192n24, 194n17
Roman d'Hunbaut, 10, 28, 30, 31, 51, 74, 77, 81–84, 178, 186n2, 189n35, 190n37
romans d'aventure, 21
Round Table, 73, 85
rustics and rusticity, 36, 40, 69–71, 72, 83, 89, 163
Rutebeuf, 120–21, 191n21

satire, 9, 39, 52, 55, 94, 147, 149, 159–69, 173, 175–76
scatological humor, 5, 97, 103, 97, 100, 103, 117–22, 192n24
Schopenhauer, Arthur, 6
scripts, joke, 7, 99, 124–25
seneschal, 29–30, 76
sermons, 40, 77, 155–58, 177
servants, and domestic service, 21, 24, 29, 36, 43, 56, 62, 64, 66, 85, 86, 87, 90, 136
Sexual Ignorance script, 7, 139, 124
sexuality and sexual activity, 1, 4, 11–12, 15, 19, 21, 31, 33, 47, 97, 99, 108–09, 112, 115, 121, 122–36, 137, 178
Sexual Opposition script, 139
  sexuality and erotic comedy, 122–36
sins, 4, 31–32, 43, 139. *See also under specific sins*
Sir Gawain and the Green Knight, 27, 187n8

slapstick, 1, 20, 115, 122
sloth, 31, 143
speech, 14, 24, 25, 33–34, 35, 36, 54, 72, 83, 94, 152
Spencer, Herbert, 8
spices, 4, 35, 42, 66, 76, 89, 119–20
Stinginess script, 7, 139
strangers, 23, 26–27, 30, 68, 70, 77, 88
students, 11, 29
Superior Theory, 7, 76, 139

table, 12, 22, 23–25, 26, 30, 33, 35, 40, 46, 47, 62–63, 64, 65, 71, 72, 90, 91, 93, 101, 102, 105, 112, 124, 127, 136, 170–71, 173, 187n8, 188n11, 191n10
  table cloth, 23, 25, 44, 62–63, 65, 135
  table manners, 1, 11, 14–15, 22, 26, 30, 33, 35, 40, 43–44, 46, 50, 61, 66–67, 71, 84, 103, 178, 179, 185n38
thieves and robbers, 11, 33, 56, 70, 76, 77–78, 89, 132, 109, 115, 139, 160, 162
thirst, epic, 38, 75
Torelore, 16–18
trickster, 30, 112, 173–74
Tristan, 24, 183n10, 191n9

Ugly, the, 5, 33, 179

vagina dentata, 125, 130
values, 14, 30–31, 72, 76, 183n2
vegetarianism, 3, 37, 45, 46, 61
Vengeance Raguidel, 10, 28, 30, 31, 50, 179, 187n4
venison, 24, 27, 35, 39, 45, 60, 61, 65, 93, 118, 126, 188n11
Viandier de Taillevent, 42

vilain, 2, 11, 16, 21–22, 29, 30, 37, 44, 47–48, 65–66, 71, 74, 75, 77, 78, 82, 86, 98, 99, 101–02, 103, 105, 110, 112, 113, 116, 119, 120, 121, 127–29, 132, 146–47, 149, 150–51, 153, 155, 159, 162–66, 167–68, 171, 173, 184n25, 195n26
Villon, François, 180–81, 184n19, 191n21
violence, 14, 16–18, 20, 25, 30, 36–37, 39, 75, 80, 82, 83, 84, 95, 99, 103, 142, 144, 153, 165, 172
voyeurism, 127

war, 17–18, 20, 38. *See also* violence
wasteland, 16, 82
water, 45–46, 48, 63, 66, 150, 170, 194n17
weddings and wedding feasts, 15, 22, 32, 47, 57, 65, 80–81, 105–06, 152, 187n9
wine, 4, 29, 32, 36, 37, 39, 45, 46, 67, 71, 88, 89, 90, 93, 112, 127, 151, 165, 169, 188n11, 191n10, 195n28

Yder, 194n23

Zola, Emile, 2

About the Author

Sarah Gordon, Utah State University, has published articles on medieval literature in journals such as *LIT, Medievalia et Humanistica,* and *Women in French*. She also taught at the Sorbonne and Ohio University and was a restaurant critic in Paris.

www.ingramcontent.com/pod-product-compliance
Lightning Source LLC
Chambersburg PA
CBHW062219300426
44115CB00012BA/2139